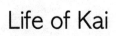

Life of Kai

LIFE OF KAI

a memoir of awakening

KAI CAROL JUD

Haley's

Athol, Massachusetts

International Standard Book Number, trade paperback:
978-1-948380-89-8

International Standard Book Number, ebook, epub format:
978-1-948380-90-4

International Standard Book Number, ebook, Kindle format:
978-1-948380-92-8

International Standard Book Number, audiobook:
978-1-948380-91-1

Copy edited by Mary-Ann DeVita Palmieri.
Proof read by Richard Bruno.
Cover photo by Jean Miele.
Cover designed by Mark Wright.
Original ink section ornament by Adrian Montagano.

Life of Kai relates factual events. The author has changed the names of some individuals..

Haley's
488 South Main Street
Athol, MA 01331
marcia2gagliardi@gmail.com

Library of Congress Cataloging-in-Publication Data pending

in memory of my Beloved
Chris Boeve
1944-2012

Chris Boeve

Be grateful for whatever comes,
because each has been sent
as a guide from beyond.

—Rumi

Contents

Preparation

On the Road

Going Home

Preparation

Into the Underworld

Whenever sorrow comes, be kind to it.
For God has placed a pearl in sorrow's hand.

—Rumi

Alone on the beach in West Haven, Connecticut, at Savin Rock, I await their return. My thirteen-year-old eyes search but find nothing. I will myself to see the boat coming back with my aunt, brother, sister, and mother safe and smiling. Despite my resolve for their safe return, the horizon gives back nothing but emptiness, and I wait. On the shore, waves lap across shells and stones. The breeze nips lightly at my skin, hot from summer sun.

It is the Fourth of July. Families and couples celebrate happily around my blanket in the sand. Still, I pay no attention to anything save keeping my mind steady and far away from thoughts of catastrophe.

The day started in a celebratory fashion. I'm with my beloved Aunt Ginny and my mother, Esther, along with my ten-year-old brother, Dan, and my seven-year-old sister, Ginger. We had come from Ohio to Connecticut for a week-long visit with my aunt, and today we were going to the beach on Long Island Sound to try out her new flat-hulled boat with a sail.

I am surprised that my mother has chosen to be with Ginny, her only sister, and us kids for this holiday. Today is a momentous day for my father. The newly formed United Church of Christ is installing him as General Secretary of the Board for Homeland Ministry, heading the Division of Evangelism and Research, a move that will bring his career in the church to new heights. I have a feeling that my mother should be with him and not us, but I don't give it much thought. I am dimly aware that she was not happy when my father decided a year ago to leave his position as a parish minister. She missed working with him as his partner in church activities when he was no longer conducting services and in the long periods when my father traveled, I felt my mother's increasing resentment and distress. No one talked about it, but his absence disrupted the peaceful energy of our family.

I miss my father on today's adventure, but I'm happy to be with my mother, siblings, and especially Aunt Ginny. My aunt lived in the parsonage with us for a couple of years when she was a resident at Yale Medical School. Until I was nine, she acted as my cultural mentor. We shared magical adventures that included New Haven Railroad trips to New York City, eating in the train's dining car, attending the New York City Ballet, and feasting at fancy French restaurants. I've missed being with her since we moved from New Haven three years ago.

Today begins my chance to be with my aunt for a whole week, and all of us are excited about going to the beach to try out her new sailboat. As we walk across the beach to the water's edge, Aunt Ginny notices that we've forgotten the life jackets. She and Mom decide that it's not a big deal, given that we three kids are competent swimmers. So, we continue toward the pleasures of the day.

As the oldest child, I am gifted with the first ride. Aunt Ginny pulls the boat with its brightly colored single sail of yellow, orange, and blue stripes into the water. I perch on one of the hollowed-out seats on the boat's flat plank. The wind fills the sail, and I watch silently as my aunt steers far from shore. Soon my family becomes a tiny speck on the beach, and I am surrounded by water. My aunt busily maneuvers the sails, and I am bored with nothing to do. I'm disappointed that the ride isn't as thrilling as I expected and am not sorry when Ginny turns the boat back toward shore.

I disembark and settle onto my blanket in the sand. I see my aunt hold the hull steady as my mother, brother, and sister climb on. As they head out into open water, I wave goodbye. They hardly look back. They have already entered their adventure. Gliding over incoming waves, the sail appears smaller and smaller until it disappears over the horizon. I settle alone on the sand and imagine my siblings having a much more exciting time than I did on my short, uneventful voyage.

I watch waves in their rhythmic flow slapping at the shore, and I hear children's squeals and parents' concerned cries as kids go too far out into the water. Seagulls fly over, squawking unintelligible messages. I do my best to feel as if I'm having a good time at the beach, but anxiety creeps in as time goes by.

My ride had been quick, a swift going out and coming back. Although worry has distorted my sense of time, clearly my family has been gone far too long. I tell myself sternly that they will appear any minute, but an hour or two goes by, and I am still sitting on the beach, alone and waiting.

I don't pray for their safe return. That would make the possibility of disaster a reality. I feel more secure imagining no danger, even though I find it harder and harder to believe.

My reverie breaks as I see a crowd gathering far down the beach. I can barely make out what is happening, and I tell myself that whatever is going on has nothing to do with me. I don't allow myself to think. Instead, I watch the sea, and I watch the sand. I watch drifting clouds in the crisp blue sky. I will my mind to go blank because to let anything in at that moment would court disaster. Only emptiness is safe, so I hold on to it for dear life while I sit and wait.

I see my brother and sister walking toward me with a woman in her thirties whom I don't recognize. She is dressed not for the beach but in a baggy blue striped dress and street shoes. As she awkwardly steers Dan and Ginger toward me, they approach, looking down at the sand, not at me. They are trembling despite the hot sun and seem shrouded in silence. Asking anything feels too dangerous. I am frozen in my fear. I don't want to know what they know. I simply pretend that seeing them appear with an unknown person is normal, even though I know it is not.

The woman stops at the edge of my blanket and without explanation or introduction says, "Come with me." She does nothing to put my mind at ease.

I rise and follow. I don't know where we are going, but it doesn't matter. I am no longer the girl I was before who might care where she is taken. I have fallen into emptiness. The woman guides us across the street that runs along the beach and takes us into her modest home.

I am far too terrified to speak and no longer aware enough to wonder what we are doing in this stranger's house. My world has contracted into a cold place inside my body. I barely look to see where we have landed.

The woman ushers us into a small room where a TV set is blasting. She tells us to sit on the couch. The three of us sit in stony silence, squeezed by our personal terrors. We haven't spoken a word to each other since the woman appeared at my blanket.

I wonder what we are doing here. My brother and sister are with me but not really. They sit quietly, not too close together, their bodies trembling while my mind stays resolutely quiet. I cannot afford to ask questions.

The woman brings tea on a tray and tells us to drink. I have forgotten what it is to drink and stare blankly at the cup.

She leaves, and the three of us sit without speaking. Hours go by, and we remain together in frozen isolation. Still, it hasn't been quiet. The TV has been blaring. Suddenly, something calls my attention. A special newscast has broken into regular programming.

The announcer's voice fills the room. "The wife of the beloved former minister of the Congregational Church on the Green has died in a boating accident at Savin Rock." The words go into my mind and out the other side. I watch myself take in and erase that horrifying moment.

I leave my body and everything I've known as I sit on the couch, staring at my cold tea.

My brother, sister, and I, frozen in forgetfulness and denial, continue to sit on that couch with the tragic news floating invisibly in the air.

My father arrives from Philadelphia. I see him in the doorway. My heart leaps in delight at the sight of him, but as we run into his arms, a feeling of dread comes over me. What is he doing here? It should be my mother, not my father, coming to take us home. Where is she? The report I heard on the TV has not lodged anywhere in my being, and I await her return.

My father kneels and puts his arms around us. In a voice that comes from far away, he whispers, "Your mother is dead. She drowned. She's gone."

* * *

The thirteen-year-old girl that I was grew up in that moment. No longer the innocent child her father described as "happy as a clam at high tide," she could not even imagine what awaited her nor how she would find her way without her mother. She could barely think about such things.

She had not been present at her mother's death. Her brother, sister, and aunt couldn't or wouldn't discuss what happened. She knew only that the boat had turned over in Long Island Sound far from shore. The sail had become waterlogged, so the hull could not be righted. The four flailed in the water for an untold amount of time while motorboats passed by, their passengers and operators waving friendly greetings. Ginger remembers watching terrified as a wave swept over our mother's head. I heard that two men on speedboats brought them all to shore and that my aunt saw foam coming out of her sister's mouth, making it evident that water had entered her lungs. She knew then that her sister had died. That is the little I learned from limited information shared over the years.

As the days unfolded, my father and siblings disappeared into their own private worlds of grief. Although we shared a home in Shaker Heights, Ohio, and a year later in Scarsdale, New York, we rarely discussed the terror and sadness surrounding my mother's death. It felt as if we were each a spinning top whirling in a large bowl that held us together in a shared space but in separate universes.

I watched my father grieve for Esther who was for him "all that was wonderful and joyful about this world." I was terrified by the endless grief I saw in him.

Since taking the new job with the United Church of Christ, my father no longer had local church responsibilities such as preaching. When not traveling, the family attended a small local church. After my mother's death, I remember sitting with him on Sundays in church, my hand wrapped around his, as his tears flowed profusely. His profound despair left little space for us three kids to grieve. We were left to find our own way.

Still, he was the only parent I had, and I felt that my very existence depended on keeping him alive and well. Without conscious awareness, I contracted with him and all the men who followed. My job was to be the healer who held everything together.

To soften the grief of my mother's loss, I turned my back on my connections with women. I was too terrified to think that I was a daughter without a mother, and I chose to believe that a thirteen-year-old girl was grown up and didn't need a mother. I pushed away from the kindnesses of women and concentrated my energies on men even at that time when I most needed motherly ministrations.

Years later, when I became a psychotherapist, I recognized that I had ritually initiated many women into womanhood and become a mother figure for others but had never been initiated myself. I wondered how I had become the one to welcome women, some much older than myself, into the larger community of women. I will never know but chose to believe that my mother guided me from the other side.

As much as I turned away from intimate relationships with women, I found myself searching not for the personal mother but for the Great Mother, a being I could trust and lean into. She came in the form of nature—ocean, deserts, changing seasons, and starry nights. I can't remember my mother's touch or smell, but I sensed her as part of the essential Mother

9

force in all that is, the energy that loves me, holds me, and knows my name.

My mother's death, a devastating catastrophe in my young life, offered a crucial yet demanding gift. The shattering of my home life banished me from the normal expectations of what life would offer. No longer trusting the safety of my family and church, I felt compelled to explore outside the limitations of accepted cultural patterns. Finding my own way as a motherless daughter thrust me headlong into my spiritual journey, a journey into the darkness that birthed my deepest self.

I wouldn't have had words to describe my spiritual journey when I was thirteen, but circumstances had thrown me into the journey of the mystic. Mysticism comes not from faith in a system of beliefs but from direct experience of the oneness of all things. My mystic path has been a lifelong journey, a calling, and a commitment requiring the willingness to die to the old and awaken to the new. My life, an ever-continuing process of letting go and being born again, has taken me into the Dark Night of the Soul and the ecstasy of union, and I am eternally grateful for all that brought me to the path.

Beginnings

You are part of a love story. You are desired and longed for.
There are thousands of witnesses before you
who would claim that you are held in the arms of love.

—Alan Jones

Thirteen years before my mother died, I entered the world on December 23, 1947, to the delight of my parents, Esther and Jerry Jud. The skies blew heavy with snow that night, and in the heavens beyond, the Sun, Moon, and Mars formed what astrologers call a Grand Trine, a configuration that promised me a solid foundation in life and an underlying sense of wholeness.

Yet, the most potent force the skies presented was not the Grand Trine but the square of Pluto and the Moon. In classical mythology and astrology, Pluto is God of the Underworld and associated with darkness, the subconscious, death, and rebirth. His pathway demands constant letting go and revisioning, requiring profound trust in the power of transformation.

The Grand Trine did not bring me a life of simple comfort as it seemed to promise. Instead, it offered grace and ease while walking in the realms of death and darkness. Events that could have broken me transformed into great blessings in my life. Even in my darkest hours, I have always felt held.

Life started sweetly for me. I was born into a vibrant Congregational Church community of fifteen hundred members. The church building was classically set in the middle of the town green in West Haven, Connecticut, a solid working-class neighborhood. The steeple served as a landmark used by local fishermen for navigation. When it blew down in a storm in 1953, they donated money to help restore it to its former glory.

I was enthusiastically welcomed as the first child born to a church pastor in more than fifty years. Fortunately for me, I wasn't a boy. Had I been male, the comparisons between the little baby Jesus and me could have been too weighty to bear.

As it was, the people in the congregation considered me a princess. My father and mother carried me around in a basket, and people felt honored that my parents allowed them to touch me. As I grew, I felt surrounded by love and a deep sense of belonging.

The church sat directly across the street from the parsonage, the big, old, white three-story house that we occupied. In it, we hosted weddings, meetings, picnics, and other gatherings. A stream of people flowed in and out all day long. Behind the house, the backyard extended into a huge garden that grew rows of corn, tomatoes, beans, strawberries, apples, and grapes that my mother preserved to take us through the winter months. It was paradise for a little girl.

As my navigational center, the church provided me with a generous and lively community energized by men coming back from World War II, marrying, and having families. In the church sanctuary with its plain white walls and lack of decoration and in the warmth of my home, adults taught me about a loving God who wanted us to make the world a better place. That God was not punishing. There were no images of hell and brimstone. The little baby Jesus, unrealistically depicted as white and rosy-cheeked, had come to teach us to be love in the world. I felt safe and secure.

My father, Gerald Jud, known as Jerry, came from a long line of Swiss and German theologians, including Leo Jud who worked with Zwingli during the Swiss Reformation in the early 1500s. My father's father, Daniel, was neither a fundamentalist nor a liberal, but he taught my father that in life and death, he was safe in God's hands and that loving one another and doing the right thing was what God required.

Jerry's mother, Aurelia, birthed thirteen children, nine of whom lived, including my father, the youngest boy. My grandmother, a woman of Texas pioneer stock, played the organ at the tiny country church founded by German immigrants in Riesel, Texas, where her husband served as minister. The church belonged to the Evangelical Synod of North America. Aurelia took primary responsibility in the household regarding organization and discipline of the children while Daniel took care of the spiritual matters of praying, studying theological texts, and preaching in German on Sunday mornings. My father insisted that his four older brothers taught him everything he needed to know while his father worked in his study.

Jerry worked his way through Baylor University and came close to going to Moody Bible School to become a fundamentalist preacher. One of his professors told him he was far too bright for such a conservative education and sent him off to McCormick Seminary, affiliated with the University of Chicago.

There he studied theology, the psychology of religion, and citified manners that would make him acceptable to an upper-class congregation. He even had a maid who cleaned his room every day. At McCormick he discovered a much bigger world than he could have ever imagined back in Texas.

He expected to go to Princeton to continue his studies when a mysterious man named Mr. Schaumburg showed up at the seminary and asked the dean if any of his students planned to study for a doctorate. The dean recommended Jerry Jud, and Mr. Schaumburg offered him a job as assistant pastor at the Humphrey Street Church in New Haven if he would agree, instead, to go to Yale.

My father altered his plans, and Yale Divinity School accepted him. He was delighted that he would have a ready-made job to support his schooling. He arrived in New Haven and went directly to the Humphrey Street Church. To his shock, no one had ever heard of Mr. Schaumburg or Jerry Jud. Enterprising young man that he was, he quickly found a job as assistant pastor at the First Congregational Church in West Haven and soon became senior pastor for the next seventeen years.

Mr. Schaumburg was never heard of again. In looking back, I wonder whether Mr. Schaumburg even existed. Perhaps he was an angel sent to change the course of my father's trajectory so that I could come into the life I know as mine.

My father loved to tell the story of meeting my mother. One day soon after he arrived at Yale, he saw a lovely young woman walking on the campus. She had long, wavy auburn hair and wore a black skirt and a white blouse. Her beauty swept him away. He followed her into one of the classroom buildings and shyly said hello.

Her name was Esther. She came from Lincoln, Nebraska, and her father worked as a railroad engineer. Her family members were all good Baptists, and she had come to Yale to study for a master's in Christian education. As one of the few women admitted to Yale Divinity School in those years, she was a woman ahead of her time and, compared to my father, experienced in the ways of the world.

Jerry asked Esther to go for a walk the next day, and that naive country boy found himself kissing her. Rashly, he blurted out, "I love you."

Regaining control of herself after the kiss, Esther explained that she was engaged to a dentist back in Lincoln.

"That's all right," said Jerry, rising to all his priestly power. "If it is the will of God, something will come of our relationship."

On the following day, they walked in the Farnham Gardens, a lovely park near the campus bursting with new life and spring color. They sat close together on a step and looked at the beauty surrounding them.

"I'm going home to Lincoln after graduation," she said. "Will you come to see me this summer?"

"Of course," he said.

"And will you take me away with you?" she asked with bright eyes.

"I will," he said without taking a breath. And thus began a great love they shared generously with all who knew them.

They married three months after their whirlwind courtship began.

I have often wondered how those two strangers recognized each other so immediately and how they knew they had work and play to do with each other. It makes me wonder about destiny, guardian angels, and contracts made before entering this earthly plane.

I entered this world three years later. When I made my appearance hospitals did not allow fathers in the delivery room. My father was attending a Christmas carol party at the church when I was born, and he raced over to the hospital excitedly as soon as he could to meet me. In those days, even Protestant ministers wore white, starched cotton clerical collars and black shirts over them so a stiff white neckpiece showed through. Looking very ministerial, he entered an elevator.

Seeing him, a woman said, "Good evening, Father."

"How did you know?" he responded joyously.

They called me Carol after the songs sung to welcome the little baby Jesus. And, so, the days of Camelot began.

The church flourished under my father's charismatic energy, and I grew and toddled in my safe, warm, loving container. Then Pluto made his first visit and perhaps shifted the trajectory of my life. I was sixteen months old, a happy toddler with a pregnant mom. Both of my parents were thrilled that a new baby would come into their lives. They laid an abundance of dreams on the child.

The day came when my mother went to the hospital. At that time, women stayed in the hospital after Cesarean sections for two weeks, a lifetime for a toddler waiting for her mother's return. My mother turned over my care to my grandmother Polly, a stern midwesterner who was practical but not particularly warm. I was helpless in my anger and fear that my loving mother had abandoned me so unexpectedly, and there was little that my grandmother could do to comfort me.

My parents named my baby brother John Mark, and his birth was celebrated with delight by family and friends. Yet, after three days, while still in the hospital, the seemingly healthy baby died of unknown causes. My mother never saw him after he died, and I never met him. Accompanied by one friend, my father buried his son on a dark and cold April day.

Despite their grief, my parents did their best to return to the old life when my mother came home. My mother cooked and tended me, and my father carried out his work at the church. But my mother's sorrow was heavy, and my father held his grief deep inside. I felt an unfamiliar distance between them that I didn't understand and wondered how I fit into this new energy.

A week later, I was teething, and pain added to my distress about the changes in the household. I was playing alone in the living room when a throbbing ache raged through my jaw. I howled in shock, which brought my mother and father running in to find me rolling on the floor. Having so recently lost one child, my parents were terrified that they were about to lose their only other child.

My pain grew until the muscles of my tiny body clenched and became rigid. Convulsions took me over as my body flailed uncontrollably. My consciousness dissolved, and I felt lifted into another realm where I floated in bliss above all pain. I drifted free and happy in the light, traveling far away from the inert body that lay on the floor next to my distraught parents.

Flying higher, I looked down and caught a glimpse of my mother's face and heard an echo of my father's voice. I remembered the comfort of being held, seen, and loved even as I found myself gripped by forces beyond anything I had ever felt before. I wanted to float forever in that pleasure, but I had been called back.

"Mommy," I called out.

Shocked at the density of my landing, I plunged back into my body. The pain in my jaw had diminished, but I felt the heavy weight of my body and the ground. I had been summoned back by an energy I didn't understand. Yet I knew I would stay despite the radiance of the light I had to leave behind.

The place I visited, that other place, has no words to describe it. I had encountered a secret realm, foreign to my earth plane home but strangely familiar.

When I returned, everything looked the same, but I had changed. I am not sorry that I decided to return, but what I glimpsed in that experience has remained as a tender and deep longing for home, my true home. Ever since my early meeting with death and the beyond, my deep-seated hunger for my true home has guided my mystical journey.

As I grew up in a household that did not embrace the darkness, life went on, and all memories of death and loss went underground. Everything looked bright in our home, but the shadow must have lurked behind the walls, under the rug, just around the corner, somewhere just out of sight. We were people of the light. For us, the darkness did not exist.

Or did it? Perhaps even as a small child I could smell it, taste it, or hear the dim echoes of darkness. I must have known that it was there but always just beyond reach. I do not doubt that I breathed in my mother's grief with the air that came through my nostrils. I tasted my father's frustrated anger with God and his bewilderment that life had not gone according to plan. All my senses cried out that something was amiss. Even as I sensed that things were not as they seemed, I only heard silence. A dark shadow had inserted itself into the happy innocence of our previous life, a shadow we never talked about in the years to come.

A year later, the family joyfully received another boy, my brother Daniel, and welcomed him as the firstborn son, thus strangely erasing John Mark's fleeting but potent presence in our lives. I often wonder what it must have been like for Dan to have been born with the ghost of John Mark unmentioned and unacknowledged. As I think about it now, if I were Dan, I would wonder if I, also, could come and go with so little notice, so little remembrance.

My sister Ginger arrived three years later, the night before my mother heard that her parents had been in an automobile accident and lay near death. They both survived, but Ginger was born to a mother grieving for yet another time.

It would take me many years of therapy, meditation, and spiritual growth to untangle the loss, mixed messages, and grief that came from meeting death at such an early age. Yet those experiences brought me in touch with the mysteries of life and death and set me on a path of spiritual exploration.

Growing Up

Live the questions now. Perhaps then, someday far in the future,
you will gradually, without even noticing it, live your way into the answer.

—Rainer Maria Rilke

In 1957 when I was nine, Central Congregational Church
in Worcester, Massachusetts, called my father to be the senior
minister. That summer, we moved, and I felt ripped away from
my West Haven community. With the new church located more
than twenty minutes from our home, I no longer experienced
the church and our home as one.

Two and a half years later, my father was invited to be one
of five executives in charge of the new national denomination
called the United Church of Christ headquartered in
Cleveland, Ohio. I had just begun to settle into Worcester
when I was uprooted again in the middle of the school year in
January 1960.

I found moving to suburban Shaker Heights, Ohio, which
my father and mother chose because of the excellence of its
school system, a terrifying transition. Not only did I have to
leave my friends and familiar life behind for the second time,
but the Worcester schools had not prepared me for college
prep courses in my new, upscale school. I had fallen far behind

academically, and although I did my best to catch up, my parents offered little support. My father traveled for his job almost half the time, and my mother had to get used to being a single parent. She took good care of us kids, but when my father returned home from his trips, it disrupted household patterns, and my mother needed to shift much of her attention to his emotional and physical needs. Not understanding her grief at his absence and the pressure his comings and goings had put on her, he responded to her discomfort by telling her that she had to find a new life for herself.

She took a part-time job as head of Christian education in our local church and put her Yale education to good use, but her previous satisfying life had changed significantly. We kept appearances up as the happy family. But she was hurt and angry at my father's absence, and her anger, a subdued rumbling, launched a new energy in our household.

My mother died on July 4, 1961, a year and a half after our move to Shaker Heights and just months after her father's death, which she grieved heavily. Her death left our family in an ocean as deep as the ocean that claimed her physical body.

On the evening of the day my mother drowned, my father took my brother, sister, and me back to Aunt Ginny's house from the home of the stranger who had taken us from the beach. We sat around the kitchen table in shock and silence, pretending we were hungry, yet no one did more than stir the soup Aunt Ginny had put in front of us.

Darkness fell, and bedtime approached. My father insisted that we four sleep in the same room to comfort each other. Two twin beds pushed together made a large bed in the center of the room. I curled up alone on a small cot tucked in the corner.

My father, lost in his own grief and undoubtedly needing comfort himself, invited the three of us to join him in the bed.

Dan and Ginger complied willingly and seemed relieved to be safe in the closeness of their father. I, however, stayed huddled in terror on the cot, which seemed so far distant that I felt I had slipped into another world.

I heard his pleading invitation over and over but couldn't move. My longing for contact and solace tempted me, yet I was acutely conscious that my father's beloved was gone and her position in the bed was empty. Should I move into her place, filling that emptiness? Should I let my just budding sexual fantasies come into consciousness or pretend that a thirteen-year-old young woman entering her father's bed meant nothing?

I listened as his gentle urgings filled me with longing and with fear. Finally, I acquiesced and entered the bed. No sexual activity ever happened that night nor any night, but it was the moment that marked the ending of my childhood. Unwittingly, I slipped into the role of surrogate wife, becoming the keeper of my mother's values, energies, and stories and the healer who would keep the family intact.

Even though my objectives limited my own development in ways that I was undoubtedly unaware of then, it was a contract I agreed to, not feeling at the time that I had any choice.

I grew to be a young woman without a mother. Years later, I started working with John Pierrakos, who with his colleague Alexander Lowen invented bioenergetic therapy, a form of mind-body psychotherapy. Looking at me for the first time, John said he saw an orphan. I had always thought of myself as having the perfect childhood, probably because that was what I was taught, but when I heard John's words, I knew he spoke the truth. I was a motherless child, and my father was no longer fathering me.

Soon after my mother's death, my grandmother on my mother's side came to take care of my brother, sister, and me when my father was working. My father moved out of the room he had shared with my mother into a spare room on the third floor. It was furnished simply with a single bed, an impressive mahogany desk, and a simple wooden prayer bench.

One day almost a year after my mother died, my father called me up to his room. I was rarely summoned to his private space, so I felt the conversation had to be something serious.

He asked me to sit, and I perched uncomfortably on a chair. Looking at him over the desk, I wondered what was coming.

"You know," he began, "now that your mother is gone, I have to marry again."

Every cell in my fourteen-year-old body screamed, "What are you talking about? That can't be." But that is not what came out of my mouth.

Instead, I said calmly, "Of course. Yes, of course." My world was shattering, yet I saw myself doing my best to hold all the pieces together as they flew away.

"I want your advice," he said. "There are six women I am considering, and I want to hear what you think."

Even at that young age, I knew there was something crazy about helping my father choose a wife. Yet, I also knew I was probably his most trusted advisor, the one who carried my mother in my body, the one who would be a bridge to the past. And so, we continued in our dreamlike conversation.

He listed the women. The first was my Aunt Ginny, who already had a committed woman partner. Another woman had six kids, which I thought untenable. The others all had children. Finally, there was Elisabeth, a Swiss woman who had trained as a psychologist at the Gesell Institute of Child Development in New Haven. She had been one of my mother's best friends and had often visited our home.

I composed myself and replied with confidence I didn't feel that Elisabeth would be the best choice. My father smiled and told me they had already set a date to meet in Ireland to discuss his offer of marriage.

I understood. The decision had already been made. My input was not the deciding factor nor perhaps even worthy of regard.

I left the room feeling dazed. My life was moving forward in directions I couldn't control. It was clear to me. I was on my own. No one else knew anything that would keep me safe.

The United Church of Christ headquarters relocated from Cleveland to New York City, and in January of 1962, my family moved to Scarsdale, New York, the third move in less than six years. My grandmother continued to live with us, but she was clearly relieved that my father was going to marry so she would be released from her caretaking responsibilities.

The wedding took place in December, 1962, in Switzerland with Elisabeth's family and friends present. We kids were not included. When my father returned, Elisabeth entered our home as a fait accompli and my grandmother returned immediately to her home in Lincoln, Nebraska. Elisabeth became our primary caretaker and took good care of our physical needs, which was clearly the contract she had made with my father. An unmothered daughter herself, Elisabeth knew little about mothering three grief-stricken kids. And I was a young teenager who, having lost my mother, had little use for a substitute.

I finished high school in 1965 when the first US combat troops arrived in Vietnam, the Beatles were taking the world by storm, and Gemini 5 launched two astronauts into Earth orbit. I had been an active member of the church youth fellowship all through high school and a good student at Scarsdale High School, which had a reputation for excellent academic standards.

Shellshocked and in grief at the loss of my mother, I stayed pretty much on the straight and narrow with no drugs or alcohol and minimal explorations into my sexuality. Looking back, I find it a sad waste of the exuberant energies of the sixties. My father's message was that all was well, even though it obviously was not.

As the school year ended, my father insisted that I get a job before college. The idea did not appeal to me, but my Aunt Ginny saved the day. Her partner, Pat, designed the lighting for productions at Turnau Opera, a summer stock opera company in Woodstock, New York. The company presented operas in English to the accompaniment of two pianos with a cast of talented young singers.

Ginny made a practical arrangement with the opera company. She donated money to Turnau, and I got a salary. I spent the summers at Turnau after my senior year in high school and freshman year at college. I sewed costumes, took stage notes for the director, swept the auditorium, sold tickets, did some walk-on parts, and learned to drink and dabble in sex. It was a life-changing experience for a good little minister's daughter.

After high school, I insisted on going to an out-of-state school and chose the competitive women's institution Jackson College at Tufts University. I spent only one year there where, after my summers of freedom in the theater, I could not tolerate rules requiring me to wear a skirt on campus and be back in the dorm by ten every night.

I was drawn to the excitement of New York City and was accepted as a student at Barnard College, where I majored in psychology. I started piano lessons and had what felt like a religious conversion experience. All I wanted to do was play the piano, and when I played, as elementary as my playing was, all earth plane cares disappeared, and I was transported into an altered state of spiritual bliss. I lived alone in a large two-bedroom apartment on Cathedral Parkway and was content to stay at home playing my piano throughout the Columbia riots of 1968 when five university buildings were taken over by nearly a thousand protesters, and the campus was on lockdown after its dean was taken hostage. I concentrated on making music and had no regrets about missing the violent skirmishes even though I lived blocks away.

During my first year at Barnard, I took Music 101 and became friends with Ken, my course professor. My love of music grew parallel to my frustration with psychology courses focused on experimental psychology and teaching tricks to rats in Skinner boxes. Conditioning rodents with rewards and punishments did not light my fires.

Transported by playing the piano, I got the crazy idea that I should become a music major. When I talked to Ken, he asked, "What does your heart want?"

The answer was clear. "I want to study music."

He signed the papers that allowed me entrance into the music department. Not knowing where I was heading, I radically shifted the direction of my life.

I see the irony in my decision to go to an Ivy League school and not study an academic subject. I might have seen it as a waste, but later in my life, I realized that my decision to sidestep a classical education permitted me to live outside the demands of the culture and my own sense of limitation. My most profound knowledge has come from my own experience and not from concepts I learned in books, and I trusted that I could follow my heart's desire and be taken where I needed to go.

As a music student who couldn't read music, I felt like an outsider, but I already saw myself as an outsider. As a motherless daughter, I felt shame and separateness from other women. By the time I got to college, I had moved five times and always felt like the new kid who didn't belong. So being a music student who couldn't read music was just another way of being outside looking in. And I learned that anything is possible, an experience that gave me the courage to take leaps in my later life.

Whatever the reason for that surprising turn in my education, I managed to graduate on the dean's list and then taught piano to kids for the next thirteen years. Despite my limited musical skills, I discovered that I knew how to teach.

I met Bernie when I was twenty-five working as a part-time secretary in his law firm. He was thirty years older than I. With a mop of salt-and-pepper curly hair, bushy eyebrows, and an irresistible twinkle in his eyes, he emanated wild energy reminiscent of Groucho Marx and Zorba the Greek. Filled with exhilaration, passion, and an insistence on doing things his own way, he danced through life. Still feeling the pain of my mother's death and my father's disappearance into his grief and his work with the United Church of Christ, I found Bernie's zest for life irresistible. I knew I had some growing to do twelve years after my mother's death and recognized Bernie as someone who could activate my deadened life force and nurture and heal my wounded child.

We met at the perfect time. Bernie was already thinking about leaving his marriage, and I was desperately looking for something to anchor me. Soon after we met, we moved in together and later married in a small ceremony officiated by my father. At first, we lived in my bare-bones fifth-floor walk-up railroad flat on West Fourth and West Eleventh Streets in Greenwich Village. A year later, we moved to his townhouse further south on Bedford Street where out of two apartments we created a duplex with two fireplaces, a spiral staircase connecting the two floors, and a deck looking out on a scrubby courtyard.

Life with Bernie was vibrant and adventurous. He taught me to folk dance, ice dance, and play tennis. We traveled around Europe, enjoyed a house by the beach in Southampton, Long Island, and hosted grand dinner parties, including black-tie New Year's Eve parties, Passover Seders, and folk dance parties with whole lambs roasted on a spit. I took on the role of the fresh, youthful companion and playmate while he took on the part of the adoring, supportive, mature man who presented me proudly to the world. It was a good match. I saw my world opening up in exciting ways.

Planting Seeds

The minute I heard my first love story, I started looking for you,
not knowing how blind that was. Lovers don't finally meet somewhere.
They're in each other all along.

—Rumi

In 1976, my father and his second wife, Elisabeth, founded the Shalom Mountain Retreat and Study Center in New York state. It was rooted in the early Christian house church, where small groups of Jesus's followers lived together, prayed together, and cared for each other.

The central purpose of the three-and-a-half-day Shalom Retreat was to provide attendees an opportunity to experience love as the great sustaining power of the Universe and practice love and healing within community. My father and Elisabeth offered retreats a couple of times a month in an old hotel they had converted into a retreat center. Fifteen people at a time gathered to sing, dance, eat, and share in the healing of childhood wounds.

A year later, my maternal grandmother turned ninety, and my father and Elisabeth invited a dozen relatives to celebrate her birthday at Shalom Mountain. Bernie and I drove from

New York City and took the narrow, winding road up the mountain to the dilapidated, mustard-colored, two-story building with its open porch. The first floor had a spacious living room, dining room, kitchen, and study. Above the kitchen, a windowed meditation room offered sweeping views of the surrounding countryside. A library connected a large meeting hall to the main house. Upstairs, ten bedrooms had plenty of room for all the relatives.

We had gathered to celebrate my grandmother, but we were all excited to catch up with each other, since our East Coast and West Coast families rarely got together. We spent an intense day filled with stories, feasting, and the delight of being together.

When night fell, everyone tucked into bed in the creaky old building, but it was still early, and I was wide awake. Bernie had already fallen asleep, so I quietly left the bed and wandered downstairs to see if anyone else was up. I saw a light in the living room and went to investigate.

I was surprised to see a handsome, bearded man with sparkling blue eyes sitting on the chintz couch. Dressed in jeans and a black tee-shirt, he had the cocky look of an outlaw taking up space in my father's living room as if he owned the place.

Puzzled, I perched on the arm of the couch to check him out.

"I'm Chris," he said with a deep, resonant voice and smile that brought color to my cheeks. "I'm one of Jerry's artisans. You know, the guys in the Shalom community who help Jerry fix things around here in gratitude for his healing work. I do carpentry, and some of the other guys do electrical work or plumbing. We help him keep the place going."

"Nice to meet you. I'm Carol, Jerry's daughter," I said, thinking it curious that Chris probably knew more about Shalom and its activities than I did, since I only came for family occasions and not retreats.

"What are you doing here?" I asked, thinking it odd that he had barged in on a private event.

"Jerry lets us guys hang out on the property whenever we want in return for our services. I had no idea there was a family gathering going on, so I just came."

His eyes were the bluest blue I'd ever seen, and they grabbed at my heart as he gazed at me.

I slipped down onto the couch next to him and felt a depth and gentleness that warmed my body and made me smile. My mind flashed on Bernie sleeping in the bedroom upstairs. I wasn't looking to bring more complexity into my life, but the man intrigued me, and I wanted to stay. *There's no harm in just sitting and talking,* I told myself.

We talked for an hour—or was it two? Time didn't seem to matter. We talked easily as we shared stories about our lives and dreams.

I wanted to stay but, finally, I said goodnight and went back to my sleeping husband.

All I remembered afterward was that the stranger's name was Chris and there was something about those blue eyes that I couldn't forget.

Finding My Work

It does not yet appear what we shall be. We are pregnant with mystery.

—Liza Gabriel
paraphrase of 1 John 3:2

After the weekend, Bernie and I returned to our lives in New York City, he to his law practice and I to teaching piano to children and adults in their homes. Although a competent teacher, I felt ready for something new, something more aligned with my natural gifts.

In 1980 when my sister Ginger was twenty-seven years old, she had a severe psychotic break and was diagnosed with bipolar disorder. Our family went into crisis as the bright fantasy of ourselves as the perfect family, happy and healthy, fell apart. I watched the ineffective treatment she received at Yale-New Haven Hospital, including family therapy focused more on blame than on healing, and decided I should study psychology. I hoped to understand how to help her heal, grandiosely thinking that I would do a better job than the professionals at Yale.

In 1983, I entered New York University and graduated two years later with a degree in social work. I began practicing therapy at a small counseling center in Dyker Heights, Brooklyn, a close-knit Italian neighborhood near the Verrazano-Narrows Bridge.

I hadn't loved school. I kept waiting for the studies to bring me to the real nitty-gritty of human behavior. I had found the curriculum dry and pedantic, but as soon as I started working with real clients, the myriad ways humans expressed themselves fascinated me. With developmental models I had learned, I had the freedom to find my own way of communicating with clients and helping them learn how to recognize and love parts of themselves, heal childhood wounds, and develop an internal observer who could bring balance into their lives.

It excited me to engage with my clients in the healing process, but I knew I needed to expand my skills beyond what I had learned in social work school. In 1985, I enrolled in the Institute of Core Energetics headed by John Pierrakos. John and Alexander Lowen had been students of Wilhelm Reich, a student of Sigmund Freud. Together, John and Alexander developed a healing system called bioenergetics, which helped people work with the mind and body to resolve emotional blockages and realize more joy in life.

I saw that John offered a four-year training designed to deepen understanding of the body-mind-spirit connection, and I signed up immediately. I enthusiastically began my studies at the institute's headquarters on Manhattan's Twenty-third Street and Park Avenue, where I also saw my private clients.

Two years into my studies, I decided the time had come for me to experience a Shalom Retreat. I hadn't been curious about my father's work at Shalom Mountain since he founded it, partly because I needed to separate from him and partly because I was busy finding my own life. Working as a therapist and student at the institute, however, I was ready to see what I could learn from my father. Not knowing what to expect, I signed up for a retreat as a participant.

I arrived at the Mountain with fourteen other people on a Thursday night. After dinner, we danced and then sat on cushions in a semicircle on the floor in the meeting hall we called the Shalom Room. My father explained that Shalom Retreats were based on the principle that we can all grow in our power of giving and receiving love. The weekend would teach retreatants the skills and principles of love and provide practice for putting those skills into action.

To help us get to know each other quickly and in profound ways, my father focused on community-building exercises throughout the first evening.

Sitting with partners, we answered intimate questions about our mothers, fathers, beliefs, hopes, and fears. After each question, we moved to a new partner, repeating the process until we had spoken with each person. In another exercise, we gazed into each person's eyes, sharing our energies and vulnerabilities. By the end of the evening, we had begun to form a trusting community.

In the morning, each person had the opportunity to tell their story in seven minutes as a way of further deepening our connections. We all felt as if we had known each other for a long time by Friday afternoon when we gathered for lunch.

After eating, we began the healing process we called mat trips, the heart of the work. The person on the mat lay down and stretched out blindfolded to begin their individual process while the rest of the group gathered around to support and witness the healing. My father, the facilitator, induced an altered state of consciousness through deep breathing designed to help the person move beyond thought and into the feelings of the body. In time, the breath often dissolved into something like a primal scream, which then initiated an altered state.

I watched as each person took their turn on the mat, facing their fears, and gradually letting go into the healing of childhood wounds that had prevented them from loving themselves and others. All the primal emotions emerged. Anger, grief, revenge, and despair arose, sometimes with violence and sometimes passivity. Each person allowed themselves to be seen nakedly in their vulnerability and ultimately in their power as they could finally let go of the past and see a new way to move forward.

I was both afraid and intrigued by what I would experience.

When it was my turn, I took my place on the mat. My father and I both knew it was delicate territory for father and daughter to explore together. Rarely do family members do healing work directly without the mediation of a therapist. We looked at each other, took a deep breath, trusting we would find our way in love and honesty with the community's support, and surrendered.

As my breathing deepened, a scream came from the depths of my belly. I was taken over by a powerful force. I didn't feel that I was screaming but that I was being screamed. As I quieted, I was taken back to a time when I was a toddler whose mother had left her to give birth to a new baby. The feelings of anger arose and then dissolved into buried feelings about my mother's death and the days that followed.

As I moved more intensely into the experience, I realized how terrified and careful I had been in my past relationships. I saw how my mother mourned the death of her newborn son in lonely solitude and how grief had broken my father after my mother's death. I realized that I believed that loving meant I would have to die for that loving and, to keep myself safe, I had chosen to close my heart. Having experienced the reality of love and the actuality of death and grief, I was terrified of true intimacy. I resolved to protect myself by not surrendering into love.

Bernie had been a good daddy to me. When we first got together, I was twenty-five years old, but inside I was still a broken thirteen-year-old who needed a parent. Bernie was the same age as my father, and he had nurtured me, taught me, and proudly presented me to the world. He shined his light on me, and I flourished.

By the end of the retreat, I realized I no longer needed the care of a daddy to keep me safe. In the fifteen years Bernie and I had been together, I had grown from a wounded child into a woman. I felt ready to find my own way in life. I left the retreat feeling like I had been reborn.

A week later, Bernie and I drove back from Canada after a four-day folk dance festival. We'd had a glorious weekend. Bernie had always been a big flirt, but that weekend, I realized I could flirt, too. I danced wildly and paid less attention to Bernie than usual. He hadn't mentioned my behavior during the weekend, but as we drove back in the privacy of our car, he said he felt that something was off about me. He said I was different.

"What's going on?" he asked.

The words slipped out without any thought. "We've grown apart. Something isn't working, and I'm longing for more."

I could hardly believe I spoke those words and was even more shocked at how quickly Bernie responded.

"Well, if you want a divorce, I am a lawyer, and I can get that taken care of in three weeks."

I had heard those words before. All through our marriage, whenever I had some childish temper tantrum or even a more mature difference of opinion with Bernie, he responded, "If you don't like it, then you can leave."

Hearing that always terrified me. I had no money of my own and couldn't imagine being away from Bernie and all alone. Before, I always gave in and made peace so we could go on without conflict. But that story was over. I was no longer the young woman who looked to Bernie for the parenting I missed when my mother drowned. I had a voice, although I didn't know where that voice might take me.

It all happened so fast. One minute we were driving along the highway discussing my standoffish behavior at the dance workshop, and the next, we were making plans to end our marriage. Before my recent Shalom Retreat, I hadn't been conscious of being unhappy in our relationship, let alone that I would be ready to leave. As we talked, I felt clarity for the first time. Before I could offer myself as a true partner, I needed to stand on my own two feet and get to know myself.

I was grateful for the years I had shared with Bernie, thankful he had put me through social work school and that he had lovingly supported me for fifteen years. But that chapter was over. I needed to trust that I would be okay on my own.

After five hours of talking while our car sped back to New York City, we came up with a plan. We agreed that I would move into the second-floor studio apartment in our Greenwich Village townhouse that I had planned to use as my psychotherapy office. I moved out of Bernie's bed the next night.

Manic in my excitement about being on my own after fifteen years of marriage, I painted the walls pink and called the space My Pink Womb. I felt pregnant and ready to give birth to myself. I was leaving behind an old part of myself and had no idea who I would become. I was relieved when Bernie found an even younger woman within two weeks to ease his grief. I was truly free.

I stayed in My Pink Womb for exactly nine months. With the help of my generous Uncle Gene, my father's brother, I put a deposit on a co-op studio apartment on Sixth Avenue and

Twelfth Street in Greenwich Village. Owning my own home and making sufficient money from my therapy practice to pay my bills, I finally started to feel like a grown-up.

The apartment was perfect for me. The open L-shaped space allowed room for my seven-foot Steinway grand, and a bookshelf room divider created a private space for my bed, which rested on the floor on one side with a living room and study area on the other. I needed only a small, efficiency kitchen, since I lived alone and ate out most of the time. The windows looked out on Sixth Avenue, which meant activity and noise at all hours. Soon I got used to the commotion and learned to fall asleep to the raucous sounds of traffic and pedestrians. I loved living in New York City with its museums, concerts, dances, restaurants, and electric energy. I had everything that I needed.

I found being on my own for the first time thrilling. It offered exciting new horizons. My private therapy practice boomed, and I loved the work and my clients.

In September of 1987, I founded the Institute of Process Therapy comprising an eight-month course for healers. I had never thought about teaching, but one day I got a phone call from a woman named Casey, whom I had never met. She dove right in. "I hear you teach."

Not knowing what she was talking about, I said, "I do?"

"Yes," she said. "Your father said that you teach about the process they use at Shalom Mountain."

Only two years out of social work school and having led only several Shalom Retreats, I hadn't had much experience, but I was curious and ready for an adventure, so I answered, "Yes, you are right. I teach, and I am getting a class ready now. If you are interested, why don't you come and bring a few friends and we can talk about what you are looking for and what I might be able to offer?"

I am not sure what gave me the nerve to take such a leap of faith, but I suspect that my experience of being a music major who couldn't read music gave me the idea, right or wrong, that I could follow my dreams whether or not I had the correct qualifications.

Casey came the next week and brought four friends with her. I asked them to tell me what they sought in training, and I took copious notes. When they left, I sat at my word processor and wrote Curriculum at the top of the document. Then I carefully fashioned all their suggestions into a coherent course of study and sent it out to the five women. They were pleasantly surprised at the coincidence that I taught exactly what they wanted to learn.

And so, the Institute for Process Therapy was born.

The eight-month program included seven weekend meetings and a three-and-a-half-day intensive in January. I offered deep ritual, healing practices, the study of bioenergetics, and exercises in the skills and principles of loving.

Ironically, the room on Twenty-third Street that I rented from John Pierrakos for my Process Training class was the same room where I studied as a third year student in his Core Energetic Training. On Friday nights and Saturdays, I participated as a not particularly brilliant student. On Sundays, when I taught, it seemed that Spirit spoke through me and led my students and me to the places we needed to go.

My first class included nine women. One woman had twenty-five years of experience. Another was a PhD candidate in psychology. Several others were practicing therapists. I had far less experience than my students, but I was the one who had the nerve to put myself out and lead. As a leader, however, I was as eager to learn from my students as they were to learn from me.

Another opportunity opened when Walter Beveridge, a Shalom community member, asked me to co-lead a retreat with him. His offer surprised me, since my only previous experience involved attending three of my father's retreats. I was terrified by my lack of preparation, but for some reason, I agreed, feeling that I already knew what I needed to know. Was the knowing genetic, or was it the wild energy that led me to study music at Columbia University when I had limited musical skills? Whichever, I said yes to Walter. After a successful weekend, I found that I loved the excitement and intimacy of facilitating healing work and looked forward to more.

Soon after, I got a call from Be Hudson, who lived at Shalom Mountain. She said that many women at Shalom Mountain wanted to share healing energies only with other women. As a man, my father could not provide such a space. None of the other women living at Shalom Mountain were trained in psychology, so even though I lacked experience, I seemed to be the best choice. With eagerness and more than a bit of trepidation, I began leading Shalom Retreats for women in October of 1987.

My father expected me to bring my own people to fill the retreats while I paid rent for the room and board he provided. Although I led the sessions with his encouragement, I felt independent as I led women only, which he couldn't do. Not being in direct competition with him took a lot of pressure off. I started leading retreats every couple of months and gradually developed a following of my own.

One of the unexpected consequences of leading Shalom Retreats was that, since I shared the Shalom community with my father, I felt awkward talking about *Dad* when clients needed to talk about issues with him. I realized that the days of calling him Dad were over and chose to call him Jerry in both professional and familial situations.

In addition to retreats and trainings, I threw myself into weekly folk dances thanks to Bernie's introduction and added swing dancing to my repertoire. My spiritual life grew as I studied Hinduism, Buddhism, and Sufism and brought the teachings and rituals into my therapy practice with clients.

Finally, my life was my own, and it was good.

Meeting My Mother

Ancient Mother, I hear you calling. Ancient Mother, I hear your sounds.
Ancient Mother, I hear your laughter. Ancient Mother, I taste your tears.
—traditional chant

In 1991, a friend asked me to lead a group of people from Shalom Mountain on a rafting trip through the Grand Canyon. I agreed, and fifteen people joined me along with Terry, my boyfriend of the moment. Tall, athletic, and boyishly handsome, Terry had short brown hair, intense dark eyes, and a rakish goatee and mustache. Right from the start, he told me he was bisexual, but I was entranced by his charismatic energy, and in my innocent infatuation, I did not consider his admission important. Ignoring the warning, I moved ahead without hesitation into yet another impossible romance. Our relationship had been rocky from the start, but I hoped the river adventure would smooth over the rough edges.

Several days into our journey on the Colorado River, my worst fears came to pass. Before the trip, I had drawn a tarot card from the ancient divinatory system I consulted when I wanted to peek into the energies of the future. Drawing the Hermit card made me uneasy. A solitary figure, the Hermit carries his own light and looks within. It was not the card of happy romantic energy I wished for, and it concerned me. A mile into the canyon's depths, Terry called me over to talk."I just can't do it," he said, turning away from my questioning eyes.

"What do you mean?" I asked, knowing perfectly well that he was finally giving up on our relationship.

"It's not working. I can't be with you. I've tried, but I can't. It's over."

What could I say? I knew he'd made up his mind, yet I loved Terry and didn't want to lose him.

"What's the point of arguing?" I asked myself. I longed for a man to want me, and Terry only wanted me to go away. What was there to talk about? I said nothing, but my quiet belied the storms that were going on inside of me. I felt shattered, lost, and embarrassed to be sharing my intimate drama under the eyes of the people I was leading on the trip, but Terry had left me no choice.

Somehow, I made it through the evening's activity, an improvised drum circle where we rowdily beat with hands, rocks, and sticks on pots, pans, and boat cushions. We danced wildly at the river's edge to our impromptu music-making as the sun began its disappearance beyond the rim of the canyon. I could feel my energy returning for a short time, but when my women friends invited me to join them to hang out and talk, I declined, as I knew I had to be alone to process the dark feelings swirling around in me.

I wanted to find a spot I had seen earlier in the day—a sandy beach facing a sparkling waterfall across the river where the sun had put on a breathtaking light show as it danced with the water. It was the most stunning of the many beautiful places I had seen on the trip, and it called me back.

As dark took over, I set off to find the place. I had easily found the beach during the day. In the dark and moonless night, tripping on underbrush, I got lost and had to find my way out of one dead end after another. I knew the danger of walking alone next to the river where I could be hurt and no one would know, but I trusted I would be safe and protected. There was so little light that I couldn't see the falls, but I could hear their music and the roar of the river. Just when I was about to give up, I found my spot.

I didn't know what I had come to do. In the chilly night air, I shivered in a light breeze. I quieted myself and listened. A voice emerged from the darkness and told me to bury myself in the mud. Not knowing what else to do, I began my ritual by sitting at water's edge and digging my feet deep into the soft sediment. Handful by handful, I covered my feet, legs, and belly with mud until I was completely buried up to my waist. Immersed in the oozy mire, I became an organic part of the river.

I began to pray to the Great Mother, "Goddess, teach me to love, give and receive, so I may celebrate you and be an instrument of your work in the world." Over and over, I repeated my prayer until I began singing a song I had learned at Shalom.

> *Ancient Mother, I hear you calling.*
> *Ancient Mother, I hear your sounds.*
> *Ancient Mother, I hear your laughter.*
> *Ancient Mother, I taste your tears.*

Above the sound of my voice mingling with the river, I heard another vibration and felt a familiar and compelling presence. Across the water, I saw a glowing form emerging from the darkness of that moonless night. I knew immediately it was my mother, and she called to me. "Carol, my beloved daughter, Carol, I am here. I live in this canyon. It is my home. I'm happy here. You can visit me here, and you no longer have to worry about me."

Her energy, bright and animated, permitted no doubt that she was in my presence. In the thirty years since she had died, I hadn't heard her voice nor felt her, but there she was with me, speaking tenderly and comforting me. I felt her arms wrap around me. I felt as if she washed me clean of all the pain of the past.

My body relaxed into the mud as my tears fell in a mixture of joy and grief.

Gradually, the vision drifted away, and I returned to singing and praying as I took in the significance of that welcome visitation.

Then I heard her again. Her voice rose up high above the roar of the river, saying, "Carol, you are free to live. All is well."

I didn't know I had been waiting to hear that blessing, but even in my sadness at losing Terry, I knew that my feelings of abandonment from so long ago had begun to heal.

I stayed awake all night listening to the teachings of the river. Before my time on the Colorado River, I had visualized that going with the flow means following a gently gliding stream. While living on the river for six days, I experienced it as an ever changing entity, never the same, rapidly moving among extremes. Sometimes it was harsh, sometimes gentle. Sometimes it hurt, sometimes it soothed. Sometimes the river flowed with tears or with love or even anger. It was never the same.

The river taught me that going with the flow doesn't guarantee gentle experience. Going with the flow requires presence and gratitude for whatever is, without judgment or control. Before the trip, I was a journeyer traveling by land with a compass and map. After the trip, I was called to learn to float, trusting that the currents would take me where I must go.

Soul Mates

You were born together, and together you shall be forevermore.

—Kahlil Gibran

A month after my trip to the Grand Canyon, I went to
Shalom Mountain for a Labor Day work weekend. People
gather at Shalom for work weekends in gratitude, freely
offering their services to fix up the retreat grounds. I arrived
ready to work and enjoy the good energy of the community.

Still lost and brokenhearted from the breakup with Terry,
I sank even lower when I first saw him. He looked radiant
dressed in white pants and a flowing, white shirt embroidered
with flowers. Surrounded by an admiring group of people,
he shined like the sun, and his beauty and happiness made
me even more miserable. To assuage my grief and jealousy, I
desperately wanted to find another focus for my attention.

Then I saw Chris. It had been fourteen years since we first
met, and we had only met one other time at a Shalom celebration. As soon as I saw him, I felt my spirits lift. His energy
warmed me as we chatted, and I fell into his beautiful blue eyes.
Our light conversation started to feel more intimate, and I began
to think I had found something to take my mind off my grief.

We talked, and the energy built. People passed by, but it seemed that a bubble had grown around us that held only the two of us. My body warmed to him as he asked, "So, do you think that you would like to hang out with me? I have a private room upstairs and I would love to have you meet me there tonight."

It was quite a brazen offer since we had hardly spent any time together, but I was hungry for connection and excited to think of the sweetness of lying naked next to Chris's body.

I heard myself saying, "Yes, but please, we have to be just a little discreet. I have clients here, and I'm not ready to share my private life with the community."

Chris agreed, and we planned to meet in the same living room where we had first met fourteen years before but with a big difference. I would no longer be meeting Chris alone in a dark room but in a room crowded with my Shalom friends.

Enjoying the buzz of the conversation after dinner, I relaxed on the couch waiting for Chris. I was startled when he walked in and loudly announced, "I've come to take you to my room."

I had hoped for discretion, but obviously that didn't fit Chris's plan. Hoping no one had heard, I got up quietly and followed him up the stairs. I knew I would have some explaining to do with my clients who shouldn't have been privy to that intimate moment, but that would have to wait.

I sat down next to Chris on the bed and wondered where the energy would take us. For a moment Chris was quiet. Then he said, "I have to tell you something."

"Oh, really? What could that be?"

"Well, after we made our date this morning, I met Susan, and I fell in love."

"You what? Who is Susan? And why am I here and not her?"

"I had made a promise to you, and I didn't want to leave you bereft," he said unconvincingly.

How could this be happening? I had hoped for an adventure that would get my mind off losing Terry, but here was yet another loss. I wanted to run, but I had nowhere to go. I had no idea how to extricate myself from the bizarre situation. I couldn't find the wherewithal to leave, but I barely had the heart to stay. So we slept chastely together fully dressed, each on our own side of the bed while my mind went crazy with confusion.

All night, I felt the tantalizing energy between us. Chris was so beautiful with his firm, muscular body, broad shoulders, and toothy smile. I longed to get close to him and find out who the fascinating stranger was, but that no longer seemed possible. I thought everything had lined up perfectly for at least a titillating escapade, but it had turned into nothing.

Even though our romance didn't blossom in the year he dated Susan, Chris and I stayed in touch through the next several years in a sweet friendship. We developed a comfortable, mutual relationship with no agenda. I was happy to have a good friend and never had any romantic inclinations. I did allow myself to fantasize that someday I might meet a man like Chris.

I went on to other relationships. Many. I chose men in good part by the extent to which they needed my healing ministrations. I began each relationship fully aware of my partner's challenges—childhood wounding, addictions, depression, anxiety. I could see it all in the first moment of meeting.

Then in an instant, I blindly fell into a state of amnesia, discounting all the energies that eventually blew up the romance. Relationships lasted between six months and a year and a half. For another six months to a year and a half after the breakup, I grieved the loss, feeling abandoned not just by my lover but by the whole universe, as I had when my mother died. With each ending, I mourned not just the current loss but all my previous losses. When my sorrow subsided, I began again with yet another wounded man.

In September 1993, I suffered through another painful breakup. I was relieved to be invited to a Saturday night party celebrating the birthday of my friend and student Cynthia in New Haven. It gave me something to look forward to while giving me an excuse to visit Chris on the same trip.

I arrived at his home late at night after the party and met his dog Dandy and his eight-foot boa constrictor, Tiamat, housed in a large glass aquarium. Chris's home was spare, very much the dwelling of a bachelor. We sat on his lumpy couch and talked a little, moving closer and closer until we began tentatively exploring each other's bodies.

His touch on my hungry body felt electric, and soon we ended up in bed together. A strange and new energy emerged in the middle of our lovemaking, something I had never experienced with a man. I felt penetrated by the love of a mother but not the love of a mother for her child. Instead, I experienced the Great Mother's ecstatic love for the entire Universe.

Strange, unfamiliar energy flooded me with love so overpowering it blew me out of my body. Embarrassed to have such seemingly unexpected reactions during the heat of passion, I became confused and frightened not knowing who or what Chris was or what I was experiencing. Should I feel that way with a man? Why did I feel that at all? I wasn't used to anything like it and didn't know what to make of it.

I said nothing at the time, and it soon became a fleeting memory as we moved onto more familiar ground, and we relaxed into intimately sharing our bodies all night.

In the morning, I awoke surprised to find myself in Chris's bed. The night had felt like a sweet and exotic dream, but it didn't seem to have anything to do with the life I led.

On Monday, after I had returned to my apartment in Greenwich Village, Chris called and, in a most gentlemanly voice, asked, "When can I see you again?"

I heard myself answer, "Never."

"Can we talk about this?"

"No," I said with anger that came from a place in me I didn't understand.

Almost pleading for me to change my mind, Chris tried to reason with me.

I deflected his appeals as I did my best to smooth over the dark energy that had risen in me. He finally gave up, and when we said an awkward goodbye, I watched myself erase the sweetness of the time I had shared in his bed as I found firm ground in more secure territory. My heart was my own. The night we shared had just been a casual meeting—nothing that would weaken my autonomy. I had nothing to fear.

Six months later after no contact, Chris called again. Despite my previous resistance, I was happy to hear his voice. We made light chatter, and all was well until he asked casually, "So, are you seeing anyone?"

I felt that disembodied anger come up again. I didn't understand the intensity of my feelings. I responded truthfully, "Yes, I am."

Chris asked tenderly, "But do you love him?"

My rage exploded as heat rose from my belly up to my face. What right did Chris have to ask me who I loved?

"That's none of your business, and we are not going to talk about it," I shrieked, surprised at the force of my energy. Confused at the anger that had risen unbidden in me I took a breath and tentatively tried to move the conversation into safer, less personal territory before saying goodbye.

Meanwhile, my relationship with Arne, the new man in my life, had gotten stormier. He was an excellent dance partner, and the sexual energy between us was powerful and satisfying. We didn't live together, but when we were together, we screamed frantically at each other all day long with unsuccessful pleas to be heard and understood. I often felt one or both of us on the verge of psychosis.

I watched myself become a person I didn't recognize. The sexual energy continued to draw me in, but the insanity of our anger made me wonder what I was doing. Feeling stuck, I called for an appointment with my trusted Jungian astrologer, Bob Cook.

I took the train out to Long Island to hear what he had to say about my fate in the second half of 1995. I explained my involvement in a dark and challenging relationship and asked if I had more to learn if I stayed.

Talking a mile a minute, he said, "Of course, there is always more to learn about the underworld, but there is an alternative coming through. Uranus is moving into a once-in-a-lifetime conjunct with Venus, and it will shake things up, possibly preparing you for something remarkable down the road.

"This Uranian experience could be the love of your life," he continued, "perhaps not forever and perhaps mixed in with death, since love and death are so inextricably bound. But still, this could be the love of your life. With Uranus and Neptune soon coming into your chart, this energy could bring a partner who would be fun, easy, and harmonious."

Fun? Easy? I couldn't believe it. I didn't know those menu items in relationships existed. I thought of relationships as schools that teach the harsh lessons of life. All the relationships I'd known had been hard work.

Bob assured me that the choice was up to me. "You can continue to wander in the realms of darkness, or you can frolic in the light. Your choice."

I didn't trust Bob's new story about the possibility of a relationship that embodied grace and ease. Still, the raging conflicts with Arne became so uncomfortable that I knew I couldn't continue even though I understood from childhood and my father that my safety and survival depended on keeping the man secure and healthy, not me.

I was dying emotionally in my relationship with Arne, and I reached the point where I knew—though terrified to leave—that I couldn't stay. I had to choose. Could I turn my back on the man and trust myself to survive on my own, or did I need to keep him happy so he could care for me?

Within days after my reading with Bob Cook and after yet one more intense screaming match with Arne, I announced that I was done, and I walked away. I felt alone and sad, but I no longer felt crazy.

The breakup with Arne seemed different from other relationship endings. I felt as if I had awakened from a trance and recognized that I needed to end my childhood strategy of attempting to heal my father and keep him safe so that I, a motherless child, would be safe. With Arne, I understood that not only was it not necessary to keep the man in my life happy and healed, but it was also impossible.

I had always thought the men I chose were too immature and wounded to commit to a relationship with me. When I decided to leave Arne, I realized I had chosen such men because I was not ready to commit. I felt paralyzed, fearing that I might be broken like my father after my mother's death, and I kept my heart closed.

For all the hardship Arne had brought into my life, I appreciated his helping me end my childhood contract with my father.

The strategy supported me as a child but prevented me from finding deep and mutual love as an adult. I didn't know how my life would unfold, but I knew I had been given an invaluable although painful gift.

By November, the grief of the breakup had begun to dissipate, and my solo life filled with the pleasure of close friends, my work as a therapist and retreat leader, contra and folk dancing, theater, and movies. I didn't need a man. I would remain single for the rest of my life, and all would be well.

Every year I hosted a tree-trimming party to celebrate my birthday, two days before Christmas. Usually, it was a big affair with fifty or more people packed into my tiny apartment. But that year, I wanted something more intimate with only people I loved dearly who were close to my heart—my most inner circle. I chose a dozen and a half of my dancer friends, work friends, and friends from my past.

And then there was Chris. I addressed all the invitations, but before I took them down to the mailbox, I removed the card addressed to Chris for a reason I didn't understand. The lonely envelope sat on my desk for days until one night, moving so quickly that I couldn't think, I took the elevator down to the street level and dropped it in the mailbox. I had butterflies in my stomach and a strange sense of foreboding. What was I afraid of? We were just friends. But something told me that inviting him was a momentous decision that could change my life in unforeseen ways.

A few days later while conducting a therapy session in my apartment, I heard the phone ring in the background but didn't listen to the message until I finished with my client. It was Chris calling. He sounded thrilled to have been invited and said that he looked forward to catching up.

I listened to the message, but in a move that made no rational sense, I didn't call him back. I had invited him and wanted him to come but was nervous about calling him. What danger was afoot? I did my best to forget the whole thing.

On the morning of the party, he called.

"So, do you want me to come? I never heard back from you, and it's a two-hour drive I don't want to make if it doesn't matter to you."

"Oh, of course, I want to see you. Please come. I really want you here. I'm so sorry I didn't get back to you." The words sounded shallow, but I really did want to see him.

He started to relax and said, "Okay, I'll see you later."

"Great! But maybe we should talk now because I will be busy at the party, and I might not have time then." I knew it sounded unwelcoming, but I was stuck between wanting him to come and feeling anxious. We were good friends. Why should this evening change anything? We talked a little longer and said goodbye.

Chris showed up at the party carrying a small frog made of green cloth, a symbol of transformation, and with great fanfare, presented it to me. I didn't know why he had chosen that gift, but I thanked him anyway and put it with other gifts under the tree.

As I had suspected, I was busy being the hostess and didn't have much time to spend with him. I saw him flirting with my best friend, Faye, and didn't have any conscious judgment about it, although she seemed a bit uncomfortable. Chris was my friend, that was all, and I was not even looking for a man in my life. Why should I care?

The lively group dove into the mountain of food, numerous dips, cheeses, and appetizers I had prepared. Everyone drank my luxurious eggnog while we decorated the tree with an abundance of shiny ornaments. My friends had brought presents and urged me to open them up in front of everyone.

I sat down on the floor in front of the tree while people gathered around me. I watched Chris look around for a place to sit. Then he walked around behind me, careful not to jostle the ornaments on the tree. He cautiously seated himself and gently wrapped his arms and legs around my body. I felt his chest warm against my back as I looked out at my guests. Something about his touch felt familiar even though we had had only one previous night of lovemaking. His intimate gesture in such a public gathering surprised me but also delighted me with pleasant curiosity.

I opened the presents, many of them beautiful new ornaments for my tree. With the gift opening ritual complete and the party in full swing again, people asked me, "Who is that man?" No one had seen or heard of him before, yet he appeared to be taking a prominent place in my life.

I said, "That's Chris." I didn't know what else to say.

My guests left well after midnight—everyone except Chris, who helped me clean up before we fell into bed.

That night of lovemaking differed so much from the first. Chris no longer felt like an exciting stranger. I sensed that I had returned home. My body and Chris's came together as if everything that happened before had led to that moment of union. I felt right and good wrapped in his arms. As I rode the energy of ecstasy, sweet calm, curiosity, and readiness, I knew. The fight had ended. My heart had opened.

Chris returned to his home for the Christmas holidays to be with his kids, Josh and Hope, who were ten and twelve years old. We decided that he would bring the kids and meet me at Shalom Mountain to spend New Year's. More than fifty people would gather for the annual weekend event.

Since my clients and students gathered in considerable numbers at Shalom, I told Chris I might not be able to spend all my time with him. He agreed and passed an important test, as I had great fears about losing myself in a man's needs. Chris seemed perfectly capable of taking care of himself. We passed the weekend gently with friends, good food, dancing, and the pleasure of sharing a bed together. Hope and Josh found activities and sleeping arrangements especially for kids. We all welcomed the New Year with joyous blessings and hugs.

As our time at Shalom ended, I asked Chris if he would take me to Monticello to the bus to New York City. Instead, he offered to take me to his home in New Haven, where I could catch the train back to the city in the morning. The little resistance I still had to loving him fully started to fade, and I sensed that if I took him up on his offer, I would be committing to a relationship beyond my imagination. I accepted his offer of a ride to New Haven, and the die was cast.

In the next nine months, our relationship moved on a fast track. After so many years of casual friendship, it felt as if we had always been together. We delighted not just in our shared bed but in the everyday tasks of living. Life felt effortless and fun, just as my astrologer had promised.

By February, I had moved enough of my belongings to Chris's home that I effectively lived in New Haven and not in my Greenwich Village co-op. With Chris came the responsibility of two young children for whom I held pseudo-parental responsibilities. Having been a stepchild myself, I knew that the last thing a kid needed was another mother. I decided instead to be a benign adult presence, which seemed to keep the kids' hostility and resistance at bay. It also helped that I had extra money to contribute to the household along with a nifty new computer and some pretty good cooking skills.

Our lives changed on a Wednesday night in April of 1996. I had just dished up plates of spaghetti for dinner for the two of us and noticed that Chris seemed unusually quiet as we started to eat. Suddenly, he slid off his chair and onto his knees in front of me. Looking into my eyes, he said, "Will you marry me? I want you to be my wife and love you forever."

I had longed for such a traditional moment, and with its arrival I grew dizzy with excitement. Tears filled my eyes. "Of course, of course I'll marry you," I said as I felt Chris's arms wrap around me, "but I feel like we are already as married as two people can be. Let's make it a grand celebration for our friends. This is going to be a party to remember."

I came down into his arms on the floor that April evening, and as we felt the heat rising between us, we melted into happiness that seemed to light up the whole room. That was the end of any thoughts of food. We returned to the table, pulled out a large writing pad, and started dreaming of a full-on autumn wedding. The dream unfolded into a plan that would include 230 guests, a formal church ceremony, a white wedding gown and veil, a seven-member wedding party, and a potluck dinner for guests topped off with a honeymoon in Paris. It didn't all come together on that first night, but we soon realized that our wedding would be an extravaganza. It happened so quickly that when Chris told his daughter Hope that he planned to get married, her first response was, "To who?"

The time between April and September was short. We had little time for preparation since I commuted twice a week from New Haven to New York to continue my psychother-apy practice and continued leading retreats and trainings. In August, overwhelmed with details of planning a formal wedding, I walked into a bridal shop. Dazzled at the sea of white gowns surrounding the room, I told the salesperson about the wedding ceremony only one month away.

She laughed and thought I was joking.

I felt like a failure at the wedding business. I didn't even know what style of dress I wanted to wear. Fortunately, she put her judgments aside as she showed me one dress after another only to create more confusion in my mind. Then I saw it, a long white gown with a lace bodice and V-neck, long sleeves, tiny pearl buttons, and a long train tucked up into a neat bustle under a bow at the waist. Suitable for royalty. I knew it was perfect.

The wedding day arrived on Saturday, September 28, 1996. The ceremony took place in Yale University's Battell Chapel, a grand architectural structure expressing the Victorian revival of medieval and Gothic styles. High, richly colored stained glass windows created a soft light in the large sanctuary seating 850 people.

The chancel behind two facing choir lofts held a sizeable open area where Chris placed sixty of the pottery cups and phallic wooden turnings he had created. He called his ritual works of art earth grails and dedicated them to Mother Earth. Another of Chris's artistic offerings was a leaded glass mirror supporting a wooden butterfly that appeared to be in flight. Set flat on a table in front of the earth grails, the mirror, symbolizing our willingness to look inside of ourselves and each other, served as our altar. The butterfly was a sign of rebirth and transformation.

In that glorious space, 230 beloveds from Chris's life, my life, and our shared life at Shalom Mountain gathered to celebrate our marriage. Our officiants were the pastor of Battell, a black man, and the assistant pastor, a white woman, who together represented the diversity we desired in our lives.

As organ music rang out in the church's vestibule, I stood alone, dressed in my long white gown with the bustle and endless buttons up and down my sleeves and back. The veil covering my face softly blurred my view and hid myriad feelings welling up in me.

I had the requisite something old, something new, something borrowed, and something blue—the new, a silver bracelet; the borrowed, a lovely pearl necklace from my friend Deborah; and the blue, a garter pinned under my dress. The old token was my mother's wedding ring pinned into the folds of my gown. I had missed her presence at other pivotal events in my life, but she had been gone thirty-five years, and I hardly remembered her. Still, I felt that a mother should be at a daughter's wedding, and I felt my longing for her at that life-changing moment.

As I awaited the resonant chords of the bridal march, I heard out of nowhere, a ringing voice in my ears. I didn't know the source of the voice, but its words penetrated my heart. I saw Chris standing at the altar, his eyes scanning the church to take in the 230 beloveds gathered to celebrate our union, but the voice pulled my attention away from Chris into the depths of my heart.

"You know," the voice said as a pregnant pause fell and I strained to listen. *"You know, you will be separated."*

I felt the words like a punch in my belly. I took a breath and swallowed hard. More to myself than to the voice, I answered, "Yes, I know we will be separated. I know that is true, yet I will say yes, yes to Chris, with all my heart."

Tears filled my eyes as I began my procession down the aisle to the altar to join with my beloved.

Rituals filled our wedding. Chris and I asked the women and men for their love and support. We addressed Chris's two children, Josh and Hope, then eleven and thirteen, and asked for their blessings. Josh played a "Vivace for Flute" by Jean Baptiste Loeillet. Hope sang the song "The Rose," and there wasn't a dry eye in the church.

After a candle lighting ceremony, we declared our intentions. I looked into Chris's eyes and said, "The poet Rumi wrote, 'The minute I heard my first love story, I started looking for you, not knowing how blind I was. Lovers don't finally meet somewhere. They are in each other all along.'

"Chris, I have known you for eighteen years. I have been your friend watching you live your life while I lived mine. A dim awareness in me knew I wasn't ready to be with you then. I still had to grow myself, stretch, explore, and live a life entirely mine. But when we met again in December, I knew I was ready, ready to come home, stop running, and commit to my soul's longing.

"I offer you all I am, all that I can and will be. I want to walk beside you for the rest of my days, growing, learning, and living together."

Chris responded in his deep, rich voice. "Dear Carol, when first we met, we were strangers living full lives, knowing that life held up variety and richness, challenge and risk, scarcity and fullness, aloneness and friendship. We didn't know then that these were things that we would now be sharing deeply with one another.

"I have loved others, borne children dear to my life, but now it is time for me to dream, build my sacred places, and dance my dance with you as my partner, my lover, and my soul mate."

We both looked into the future and asked that we would dare to dream dreams not yet imagined. We vowed to work through challenges and find rewards as we pursued the ongoing adventure of learning who we were and who we would become. We vowed to remember our unique sense of our mission in life together and the endless possibilities of exploring our shared existence. We offered ourselves without reservation to each other.

So started a grand adventure, a love story with no beginning and no end.

New Life

"You will change," says the stars to the sun, says the night to the stars.
—Kathleen Jessie Raine

Settling into my new life in New Haven with Chris marked a significant transition for me. Suddenly I—an unattached, urban woman—faced responsibilities for two children, a dog, a house, a husband, and, on occasion, a mother-in-law more than a little ambivalent about me. I hardly had time to remember my past life.

Each day presented numerous demands and little time for thought. As I made frequent runs in my Volvo station wagon to the grocery store, I wondered how I had ended up in the alien world of suburbia, so different from my life in New York City. Gradually, I got used to driving my car rather than riding the subway and to living in a large suburban house rather than my tiny New York City apartment. As I embraced my roles as wife and mother, I had to let go of the freedom I had enjoyed in my previous ways of living.

Our love for each other blossomed. Chris was the first lover I had who shared a similar family history. Most of my partners in the past had come from vastly different backgrounds, religions, and interests. I had been with an older woman when I was in college, several Jewish guys, one black man, a drummer, a chicken farmer, and a writer, to enumerate a few. Judy taught me about the pleasures of my woman's body. Bernie helped me grow up. Mark inspired me to write poetry and essays, Barry taught me the joys of farm living and MDMA (methylenedioxy methamphetamine, commonly known as ecstasy), Al helped me become an accomplished swing dancer, and Terry taught me how to be with children. Each relationship brought gifts as well as challenges. I valued the rewards despite the often high emotional price.

I couldn't believe that life with Chris could be so easy. We knew the same songs and prayers, our family traditions were familiar, and our dreams were similar. We both came from church-going families and were on a spiritual path focused on love, healing, and connection to the universe's creative, intelligent source energy. We saw ourselves as soul mates destined to live in love and share that love with the world.

Beyond our day jobs, we focused on Hope and Josh, who lived with us every other week. We collaborated well, and family life became an added gift in my relationship with my beloved. A bonus was that when I moved in, Hope was thirteen, the same age I was when I lost my mother. I relished watching her experience the teenage life I had missed. And then there was Alia.

Alia, a purebred Akita, was already part of Chris's family when we got married. She had been raised in a pet shop and was still unclaimed at six months old. One Saturday morning, Chris took Hope and Josh to the pet store to buy hamster food. He was drawn to a cage where a puppy gazed out longingly. The sign on the cage read, "Reduced $500."

"Reduced five hundred dollars? What could that possibly leave?" Chris asked in amazement.

"Three hundred dollars," the clerk said. "There might be a better deal in the future, since the puppy is getting too old to stay here. Give me your contact information, and I'll let you know if anything changes."

At the time, Chris's finances on his teacher's salary were less than stable. He had just bought a Harley-Davidson motorcycle at a moment when paying for food was iffy, so even thinking about purchasing a pedigreed dog was outlandish. Chris returned to the car where the kids waited and asked them what they thought about bringing the cute puppy home.

"Well, Dad," Hope answered in her most earnest then twelve-year-old voice, "if you get a dog, remember, you'll be the one who has to take care of it."

The following day, the phone rang. The voice on the other end of the line sounded inviting. "Come into the store, and let's talk about the dog."

Chris arrived at the pet store and found the puppy packed up and ready to go. They agreed upon a price of $150, but after cage, leash, and other paraphernalia, the tab was right there at $300—money that Chris did not have and a detail that did not concern him.

Hope named the new family member Alia after Princess Alia in the Frank Herbert's *Great Dune Trilogy*. Alia was barely a dog but more like a human with four legs. Since the puppy had only been out of the store to pee in the parking lot, she had never seen grass and didn't know how to climb stairs, play with other dogs, or understand what it meant to fetch. But she had an intense presence that made it seem more appropriate to have a philosophical conversation with her than a romp in the park.

Fortunately for Alia, she found a four-legged tutor. Chris taught art at Hopkins School in New Haven, and one of his colleagues had a puppy who taught Alia the basics of Dog 101.

When I met her, Alia was a year and a half, and I fell madly in love with her. I had never owned a dog, although I can't say honestly that she allowed anyone to own her. She was patient with me and taught me what I needed to know about being with her.

In spite of that, she was one of the most willful beings I'd ever met, and I soon learned that Alia did things her way. Sometimes when we crossed a street, she sat all of her seventy-five pounds down in the middle of the road and refused to budge. Even as cars whizzed around and drivers smirked at my distress, no amount of coaxing brought her to action until she was ready to move.

I continued to commute to New York City twice a week to see my psychotherapy clients. On Monday mornings, I woke up at 6:15 a.m. Chris drove me to the New Haven train station, where I took the Metro-North to Grand Central and then the subway to my office on Twenty-third Street. I began seeing clients at nine and usually saw ten clients, one after the other. At the end of the day, tired but eager to return home, I grabbed takeout food and raced to Grand Central to get on the 8:30 p.m. train back to New Haven.

Tuesday mornings, I repeated the process. I loved my work. Grateful that my clients trusted me to share intimately in their lives, I felt honored to witness their struggles and the magical moments of healing. I had finally found my calling.

I could have made it easy and stayed with a friend when I worked in New York, but newly married, I wanted to spend my nights with Chris. After my long day, I didn't want to miss curling up with his sweet body in our bed. So the extra traveling never felt like a burden.

Chris met me at the station at 10:30 p.m. when I arrived, exhausted from my day. He always greeted me lovingly and thanked me without fail for doing the work that helped support the household when his finances were a little shaky. I wasn't used to being praised for doing what I would have done anyway, but Chris showered me with his gratitude and appreciation. He expressed his love with ease and from his most profound essence.

In June of 1997 Chris and I bought a sprawling Cape at the top of a hill minutes away from Hopkins School where he taught. We called our new home Knollwood. Hope and Josh spent every other week with their mom, so the five bedrooms and large finished basement which we called the Shalom Room allowed us to sleep twenty as long as people took one of many foam mattresses to a comfortable spot in the house.

When I led a Shalom Retreat or taught Process Training, I also cooked meals and tucked people in at night, thus giving a mom-and-pop aspect to our offering. I loved having Chris at my side as I cared for the participants.

After years of renting office space in New York City, I appreciated working out of my own home. In addition to seeing clients and leading retreats and weekend trainings, Chris and I hosted monthly potluck gatherings, drumming circles, and spiritual video nights featuring Brianne Swimme or Eckhardt Tolle. We had a hectic schedule, but we enjoyed our shared projects while following our separate careers.

In spring 2001, fatigue set in. I was worn out and realized I could no longer commute to New York. I found it hard to say goodbye to clients I had seen for almost five years, but I had no choice. I needed to take care of myself. I closed my practice and ended the twice-weekly commute to New York City.

As I cut back on my schedule, Chris simultaneously expanded into new arenas. He was already a well-loved art teacher at Hopkins School, a prestigious prep school, where he taught pottery, photography, furniture making, and an innovative architecture class for eighth-graders. His schedule included working on a committee planning his school's future and one that interviewed prospective students.

He even made the dubious decision of becoming chair of the art department, a curious job for someone who didn't enjoy paperwork or rules and one that brought him a fair amount of distress. Every morning, he left the house early, sometimes when I was still in bed, and often returned late in the evening, exhausted and stretched to his limits.

I felt lost and bereft. I had loved my work in New York, and with clients no longer coming back-to-back to see me, I felt useless.

Hope and Josh came every other week, and although I cooked, cleaned, chauffeured, and helped with homework, those activities did not sufficiently keep me stimulated and fulfilled. I found weekend retreats and gatherings intense and satisfying, but they came and went quickly, and after everyone left, I rumbled around our big house alone.

One morning early in September, Chris left for school as usual. I was still drinking my morning coffee when he called and told me to turn on the TV. I saw shocking images of planes flying into the World Trade Center in my beloved city. I watched in disbelief as buildings crumbled before my eyes. I tried to make sense of the images I saw on television, but my brain fought back saying it was impossible.

Deep in my soul, I knew it was not make-believe. The attack was real. People were dying, lives were ruined, and children's lives were shattered. The life we had known would never be the same.

I shed tears, but they couldn't wipe away my grief. I couldn't even find my anger. I was overwhelmed and powerless to understand the meaning of such disastrous loss of innocent life.

I felt how easily the United States could move into a place of revenge and retaliation. To do so would only escalate the evil that the terrorists had begun. There had to be another way.

Chris came home and, not knowing what else to do, we took Alia and walked the several blocks up to his school, its parking lot empty of people and cars. We wandered into the woods behind the school. Everything seemed quiet and peaceful. We breathed in the earthy smell of the ground beneath us, watched branches of trees waving in the wind, and glimpsed deer that looked up and then bounded away. All appeared the same, but something had changed. In the clear, bright sky, we saw not a single plane. In the fresh and clean air, all was silent.

Did the silence warn of even more attacks? No one knew. But as hours and days unfolded, people from all over the world sent love and compassion to New York and the United States. The nation mourned, and people around the world grieved with us. Chris and I joined others to walk in candlelight vigils in downtown New Haven. We sang and chanted, talked with friends and neighbors, and gathered in moments of silence.

We watched the love coming together, hoping this might be the moment when we, on this planet, might begin to move into a new world that would understand that no matter what happened, we were all in it together.

On September 20, addressing Congress nine days after the attacks, President George W. Bush announced the launch of the

Global War on Terrorism, saying, "Our war on terror begins with al-Qaeda, but it does not end there. It will not end until every terrorist group of global reach has been found, stopped, and defeated."

The fragile moment of potential global healing passed with that declaration, almost unnoted, and soon we were at war. Chris and I were both acutely aware that such a war would bring no healing.

I was suffering not only my pain for the people who had died and for those left grieving. There was another more personal loss. I was embarrassed to admit such a superficial and egocentric response, but I felt my own identity shatter amid the chaos and devastation of 9/11.

Since entering Barnard College in 1966, I identified myself as a New Yorker. When Chris and I traveled and people asked where we lived, Chris said, "New Haven" while I blurted out, "New York." People looked at us strangely, wondering if we lived together or even knew each other. I identified so deeply with New York City that I continued to consider New York City my true home even after five years of living in Connecticut.

After the attack on the World Trade Center towers, I realized that real New Yorkers had experienced something that would forever separate them from those who had not lived through the terror of 9/11. When I left New York to move to New Haven with Chris in April of 2001, I remained connected to my identity as a New Yorker. Following 9/11, I felt irrevocably severed from the place I had inhabited for thirty-two years, and I grieved for a wounded city no longer mine.

Feeling powerless and useless while my New York friends volunteered as healers and helpers, I sat alone in my house. I had left New York City just months before, aware that a chapter of my life had ended. I knew I would move backward if I embedded myself into the city I had so recently left, so I felt stuck with nowhere to go and nothing to do despite my unbearable grief.

I kept waiting for Chris to save me as men had in the past by coming up with ideas for travel and adventure. Busy with his work, he listened but didn't seem to understand the depth of my pain. Quietly raging, not knowing where to turn, I felt alone and miserable.

One afternoon as I sat on the deck in the late afternoon sun, I asked Spirit to help me find a way through the darkness. I closed my eyes and did my best to quiet the chatter, preventing me from listening.

I heard the quiet inner voice say, *"Chris can't be your savior. He loves you, but you need to find your own way."*

Reluctantly, I accepted the unwanted truth and started digging deeper to find the root of my stuck feelings.

The voice went on, *"So much has changed since you left New York. You have endured many losses even though you have a beautiful new life. Your fire has become damp and dim. Your love for Chris is strong, but your passion and erotic energy for your own life needs new energy. You can't find answers in Chris. You need to discover them for yourself."*

I did not want to hear that message, but a surprising thought arose as I dreamed of possibilities. Perhaps I should attend a weekend training at Body Electric. Founded in 1984, the Body Electric School incorporates an innovative process in healing and integrating sexuality and spirituality. Initially created for gay men to provide a safe group setting where participants are supported in getting to know their bodies, erotic energies, and spiritual centers, it later expanded to include women.

Several years before I married Chris, I experienced my first Body Electric workshop in a mixed-gender group. I found the experience transformative in connecting my bodily sexual energy with my spiritual self. However, in my grief after 9/11, I wanted to be with women where I would have a chance to connect more strongly with my own feminine body, activating my feminine erotic energy and individuality.

I couldn't wait for Chris to come home from work to share my excitement about my plans. I knew my desire to go to Body Electric was not because I was dissatisfied with Chris. At that time of inner confusion and loss of identity, I sought a new relationship with myself. I longed to light an inner fire that had grown dim. I felt certain that Chris would encourage me in my desire to attend.

When I told Chris about my plan, he gave me his full support.

I excitedly registered for the course, and we went to bed. The following morning, Chris woke up with second thoughts.

"What's wrong? Am I not enough for you?" he asked sheepishly. "Couldn't you find another way to feel better and more alive without being sexual with other people?"

I reassured him that I wasn't interested in other people. I needed to find a new relationship with myself. Rather than harming our relationship, I hoped that by going to Body Electric I could bring new energy to us both. I knew that Chris didn't like the idea, but I was desperate to do something to get my energy moving again. Still, I didn't like causing him concern.

At the last minute, I heard that one of my more fragile clients would be at the retreat. I didn't feel comfortable being with her in such an intimate experience, so I had an excuse to tell myself and Chris, in complete integrity, that I would not go. I knew that the circumstance didn't settle the matter, but I willingly let go of attending the workshop.

My desire to participate in a Body Electric workshop lingered, and six months later, I received an invitation to another Body Electric women's retreat. By then, Chris's concerns had dissolved sufficiently for him to encourage me to go despite his misgivings. Relieved that we could trust each other enough to experiment outside the box, I signed up quickly before he had a chance to change his mind.

The retreat incorporated everything I had hoped for and more. Fifteen women, including me, gathered at a small retreat center in Vermont for three days. We vulnerably shared our stories about our bodies and sexuality, worked with our breath, and practiced expanded awareness with movement, touch, and communication. We learned to go deeper into our bodies, hearts, minds, and spirits, thus increasing our pleasure and connection with ourselves, each other, and with Spirit. Two experienced leaders taught the skills of conscious touch required to give and receive a full body massage, and on the last night, each one of us offered and received the gift of an erotic massage as we experienced our arousal as sacred spiritual energy.

When I returned home, once again juicy in my own body, the first thing I did was ask Chris if he wanted to practice the erotic massage I had just learned. Happily, he realized that we both had much to gain from the gifts of my weekend. We pulled out our massage table and put on sensual music.

Chris delighted in the liveliness and passion in my body. We spent many happy hours playing with erotic touch and experimenting in new ways with our bodies.

Yet, even as I melted blissfully into Chris's body, I still had no idea how to bring that passionate, life-force energy into my own life.

Each year, Chris went away for five days while chaperoning a hundred Hopkins students on a ski trip to Vermont. My job always meant staying back to take care of the house and Alia, but I felt myself too restless to stay home that year. I needed something different.

I called my friend Faye and suggested we take a trip to Puerto Rico. She agreed, and we planned a vacation in the sun while Chris skied. We found a caretaker for Alia and booked a hotel on the beach where we enjoyed swimming, playing tennis, sightseeing, and eating fresh local food. I enjoyed the time with my friend, and my body started to come alive.

On the last night of our trip, I had a dream. In it, I walked through a street fair and saw a vendor selling thin silver bracelets. One of the bracelets pulled me magnetically with a tantalizing energy. I paid the vendor, but instead of giving me the bracelet, he gave me an envelope filled with three tiny black seeds. The seeds danced with lively energy and an intriguing pulsating glow.

"There's been a mistake," I told the vendor. "I wanted the bracelet, not a bunch of seeds."

"You don't understand, my dear. This is what you want. This is what you need."

He turned away from me, and I knew there was no use in arguing. I found no instructions in the envelope, only the three mysterious seeds throbbing with energy. What did it mean?

The dream continued, and I noticed a large rambling house on the same street. I recognized it as the house of my ex-boyfriend Terry. Although we were no longer lovers, we had stayed friends after the breakup in the Grand Canyon. Terry had recently bought a small rundown hotel near Shalom Mountain that he planned to use as a retreat center. I had visited him once but had never explored his new dwelling. In the dream, eager to show him the seeds I had bought, I walked through the door of the hotel and called for him. Getting no answer, I went up and down the stairs and into the rooms but couldn't find him anywhere.

I awoke in the Puerto Rican hotel room where we were staying and couldn't wait to tell Faye. I didn't understand what the dream meant, but I felt a significant foreshadowing of the future. Something about those vibrant-looking seeds made me think I was on the right track, even though I didn't know where I was going. I felt the promise of new birth, and my curiosity was aroused.

I came home from my trip renewed. The time in Puerto Rico allowed me to remember that I could do what I needed to do even if I didn't include Chris and I could still be myself while in an intimate relationship with him. I could have my own friends, activities, and desires, as could Chris. Our partnership constituted a balancing act, but I trusted that Chris and I would meet any challenges we faced.

The adventures with Body Electric and Puerto Rico helped me understand. Not only did we have permission to take risks in our relationship, but there were times when we needed to take risks in order to keep our love alive.

When the Student Is Ready

There are no edges to my loving now.
The clear bead at the center changes everything.

—Rumi

My hope that things would magically fall into place after
my dream in Puerto Rico did not materialize. Clients started
coming, and I made a few new friends. I didn't feel so desperate, but I continued to feel that something new was just around
the corner.

There was no hint of what that might be.

One afternoon in May of 2002, I sat out on the deck after
seeing clients, and the phone rang. I picked it up, and it was
my ex-boyfriend Terry. He got right to the point. "Shamans are
coming to town. Do you want to come?"

"Of course," I said, my heart beating fast. I had no idea what
I was saying yes to, but I felt that the moment I was waiting for
had finally arrived.

Years before, an acquaintance had invited my friend Faye
and me to a healing ceremony at her home led by two shamans
from Ecuador brought to the States by John Perkins. John had
called himself an economic hit man who induced developing

countries to borrow vast sums of money to pay for questionable infrastructure investments. After he learned about the wisdom of the Indigenous cultures of the Amazon, he shifted gears and dedicated his life to bringing traditional knowledge to westerners.

The shamans asked for a volunteer, and I offered myself to receive a healing of my wounds around relationships. I was asked to sit on a chair in the center of the room. In a practice called Ch'allay, the shamans sipped alcohol and rose water and sprayed it from their mouths over my body to cleanse my energetic field. They gently tapped rocks and unbroken, raw eggs on my head while chanting words I didn't understand. When they completed the ritual, they prescribed baths filled with flower petals for three nights after I returned home.

I wasn't sure what to make of the ceremony, but they did tell me that I needed to meet a shaman in the future to finish their work. Up until Terry's phone call, that had not happened.

"What are they going to do?" I asked, returning from my memory of that long-ago ceremony.

"I can't really tell you. All I know is that their names are Carlos and Maria. A group booked my retreat center and said they would be using medicines. The person coordinating the weekend called and said that every one of the participants had canceled. I told him that I was interested and offered to fill the workshop with my friends. The shamans had never worked with people they hadn't met personally, but for some reason, they accepted my offer and said they would come."

"Medicines? Do you mean drugs?" I asked.

"These medicines are actually psychedelic drugs that induce a spiritual experience rather than a merely recreational one, so this is not your usual drug trip," he explained.

My interest in medicines was sparked when I read Carlos Castaneda in the sixties. He wrote about his apprenticeship with Don Juan, a Yaqui shaman, and the realm of "non ordinary reality" accessible through magic rituals, shamanism, and psychoactive medicines. His books planted seeds in my consciousness that seemed to be quietly waiting for the proper time to bloom. Perhaps my moment had arrived.

"So, who are these shamans?" I asked.

"All I know is that they are a husband and wife from out west. I don't know anything else."

"I'm in," I said.

"That's great. You're always ready for an out-of-the-box experience, so I thought you would be up for this. One of the shamans will be calling to interview you and will answer any questions."

I didn't need to hear more. I had a fierce intuition that destiny was tapping me on the shoulder. I felt ready to pay the price of admission, which I suspected would require giving up the familiar comfort of the life I was living at the time. I felt primed to be cracked open and wrote down the dates.

I waited anxiously for Chris to come home from work.

I could hardly keep my excitement at bay when he walked through the door. Before he had a chance to sit down, I blurted out, "Guess what, Chris? We're going to see a shaman!"

"Shaman? What do you mean?" he asked with a little more edge in his tone than usual.

"Well, I don't really know, but we're going."

"Is this something about drugs?" he said quietly as he started to pace.

"I guess so, but I don't know the details."

I saw that I hadn't done anything to quiet his anxiety. He was still for a moment, perhaps trying to find a way to help me grasp the danger of what I suggested.

"Well, you know," he said, "I've got a job that makes having anything to do with drugs hazardous. Remember when my student reported me to the headmaster and said I was smoking pot outside my studio? I was only smoking a regular cigarette and was lucky that the headmaster believed me, but I can't be taking a chance with my job."

"How would anyone know?"

"I just can't risk it. You know, things get around."

He dug in his heels, but I continued. I wanted him to come with me. But truthfully, I was afraid of going by myself even though I was determined to go.

"I know you've always been a bit outside of the box, which is one of the things I love about you. This is our chance to break old patterns and move into new and exciting territory."

"Yes, but . . . "

My heart leaped when I heard the "yes," but as his voice trailed off, I began to feel the conversation ending.

I was just about to give up when he said, "Okay, I'll go if you say I have to."

As much as I felt his resistance weakening, I knew it wasn't right for him to go just to please me. I sensed that meeting the shamans was a decision of a lifetime and that Chris needed to make it independently.

"No, Chris. If you come on this adventure, it must be because you want to come for yourself. This is too important. You have to be the one to decide."

"Well, then, I've decided. You go, but I will stay."

I wasn't ready to give up and thought that learning a little more about the medicine would help me plead my case.

"Terry said we'd be using a medicine called DMT," I told him. Neither of us knew anything about it, but I convinced Chris to look with me and see what the internet would say.

We discovered that DMT stands for Dimethyltryptamine, a powerful psychedelic drug with a long history in many cultures for ritual and healing purposes. According to the United States Drug Enforcement Agency, it was a Schedule 1 drug, illegal to buy or use and supposedly having no then-accepted medical use.

We also learned that every human body naturally synthesizes and releases DMT in the pineal gland, making all humans illegal drug producers. The internet mentioned vivid, mystical experiences involving euphoria and powerful hallucinations of geometric forms, higher intelligences, extraterrestrials, elves, and God. The more we read, the more uneasy Chris became.

"Don't worry, Chris," I said, determined to find a way to get him on board. "Carlos is going to call, and he will answer any questions you have. You'll see. Everything will be fine."

Carlos called a couple of nights later and outlined the structure of the weekend. "There will be seven participants in the group, and we will be creating a safe and loving container that will allow full expression of each person's experience," he said. "We'll drum and say prayers to strengthen the group energy. The medicine used is an entheogen, a substance that generates the divine within. This will be a sacred ceremony whose primary aim is to connect each of us individually with our deepest spiritual nature."

Everything I heard made me more excited, but I saw Chris getting more worried. When Carlos finished his explanation, he asked if we had any questions. In a tone that sounded more argumentative than questioning, Chris asked, "So what is this really about?"

Carlos answered, gushing, "It's all about love. It's awesome."

Chris rolled his eyes at the answer. It became apparent that I would be going on the adventure alone.

Days later, when I had almost given up on his joining me, Chris came and said he wanted to talk.

"You know, I've been thinking," he said in a cautious tone.

"Yes? What have you been thinking?"

"I know how excited you are about this experience, and I know you really trust Terry."

I felt Chris's resistance breaking and did my best not to interfere with his fragile thoughts.

"And so . . . " I drew out the last word, hoping that it would invite Chris into his next step forward.

"And so," he said quietly, "and so, I want to be with you on this adventure, whatever it will bring. If it's a leap forward for you, I want to share that leap with you. I want to feel that we're doing this together. Yes, I want to come with you."

Feeling so excited that I could explode, I took a deep breath. I pulled Chris toward me and held him tenderly. I hardly knew what we had said yes to, but I knew we were entering a new realm together, and my love for him filled me with pleasure.

Seven of us with the two shamans, Carlos and his wife, Maria, gathered at Terry's lakefront retreat center a month later. Although I had visited the place once, I had never explored the entire building. When Chris and I went up the stairs to our assigned bedroom, I was shocked to see that the house had a strong resemblance to the building I had seen in my dream in Puerto Rico. Perhaps meeting the shamans had something to do with those three seeds I bought from the street vendor.

Participants met in the living room, where we spoke about our intentions, concerns, and previous relationship with medicines. Carlos provided most of the leadership, while Maria, a skillful and powerful feminine presence, brought soft, loving energy.

Neither Chris nor I had much experience with recreational drugs and none with entheogen medicines. As we spoke around the circle, it became evident that none of us had experience with drugs or shamans. We were all in for a new adventure.

Carlos told us that we would be using a powerful form of DMT called 5-MeO-DMT and that we would smoke it in a pipe. Rather than calling it by its scientific name, he said we would refer to it as Rumi after the mystic Sufi poet.

Rumi was not the form of DMT we had read about on the internet, which described NN-DMT, a medicine that often invited an experience in the form of mechanical elves. Rumi was very different and had the reputation of taking the journeyer straight to Oneness. Carlos and Maria told us that the journey would last about twenty minutes and that we would be invited to smoke the medicine one at a time while others silently held space.

Quietly holding our own terrors, we came together in a circle in Terry's meditation room. A large golden cloth with an Om sign hung from the ceiling above a mattress on the floor. Terry had filled the room with altars holding crystals, feathers, and statues of gods and goddesses.

Ganesha, elephant god, remover of obstacles, and one of the most favored gods of our shamans, was well represented. As we entered the room, Maria smudged us with sage to cleanse our energies and connect us to the spiritual realms. The shamans assigned each of us to a seat in a circle on the floor. I felt nervous, seeing I was not seated next to Chris.

We had all brought Native American drums, and the ceremony began with group drumming to raise the vibration of the room and our bodies. As the sound of drums died down, Carlos called the first person to the mat.

"The pipe is offered to . . . " Carlos said as we waited nervously, wondering who would be called first.

Mark, a young man I had not met before the weekend, was called, and the rest of us were relieved that someone would show us the way. He stepped onto the mat and sat cross-legged as Carlos placed minute crystals of the medicine in a red stone pipe with a long stem in front of him. The gravity of the upcoming journey was evident, and Mark hesitated before picking up the pipe. I was grateful that I had not been chosen to be first. I still had no idea what I had gotten myself into.

As Mark lifted the pipe, Carlos raised his arms and asked us to take three breaths with him. Carlos held the flame just above the Rumi, and we watched Mark take a deep pull. By the end of the exhale, Mark had fallen back onto the mat, already traveling in another world.

Mark's journey lasted about twenty minutes while the rest of us sat quietly, holding space. As Mark came back into consciousness, it was apparent that something significant had happened, although we did not take time to hear from him since he needed quiet time to ground and integrate.

We sat silently with him and waited.

After a short break, Carlos offered the pipe to Chris. I watched as my beloved surrendered to the medicine, at first moaning loudly and moving his arms and legs around the mat before quieting. When he returned, he called me to where he lay. Still in his ecstasy, Chris wanted to share the love and gratitude radiating from him. Folded in his arms, I felt immense gratitude that he had dared to face his fears and say yes. Even before I had my chance on the mat, I knew our lives had forever changed.

When my turn came, I seated myself on the mat and gazed at the red stone pipe placed before me. The group took the prescribed three breaths with me, and then Carlos told me to pick up the pipe when I was ready. Fear went through my body, and I silently asked my teachers and guides to support me for my highest good and the highest good of all other beings as I entered the new experience.

I inhaled, and as I fell back, the room disappeared and my ego dissolved as I moved into cosmic space. All fear faded, and I found myself in a place of beauty and harmony that included everything, even negative energies I had once identified as destructive. In that space, everything was necessary, and everything was held in love. There was no outside. All was part of the One.

I saw a map for all reality embedded deep in my body. I remembered that lifetimes ago, I held a shamanic view of the world and was a medicine person who brought healing to my community. I celebrated returning to a part of myself left behind.

For much of my journey, I had no awareness of ordinary reality and no longer inhabited the room where I had taken the pipe. I felt an internal landscape infinitely large and flew around the cosmos at high speed without need of a body, although my senses were fully active.

When I returned and grounded from my journey, I was surprised to hear from Carlos that I had flailed wildly, belying my internal state of ecstasy. He asked me to tell him about my experience, but words didn't come close to expressing my expansive journey. All I knew was that I had stood in awe and wonder at the gate between the worlds.

The next day, I watched a young woman named Dana taking her second turn. Most of the time, journeyers closed their eyes since ordinary reality had little relevance in more expanded states. I watched as Dana's eyes suddenly opened wide, lost in worlds far away in what we called guru eyes, eyes that see far beyond what we call reality.

My eyes locked onto hers. As I gazed deep into Dana's eyes, I felt like I had smoked the pipe again. I saw something move in the corner of the room and was stunned to see an image of my mother sitting and smiling at me.

As I gazed into her eyes, I understood that her purpose in life meant dying at just the time she died.

It wasn't that she died because she was mad at my father for taking the new job or because he had betrayed her with his patriarchal attitude, as I had previously thought. She didn't die because she had to save my sister and mothers must sacrifice for their children. She died with consciousness and courage because it was her time. I didn't need to identify her death as a burden I had to take on. Given as a blessing, her death had initiated my spiritual journey, even though it came with a high price.

I heard again the words she had spoken to me in the Grand Canyon: "You are free to live. All is well." Surrounded by Spirit energy in that room, I felt guilt and grief dissolve into nothingness. Happiness pervaded my being.

When Chris and I went to bed that night, we met in union and ecstasy unlike anything we had experienced before. We made love not only with each other but with all of creation. The earth plane no longer bound us. We had entered new realms of experience.

Before the weekend ended, all seven of us shared our experiences, learning from each other. We still felt the expansive and spacious energy of our journeys, even though the medicine had long since left our bodies.

Carlos and Maria stressed the importance of grounding to assure safe travel back to our homes where we would begin the reintegration. They urged us to walk outdoors and watch our breath to ground before stepping into our cars.

They explained that expansion and contraction are natural processes. DMT had thrown us into extraordinary, expanded states, and we undoubtedly would feel a contraction at some point. It didn't mean something had gone wrong. It simply meant our bodies and minds were doing the hard work of processing a non ordinary experience.

Grateful for the experiences that we had shared and amazed at the intimacy that had grown among us in a short time, we said goodbye to our friends.

Arriving at our house after the weekend, we stopped in the driveway to reflect. Chris and I looked deep into each other's eyes.

"I don't think I know how to do anything anymore," he said haltingly. "I don't know how to eat or sleep or work. We're going to have to start over from the beginning."

I understood. We were no longer the people who left just a few days before, thinking that we knew who we were. Our minds had been blown, and we were on new ground. Everything was new, waiting to be met with fresh energy and information. We could no longer take anything for granted from the old life. Chris and I both had to make space needed for things not even on the screen a week before. Activities that seemed necessary a mere week before seemed irrelevant. I had no words to describe the gratitude I felt for Carlos and Maria and for the impeccable attention they brought to the work. They created a safe, sacred, and alive place for us to die metaphorically and be reborn.

I had no idea where I would go with the work nor where my unfolding would take me. Still, even as I took care of the mundane necessary tasks of life, I basked in joy and gratitude when I saw my clients, worked in my garden, made love, walked our dog in the woods, shared time with our teenage son and daughter. We were in a new relationship with the past, the present, and all to come.

Grandfather

There is nothing to do and nowhere to go.
Accepting this, we can do and go anywhere.

—Mark Nepo

Chris and I were hooked. Our medicine experiences had
blown up our understanding of reality, and we wanted to
continue our explorations. We agreed to meet Carlos and Maria
in the Utah desert to work with them for two days and a night
during Chris's spring break the following March. We had no
idea what we were signing up for, but we didn't care. We were
ready to let the spirit medicines work on and in us, trusting
that we were being called into a journey that would open us up
to new horizons.

Bleary eyed from the plane ride from JFK, we met Carlos and
Maria at our hotel in Salt Lake City. We hadn't seen them since
the summer and were excited and terrified at the adventure
we were embarking on. We piled into their van, which towed a
pop-up tent that would house us through the night.

As we got off I-80 onto smaller and smaller roads, we left
civilization far behind and entered the land of the desert. We
turned onto an almost hidden dirt road, where Carlos stopped

the car. Maria rolled down her window and poured water on the barren earth below as she offered prayers to the spirit guides. She especially invoked Ganesha, asking that he would support our growth and healing for our highest good and the highest good of all beings.

As we drove the long, bumpy, desert road littered with dancing tumbleweed, I felt uneasiness in my belly. "What have we gotten ourselves into?" I wondered. The road led to a secluded spot surrounded by juniper trees. A seventy-foot rock face rose high above the sand below, and an enormous Native American Indian face appeared to be embedded in the stone. Our teachers called that face Grandfather. I felt the powerful energy of the ancient ancestor soaring above and trusted that we were in the right place.

Cold winds blew, almost knocking us down as we wandered around our new desert landscape, a scrubby expanse of sand dotted with boulders and cactus beneath magnificent, blue-tinted mountains in the distance. We helped set up the pop-up trailer tent with two bunk beds on one end, a fold-out table in the center, and a hotplate on a counter. Chris and I laid out our sleeping bags on the upper bunks and piled on layers of clothing to protect ourselves against the frigid March temperature.

Sitting on blankets on the sand outside the tent, we watched Carlos prepare a fire with the tiny scraps of bark, wood, and fragrant plants that Maria had fashioned into a delicate nest. Placing the nest in the center of the firepit he had built with stones, Carlos lit the fire and blew tenderly on the tiny flame as he added small and gradually more substantial pieces of wood. Soon, it grew into a blaze that would support us through the night.

Chris and I had come to meet Spirit and fly into the unknown. But feeling our nervousness compounded by the bitter cold, we waited awkwardly while Maria tended the fire.

Once the fire blazed, Maria began the ritual with a sacred Native American pipe ceremony, a form of prayer that calls in the spirits of the seven directions. She explained that in addition to asking spirits for support and guidance in our journeys, we were giving the universe our address so that we could travel out into the cosmos and return safely home.

In her left hand, Maria held the red soapstone bowl of her pipe representing the feminine principle. In her right hand, she held the wooden stem representing the masculine principle. Bringing the two pieces together, she said, "We honor the feminine and the masculine, the mother and the father, the source of all creation."

Holding the pipe in the palm of her left hand, she asked us to close our eyes as she placed pinches of tobacco into the bowl. Honoring each direction one by one she said, "Thank you to the Spirits of the East, to the South, to the West and the North. Thank you, Spirits of the Below, Great Mother; Spirits of the Above, Great Father; and Spirits of the Within."

She prayed for the beauty around us, the process of life and death, and the spirits that would support our journey. Her prayers sounded like poetry and music, and I felt her weaving a web that would hold us safely as we entered the journey. With her prayers complete, she asked us to open our eyes, and we watched as she blew smoke to the seven directions, each of us, the medicines, and to the fire, until the tobacco had all burned to ash.

As she brought the pipe horizontally in front of her heart, she looked up into the sky. Saying, "Aho," she emptied the ash into her palm and then dropped the ash into Chris's waiting hand. He passed the ash to me, and I passed it on to Carlos. Rubbing it onto our skin, we connected our bodies to the energy of the prayers. She gracefully returned the pipe to her bag, and the ritual was complete. It was time for our journey.

Before Chris and I drank the medicine, Carlos asked us to share our intentions. Gazing into the fire, I shared my heart's desires for the journey. First, I wanted to feel grounded in my center rather than in the outside world's expectations. Second, given that as a Capricorn I tend to be concrete or even what I consider *too* concrete, I wanted to learn to bring Spirit more directly into my everyday life. Third, I aspired to enter the journey with a beginner's mind, willing to be a student so that I could let go of knowing and receive whatever gifts Spirit offered to me.

Carlos handed us capsules of Syrian Rue, an MAOI or monoamine oxidase inhibitor. Although best known as effective antidepressants, especially for treatment-resistant depression and atypical depression, MAO inhibitors are also used to enhance and prolong journeys with hallucinogenic plants. Carlos explained that the dye used to make Oriental carpets had the same active ingredient as the pills and that Persian rug makers saw images of elaborate patterns when drinking it.

He gave steaming mugs of mushroom broth to Chris and me and asked us to convey our intentions into the medicine before we drank by holding the cup to our hearts.

I sipped the earthy and slightly astringent tea slowly, feeling the hot liquid slide down my throat into my belly. A vague feeling of nausea arose but eased as I focused my breath on my intentions. It was time to be still and allow the medicine to take effect. We returned to the tent and climbed into our sleeping bags while Carlos and Maria returned to the fire.

The minutes moved slowly as I waited, not knowing what I was waiting for. Wind pressed against the side of the tent where I lay, and I felt its arms reaching out as if to hold me as I began my journey.

At first, my fingers tingled almost imperceptibly. Without warning, I heard a noise from inside my chest like the sound of a surprised bird. I watched as I slipped back into a wild explosion of intricate patterns and intense colors. I found myself inside a sumptuously beautiful oriental carpet that spread out endlessly and spoke to me in a language I didn't know. I was fascinated and awed by the beauty all around and inside me. It felt like a familiar place, although one I couldn't quite remember. I sensed ancient ancestors around me who knew the mysteries of nature, healing, and reality. In their presence, I felt supported and at home.

Suddenly, I was back down to earth and started to obsess that Carlos had promised two cups of tea when I had gone off after drinking just one. The thought kept going around in my head, tormenting me with the idea that I would miss something by not drinking the second cup. Carlos came back into the tent, but I felt shy about asking. I raised my head several times to see if he would notice and read my mind, but he didn't, and I finally allowed myself to surrender to whatever was going to happen.

Then I was back in. The tent began to shake violently. Winds howled, and an eagle came soaring into my consciousness. "Come fly," it said. I spread my arms, which became my wings allowing me to ride the air currents. Flying high above the desert floor, I watched as the earth dissolved into color and then into white light. My body disappeared into the luminescence, and I felt the divinity of all things, myself included.

I knew from my studies of animal totems that eagle medicine represents the power of the Great Spirit, the Native American vision of life force, Supreme Being, or connection to the divine. Flying high above the earth, Eagle lives in the Spirit realms but remains connected and balanced in the earth realms. Eagle represents a state of grace through hard work, understanding, and the completion of initiatory tests, leading to owning one's personal power. I wanted to dive quickly into the mastery of the medicines, but Eagle counseled that I needed balance and patience to do the deep work of bringing my connection with the divine into my earth plane life.

My bladder informed me that I needed to pee, and I was thrown back into my body. Although I knew I had to get up, I felt pinned to the bed and couldn't move. I lay in my discomfort for what seemed like an eternity. Finally, I found the energy to drag myself out of my sleeping bag and out to pee. When I stood up and looked at the image of Grandfather embedded in the rockface above me, he broke into a multitude of golden shapes and patterns that appeared to manifest celestial music and the sweet smell of earth.

I returned to my sleeping bag and heard Chris moving in the bunk across from me. Even though we weren't touching or talking, I felt him penetrate my space.

A book inscribed with our many shared lifetimes appeared before my eyes. I flipped its pages backward, and as the pages turned, I saw the many roles Chris and I had played together. In one lifetime, I saw us raising children. In another, I saw us living chastely together in a monastery. I saw us old and young, dying, missing each other, and finding each other again. Sometimes I was a man, and sometimes he was a woman. Sometimes we were parents, children, friends, or even enemies. Our lifetimes went back as far as I could see. I experienced the eternal connection we had shared in joy and pain and the countless ways we had met.

With nausea churning in my belly, I left the tent to purge. I looked up at Grandfather and felt his loving gaze. A golden liquid rose up through my body, and I sensed I was offering a gift up to the Earth. As if to celebrate my letting go, Grandfather broke into a myriad of golden shapes, and I rejoiced in the beauty everywhere I looked.

I went back into the tent to lie down on the floor. Deep love and compassion flooded my body. As I climbed back into my sleeping bag, I experienced myself as Jesus praying in the Garden of Gethsemane. I saw that my friends had abandoned me in my hour of need, and grief filled my being. I allowed the feelings of betrayal to penetrate my heart until it became clear to me that the Garden of Gethsemane was not about betrayal. It was about the need for compassion for all of us, the betrayers and the betrayed. I welcomed the invitation to compassion for myself and others as I saw how much judgment had filled my life.

I went out behind the bushes to pee. When I finished, Maria brought me to the fire she had been tending. She held me in her arms, and I felt safe, received, and comforted by her woman's body. Snow fell, and I sat by the fire watching the golden sparks fly up to the sky and explode like fireworks as they met the falling white flakes. I wanted to taste and eat the snow and the fire. I had melted into everything.

Maria continued to hold me while she taught me about the fire. She asked me to focus and listen. I could feel the fire's energy as heat pressed against my hands and body. A door appeared on the side of the fire pit that seemed to be calling me. I couldn't get through it, but I knew it would be there when I was ready.

I returned to my sleeping bag in the tent and focused on the sacred Native American and Hindu meditation music Carlos had been playing on a CD player from the beginning of the ceremony. Whenever a track finished and a new one began, it triggered a new chapter in my journey. When an image felt important and worth exploring, I slipped down into my sleeping bag, covered my head, and listened in the darkness. Sometimes I understood what was being taught right away, but sometimes I couldn't comprehend the message.

Carlos left me alone in the tent much of the time, but when he returned to put on new music or to check on me, I often found an insight that had eluded me. He burned eucalyptus and lavender, which helped me sink into the utter beauty of all creation. My heart overflowed with the glory of it all.

I knew it was impossible, but it seemed that Carlos had entered my body and knew everything going on inside me. He knew when to leave me alone, what to play, when to change the music or ask a pertinent question. He was undoubtedly just coming and going, taking care of what needed to be taken care of, but I attributed the revelations I received to his magical interventions.

I felt ready to leave the tent, and Carlos accompanied me to the fire, where I sat mesmerized by falling snow as it merged into the flames. Wrapped in a colorful Indian blanket, he circled around the space and finally stopped above me and stood, looking ageless as he leaned on a tall wooden staff.

Warming myself by the fire, I wondered if I had been taken back to a long-ago past or if I were seeing a new beginning after the cataclysmic destruction of our world.

I had not dressed for such bitter cold. I was happy to feel close to my teachers and the beauty of the surroundings, but I wanted to return to the warmth of the tent. Before I got far, a plane flying very low overhead and then another disturbed my peace. Ripping me away from the ethereal visions I had enjoyed, dark fear entered my body.

Our solitary place in the desert was not far from a military base, so I was not surprised to hear planes above. But something felt different. As soon as the second plane flew over, I knew that the planes were not engaged in a routine military maneuver. It was war—the beginning of the 2003 invasion of Iraq we had hoped to avoid.

Countless protests had occurred as President Bush continued to press his case that Iraqi dictator Saddam Hussein already possessed or was in the process of building weapons of mass destruction. Worldwide opinion protested that the seemingly inevitable war made no sense. A month before, demonstrations in February had attracted millions of people in more than eight hundred international cities, making it one of the most massive anti-war demonstrations in human history. Now, our hopes for peace were being dashed.

Crushing grief came over me not from anti-war thoughts nor political fears but from deep in my heart. I felt like a mother crying over her lost children, a mother knowing there was nothing she could do to stop their foolishness. I was not gripped by anger or recriminations but rather overwhelmed by the suffering that war creates for women and children, families, and young men. I grieved for soldiers who, never having met each other and not even knowing each other's names, would try to kill each other for the sake of ideas they might not even understand.

Tears poured out of me. Maria and Carlos held me and rocked me.

It was a strangely impersonal spectacle. I felt like I was looking down onto the earth from another planet, watching the drama, genuinely caring, yet knowing I was powerless to intervene. I cried bitter tears as my body wracked with anguished heartbreak at the death, destruction, and uselessness of it all. It seemed like my despair would never end.

"It is so sad. It is so sad. The earth is so beautiful, and she is going to be destroyed." Over and over, I repeated my doleful lament. Carlos and Maria held me as my body writhed with heartbreak. I heard Maria whisper into my ear, "All is well. This is simply what is happening now, and we have to be with what is. All is well."

I tried to let her words comfort me, but the grief was too fierce. I didn't want it to be like this. I wanted the war that had just begun to be over, but I knew I was helpless. There was nothing to do but surrender.

I struggled with Maria's words. "All is well. All is well."

The dozen planes that had flown overhead were now far from our desert fire, and the storms in my own body began to settle while my mind continued to struggle. How could I live in peace with the world at war?

I went back to the tent with that question and found Chris ready to go outside and move. He gave me his toasty warm sleeping bag, and from inside my cozy nest, I could hear him talking and laughing with Carlos and Maria around the fire. I realized I was missing something but had no desire to go out to join them.

Carlos came back in and asked if I needed anything, but nothing came to mind. He put on a Jennifer Berezan CD, and I listened to her voice sing, "Returning to the Mother of Us All." I was content to feel the Great Mother holding me.

Still deep in the medicine, I drifted in and out of ordinary consciousness. I was reluctant to leave the beauty of the journey and did my best to drown out the sounds of Carlos, who seemed to be noisily packing things up. We had planned to stay for the night, so I was curious about the disruption, but more than anything, I just wanted to keep warm and cozy in my sleeping bag while I floated in the other world.

I heard a flurry of activity around the foldout table in the center of the tent, and the pungent smell of food reached my nostrils.

"Come on, Carol. Come on down from your bed. It's time to eat."

I didn't think I was hungry, but the aroma took me out of my reveries, and I climbed out of my sleeping bag to join the others. Maria placed foil packages in front of us, and as we opened them, steam rose carrying such deliciousness that I got lost in the smell and forgot to raise my fork to eat. Chris lovingly fed me a few bites of stew, which I rolled around in my mouth, overwhelmed by the sensation as if I had never eaten before.

The taste, smell, and texture were new and intriguing. Eating wasn't just eating but an intense and surprising sensory experience. A deep warmth flooded my body with gratitude.

I was still too far out of my body to consume more than a few bites of my meal. Still picking at my food, I noticed Carlos and Maria packing up to go home. I was confused and still altered. All I could do was watch as the others busied themselves with preparations to leave.

I was far from ready to depart, but our time in the desert was clearly coming to an end. Carlos explained that the heater in the trailer tent had broken down, and he and Maria had decided it unwise to spend the night in such frigid temperatures.

To end our ceremony, the four of us stood shivering around the fire, which had burned down to glowing embers. We offered prayers of gratitude to the fire for the loving care we had received during our journey and in silence watched the remnants of logs burn to ash in the firepit. I took a last look at Grandfather, and we began our journey back to our hotel.

Making the Medicine Ours

Once you know the way, the nature of attention will call you to return.
—*The Radiance Sutras* by Lorin Roche

Over the next year, we continued to work with Carlos and Maria individually and in circle with others. In February of 2004, they trusted us enough to give us mushrooms for independent practice. Chris and I were instructed to journey one at a time while allowing the other to hold space. That way, we would learn to use the medicines safely and share our observations.

We put aside a Saturday afternoon and night to explore on our own for the first time. We carefully measured out the mushrooms for the tea. Before drinking, we took an MAO inhibitor to make the mushrooms active when we ingested them orally.

As I watched the water bubble on the stove, I fell into a bout of fear. My day had been busy, and when I headed out for some last-minute shopping, I grabbed some chocolate on my way. There are specific dietary restrictions with MAO inhibitors, and chocolate is one of them. As I drove home, I began to worry that the chocolate I ate would react badly with the MAO inhibitor and would create a dangerous situation during my journey.

I trusted that our teachers would have warned us if there had been a great danger. I even remembered eating chocolate chip cookies before and after journeys when we had been together with them, but I watched myself chewing on the fear. I called my old boyfriend Terry, who had more experience than I did, and I became even more apprehensive when he didn't answer his phone.

Without a definite answer, we began our preparations for the ceremony in the large downstairs room where I taught my classes and led retreats. At one end of the room, we lovingly created an altar with crystals, feathers, and statues of gods and goddesses, especially our beloved elephant god Ganesha. Our eclectic altars drew sacred objects from all the world's religions. Since I believed that all was one, I didn't need to hold fast to one religious tradition. Each had a piece of the truth.

We saged the room and called in the directions as Maria had taught us to begin our ceremonies. We called the Spirits of the East: Wiyohayapa, home of the rising sun, new beginnings, and the place of water and our sweet emotions. We called the Spirits of the South: Itokaga, home of the body, the child, and fire. We called the Spirits of the West: Wiyopeyata, home of earth, the setting sun, endings, dreamtime, and death. We called the Spirits of the North: Waziya, home of air, the ancestors, and prayer. Then we called the Spirit of the Below—the Great Mother, Inamaka, thanking her for her love and abundance. We called the Spirit of the Above: Makapyate, the Great Father God who holds the matrix of all reality. Finally, we called the Spirits of the Within—all the spirits, guides, and teachers along with the energy that moves us forward in our sacred journeys.

Our prayers complete, we each drew a card from the Sweat Lodge tarot deck. Each card represents energy asking for attention in the Native American traditions. I pulled the card Iktomi, Spider, which speaks of fear of the unseen. In Lakota tradition, Spider deceives, and I interpreted the card as counseling me to detach myself from fearfulness by recognizing and renouncing it.

When I went back upstairs, I was relieved to see the answering machine blinking with a message from Terry. I called him right back.

"Thank heavens you called," I told him. "We were just about to begin our ceremony, and I got scared because I had eaten some chocolate. Is that going to be dangerous? We're taking Syrian Rue with the mushrooms, and I've been obsessing about the danger ever since."

"It's okay. Not to worry. The amounts you're taking couldn't cause you any problem, but it sounds like you have fears that have nothing to do with that. What's really going on?"

"I thought it was about the Syrian Rue, but I guess I'm terrified of dying."

"Well, that is a big fear to overcome," he said gently. "Are you ready?"

"As ready as I'll ever be," I said with more confidence than I felt.

"You're going to be okay. You've been through this before and will go through it again. Just keep watching your breath and stay awake."

Chris was the first to journey, and I watched him drink the tea in several slurps. I hadn't taken anything, but I felt myself falling in, away from Chris and out into the beyond. I managed to keep myself present because I wanted to be there for Chris, but it wasn't easy. I took a breath and brought my focus back to him.

In my role as observer, I learned what it meant to love intentionally. I watched myself moving into judgments about how Chris navigated the journey. He seemed to resist letting go and stayed on the surface. I realized that my job was to hold him in love, exactly where he was, and not where I thought he should be.

I felt helpless. Chris seemed stuck and unable to move through to a place of learning or bliss. He moaned and groaned, but I didn't get any clear messages to act and move in. I returned to loving him as well as I could and trusted that I would get a more explicit message from Spirit if any action were necessary. I knew that I still had a lot to learn about holding space for a person journeying, but I showed up the best I could.

When it was my turn, we started by drumming to raise the vibration of the space. I was so entranced with the sound of my drum that Chris had to remind me that I had taken only the MAO inhibitor and not the tea. I felt the medicine people were so happy to see me that they couldn't wait. Neither could I.

Even though I was a novice in this lifetime with the mushrooms, I felt we knew each other long ago. I drank the tea and heard the mushroom people telling me they were already in me. I just needed to learn to call them.

I began my journey by singing a Rumi poem that we often sang in my Process Training class. It became the seed of my adventure.

> Out beyond ideas of right and wrong,
>   there is a field,
> I'll meet you there.
> And we shall let the beauty we love,
>   be what we dare.

Soon, I heard a voice saying, "It doesn't matter."

I wasn't sure what to make of the message, but it resonated with me. Not mattering wasn't about not caring. It was about understanding that everything was Godstuff. Everything was there for me to eat, take in, and integrate. It didn't matter where

I looked. It was all God. I sensed that unlocking that phrase might be the work of a lifetime.

Since my mother's death, I have worshiped Kali, Hindu Goddess of Creation and Destruction and the Divine Mother. Kali is believed to eat the pain of the world. When in the depths of the medicine, I experienced eating the world's suffering along with its blessings. I saw starving children and young soldiers trained to kill. I felt the pain of illness, the grief of loss. I saw animals and plants going extinct and the waters and air of the planet polluted.

I cried, and I raged. Then I remembered the words that Maria had whispered in my ear in the desert. "All is well. All is well. We have to be with what is. Then you will know what you have to do."

I watched my breath, and my body quieted and relaxed. I began to understand why some Indigenous cultures say that the earth wants to eat our pain and tears. In my Kali role, I ate a strange kind of honey—bitter and sweet, destructive and creative, all at the same time. I didn't analyze but just ate that strange honey.

To my amazement, many teachers, spirits, guides, and great masters came into view. Jesus, Buddha, Ganesha, Kali, Carlos, and Maria crowded around me. Then, my students appeared and my clients and friends, each in the form of a great master who had given me remarkable gifts by sharing their lives, love, vulnerabilities, and wisdom.

I saw them beyond their human stories. Each one said, "I know the story that I was living was just a game. I had the opportunity to experience what I needed to experience, and I am grateful. Wasn't it a great show?"

At that moment, I knew I had gathered the perfect people around me in my life to provide the lessons I needed.

I looked at the abundant gifts and offered my gratitude to those who had blessed me. On the one hand, it felt like I was gathering my people. On the other hand, it felt that my beloveds were mirrors reflecting parts of me, and I was looking at myself. "I can't believe that they all came. They're all here," I exclaimed with delight.

I saw myself and the people in the room as seeds that would eventually be shot out into the universe to start growing something new. I felt good to be a seed. Seeing myself as a seed felt bigger than any ego story that I might come up with about my purpose. I felt comfort in knowing I could be in service without having to understand or be in control. The perfection of every detail overwhelmed me. All the pieces of my life seemed to fit together perfectly.

My delight dissolved as I felt the life force seeping out from me. I was dying and could do nothing to stop it. I had the dark feeling that I would not come out of the journey alive, that I would literally die. My heart thumped out of my chest, my breath came with difficulty, and beads of sweat rolled down my face. Yet, I felt peaceful and complete with my life. I let go of everything—my possessions, relationships, identity, and, eventually, my attachment to my body. I could stay or go. It didn't matter. I watched as I let go and felt myself float free, free at last.

And then, as if waking from a dream, I was back, filled with energy and a quiet sense of happiness. I felt wildly empty and free.

A part of me wanted to stay in pure spirit without worrying about the demands of a body. Another part was drawn to the elegance and complexity of the temple I called my body. I experienced a myriad of spontaneous movements and different forms of breathing.

I practiced the fire breath, a cleansing and energizing yogic breath, which brought a feeling of warmth and energy, filling me with Spirit. My boundaries dissolved, but I had no fear. The slightest sound, color, or texture fascinated me.

I felt a web surrounding and enclosing me on the inside of a crystal. When that image melted away, butterfly wings held me gently inside. Suddenly, I was a butterfly flying lightly from flower to flower, tasting the sweet nectar.

Just as unexpectedly, I got thrown back into my own body with a thud. There, I journeyed through human evolution, starting at the moment humans made the leap into consciousness. I listened to shamans tell stories and sing songs about our beginnings and connections to Spirit. I watched mothers rejoicing and grieving for their children. I heard that all the information I would ever need was available and that I wouldn't need to carry what wasn't necessary. I felt connected to a long lineage of shamanic healers.

The weather outside my window put on a great show as I journeyed. A snowstorm had started soon after I began, and the world was transformed into a magical, shimmering, white wonderland.

I sat transfixed in front of the French doors that opened into the garden. Watching the snowflakes, I dissolved into the most vibrant bliss.

Chris said that he had never seen me so peaceful. I stayed in the stillness for more than an hour while he held space. Coming back into my body felt gentle and graceful despite the onset of an intense headache.

Carlos and Maria had taught us to honor marijuana by calling her Mother. Chris reminded me that they said that she would help us transition back into our bodies after our journey. He filled the pipe and offered it to me. I invited

Mother in with offerings of deep gratitude. She kept me company for the next hour until dawn. With the sun's light, I felt the medicine leaving my body, and I landed back on the earth despite my reluctance to return.

Fortunately, I had the whole day to be quiet with myself and remember. I felt enormous love and gratitude for the medicine people and felt eager to take next steps, whatever they might be, in the magnificent journey.

On the Road

Leaving Home

Between two waves of the sea.
Quick now, here, now, always—a condition of complete simplicity
(costing not less than everything)

—T. S. Eliot

Blown apart and clueless after starting work with Carlos and Maria, Chris and I were excited beyond all measure. Lifeforce energy raced through us with increased power as did questions. Where were we going? Who knew? It was hard enough for us to know where we were at any given moment. Everything moved too fast to track. All we knew was that we couldn't go back to the old life.

Sadly, we had no one to share the new energy with. Our newfound knowledge came from an illegal substance even though we had consumed it in sacred space. If we talked about what we had experienced, we feared people would not take us seriously and that they might think us simply ungrounded druggies who had gone around the bend. Furthermore, our teachers had asked for a vow of confidentiality to protect them and us. Chris and I kept the details of the new world to ourselves, although we longed to share our story.

We felt grateful that we had experienced such a mind-blowing opening together and could support each other as we both integrated the many changes that had affected our bodies, minds, and souls. Our teachers checked in often, and we could always contact them by email when questions arose. Although in new territory, we felt held.

As medicine became part of our lives, we created our own ceremonies to explore the mystic realms. Once a week, we made an altar in our bedroom with flowers, crystals, and sacred statues. We shared Mother Cannabis and although those journeys were not as potent as our Rumi journeys, they helped us gently integrate our intense experiences of the holy into our bodies.

I had lived through the riotous days of the sixties but had not engaged with alcohol and drugs. As Mother became part of our lives, I was concerned that we might become addicted to the high of the journeys. To feel safe, I felt the necessity of making grounding an essential part of the process.

Chris and I committed consciously to incorporating insights we received from our journeys when we returned to earth plane. We deemed integration and grounding of the information as crucial as the journey. Night became our time to travel and explore. During the day, we digested, integrated, and embodied.

Integration required naming what we had experienced, seeing how it affected our lives in the moment, looking at obstacles that prevented embodying received information, and removing barriers. That process needed to take place in the light of day outside the influence of medicines. Chris and I set aside time to process together and separately.

Day-to-day life changed in concrete ways. We decided we no longer needed to subscribe to cable TV and took the money to rent a marble sculpture from a local artist. We continued to play tennis, but we no longer competed. We enjoyed hitting the ball back and forth and improving our skills, but we no longer needed to win.

Our night journeys expanded our intimacy and our trust in each other. Often, we moved into sexual activity, sometimes with a gentle touch and other times with fiery, passionate lovemaking. Either way, we brought our knowledge of Tantric sexual practices to the moment.

Tantra is an ancient practice connecting the spiritual with the physical. It focuses on mindfulness in the body, breathing, and connection with the partner and self to expand conscious-ness beyond the physical and ego into the spaciousness of unity with all that is.

Chris and I were not skilled students of Tantra by any means, but we appreciated being able to bring together our spiritual and sexual energies in a way that brought us enormous pleasure, expanded our awareness of the universe, and allowed us to feel our love spread beyond our individual bodies. We were not actually practicing Tantra but inventing our own way of exploring our erotic and spiritual energies.

With the help of Mother Cannabis and our erotic spiritual practices, I felt my body and sensations in new, subtle yet intense ways. The boundaries between Chris and me dissolved and created a new sphere open for exploration without judgment or separation. We included everything and trusted that all was well.

Meeting with Mother became a part of our spiritual practice. Every ritual began with gratitudes before we took our first puff. We thanked the Universe for each other, our family and friends, the beauty of the earth, and for healing. We always asked that the journey be for our highest good and the highest good of all other beings. I trusted that the work we were called to do was to bring love, gratitude, and ecstasy to our world. I couldn't think of a better task.

Even as my spirit continued to feel more and more at home in the place of ultimate surrender, I observed my body and ego as they continued to struggle valiantly for control. Chris and I each had to work with the masculine and feminine energies in ourselves, in our relationship, and in our lives.

My energies were far more linear, goal centered, and mind oriented while Chris was more heart centered, emotional, and less aggressive. Sinking into a more receptive feminine felt challenging to me. My competitiveness and fierce need to get things accomplished often exhausted Chris. Still, our trust in each other created a gentle arena where we could explore. Every day, we had new opportunities to watch our efforts toward living into more love while being as awake as we could be.

It wasn't easy for me to stay in the box that had been blown apart. I continued seeing clients, leading retreats, and teaching my Process Training classes, but I no longer felt that I was the one in control. In my classes, I found myself singing shamanic songs, providing psychic healings, and creating nature-based rituals I had never done before. Spirit took me into surprising and unfamiliar domains, and I had to work hard to trust the unfolding process. New insights flooded into my conscious-ness and excited my mind. Many of my students were also intrigued, but a few wondered where such strange ideas were coming from.

I was used to observing my inner process, but Chris, less conscious than I of tracking his own behavior, had trouble holding back his enthusiasm. He had been raised to be a good boy, but beyond appearances, it never took. It wasn't that he did terrible things. Quite the contrary. His mother named him Christopher, which means Light Bearer.

Chris identified with the Christ consciousness, not the sappy Sunday school stories but the awareness that we were meant to be embodied carriers of love. Chris knew that love had no bounds, so there would be times when love trumped rules, and sometimes that got him into trouble. He met his students at his art studio at the edge of the campus, where he had free rein to do much as he pleased without interruption from nosy administrators. The kids loved him for his unconventional style.

He taught a class called History of American Construction Techniques where eighth graders built tiny houses one-foot square, complete with furnishings, from plans they had designed and drawn themselves. Then they graduated to even fancier architectural structures made of small strips of wood the size of popsicle sticks. One student made a model of the Sydney Opera House, far beyond what one might expect from an eighth grader. Inspired by Chris's support, many of his students became architects in their later lives.

One year, all the students in HACT were boys, and Chris helped them build a sweat lodge together in a remote part of the campus, deep in the woods. Believing that if you want to do something, you don't ask permission first, Chris arranged for an all-night sweat lodge for his students, followed by breakfast made in the shop. He got the necessary approval from parents but skipped over informing the administration.

It probably wasn't the wisest idea to cook bacon under the fire alarm, because when it went off, engines with sirens blasting showed up at three in the morning to put out a fire. Chris talked his way out of the situation because he was such a beloved teacher, but it didn't look good on his record.

Then there was another misstep. As chair of the art department, Chris gathered the teachers at a fancy French restaurant in town for Professional Development Day. A drama teacher reported him to the administration after he, in what to him was an act of love, asked them all to hold hands and pray, not to any specific God but as an act of communal gratitude.

Who knows what tender spot his request triggered in the drama teacher, but she carried her outrage to the headmistress, who told Chris sternly not to hold hands with colleagues or express gratitude in public. Another warning letter was added to his record.

He came home from work a week later and told me he needed to talk. We settled snug into the living room couch with the late afternoon sun streaming in. I waited to hear what was on his mind.

"I can't do it anymore," he said.

"Can't do what?"

"I just heard that Bill is leaving." His friend Bill was assistant headmaster and always supported him. "Without him, I can't stay in my job. I'll be worrying all the time that I'm going to be caught doing something wrong. It just isn't safe for me anymore. I don't want to do it."

I was aware that he was not asking me. He had decided, and I knew his decision was the right one.

"You know," he said, "I've taken hypnotherapy courses and your therapist training for five years. I'm ready to start taking clients and being more active in the retreat work that you're doing here. I'm ready for something new. It's time for me to leave Hopkins, and it's going to be okay."

I wasn't surprised to hear his news. In some way, I was prepared, but since Chris was only sixty, I thought that I had at least five years before he would be thinking of retirement. Yet I, also, held a secret dream, one I barely acknowledged. It started a couple of years before when I attended a writing workshop with Deena Metzger, a shaman, writer, and teacher in California. One day, the assignment was to wander alone in the canyons. We were invited to write, meditate, and follow wherever the winds blew us on a hot, clear day. I was happy to be on my own.

I found a spot near a creek where I watched ladybugs hatch and cover the ground with so many bodies that it looked like a red splotch. I watched the clouds shapeshift and let myself dissolve and reshape with them. I gathered my courage, walked over a downed tree that spanned a creek, stretched out in the center of it, and became part of the log, the water, and the sky.

Waking from my dream state on the log, I noticed a steep hill dotted with scrubby brush. I left my peaceful spot on the log and scrambled clumsily to the top. I felt triumphant at my accomplishment but terrified by the challenge of finding my way down. The descent felt so precipitous that I gave up trying to stay upright and tumbled down the rest of the way. When I reached the bottom unharmed, I checked my pockets. Two items had disappeared. My clock and my pencil were nowhere to be found. What did that mean?

One aspect of the writer's workshop was to study dreams, so I decided to look at my afternoon as if it were a dream. I had dreamed through a timeless afternoon, and I had literally lost my clock. As I thought about my dreamlike day, a question emerged. How could I maintain my glorious sense of freedom and timelessness once I returned to my ordinary world of home and work?

As I pondered, I saw Chris and me surrounded by beauty in nature, free and unencumbered by the tasks of daily life. How could such radical change come to two people who were locked into jobs and responsibilities?

An answer came to me. When Chris was ready to leave teaching, I would leave my work-related responsibilities, and we would go off somewhere and begin a new life. Since we both loved our work, leaving seemed far in the future, but the time had come sooner than I had expected, and I began sharing my plan with Chris.

"Well, long ago, I had a dream, too," I said. "I decided then that when you were ready to leave Hopkins, I would stop working, too, and we would figure out what to do next." There was a moment of silence between us as I relived that moment of dreaming and decision making two years before in the hills of southern California. With excitement, I began to share the dream that had emerged then. Chris listened, and I saw a spark of curiosity as he considered the possibilities.

"Wow. Just picking up and leaving. We could do that. The kids are out of the house and on their own. There's nothing that says we have to stay here. I'm ready to leave my job, and it sounds like you could be ready, too. What can we do to make it happen?"

"Well, we could take a sabbatical for a year and test the waters," I suggested.

"We could rent the house, and there would be some money coming in, so we could go wherever we wanted," Chris responded.

"Yes, but there are some problems with that," I said. "First, don't you remember? When we rented our other house, the woman betrayed our trust and trashed the place. If we rent our house for a year, we would have no way to pack all our belongings and protect the safety of the house. Secondly, I need to do the publicity for my training program months in advance of the September starting date, so we would only be able to travel for nine months before I would have to come back and get back to work. No. A sabbatical won't work."

"How about looking into the possibility of moving into the cottage on your father's property?" he asked.

My father, Jerry, and his current wife, Georgeanne, lived in a large, rambling house they called Timshel, which in Hebrew means "thou mayest." The house sat on a twenty-five-acre property in northeastern Pennsylvania and included a two-bedroom cottage on a hill above the main building. The year before, Jerry had offered Chris and me the cottage, hoping we might move in and start leading retreats at Timshel. We did not consider moving then.

"Maybe we could talk to him again," Chris suggested.

"Yes, but don't you remember? As soon as we showed the vaguest interest, he retracted his offer. So that plan is not going to work, and I'm not sure it was a good idea anyway."

"I guess there's only one thing to do then," he said. "We can sell our two houses, give away or store our belongings, and set forth on a journey to 'we don't know where.'"

We made the decision in a matter of days, and once made, everything unfolded quickly with a kind of sureness that belied our cluelessness.

Chris left his job at the end of the school year in 2004. In September of that year, I told my Process Therapy students that I planned to leave at the end of the following year. We were fortunate that Chris was given a golden parachute deal when he retired that gave him half salary and health insurance for two years, providing us with some financial stability. During our final year before moving from Knollwood, our beloved home in New Haven, Chris began his hypnotherapy practice and helped me with retreats and trainings at the house.

Although ready to leave home and start a new adventure, a big challenge was to find a home for our beloved dog Alia. At eleven years old, she had had two surgeries on her cruciate ligaments, her canine knees. We knew she would not be able to withstand the rigors of living out of our Volvo station wagon even if there would be room for her in our fully packed car. Furthermore, Chris and I understood that we were being called to let go of everything for our upcoming journey, and Alia was part of that letting go. We felt confident we could easily find a safe and loving home for her, since she was so loved.

Our year of transition went by quickly. By the middle of May, we had found a buyer for the house with a scheduled closing date of June 15. The arduous packing process proceeded as we sorted, boxed, gave away, or discarded the mountains of stuff we had collected over nine years in our home with five bedrooms, five bathrooms, and fourteen closets. Things progressed in a we'll-never-get-everything-done-in-time kind of way, but we knew that eventually the house would be empty, and we would be ready to leave.

A week before the closing date, we were down to the wire. After packing for three weeks, boxes filled with our belongings were piled high all over the house. We had just one problem. We still hadn't found a home for Alia. Everyone had assured us that finding a home for her would be easy, but no one had stepped up. At the last minute, we faced the reality that we would soon leave in a fully packed station wagon with no place for her.

I was panicked. I was ready to be on my way and desperate to leave everything behind and start a new life, yet our four-legged beloved seemed to stand in the way. I took time off from the frantic packing to meditate. I sat quietly and asked, "What is preventing us from finding her a home?" I heard the answer in a flash. "Me! I am the one. Even though I am leaving her, I still don't want to give her up." I felt the painful push/pull of holding on and letting go, ashamed to see that I was the one holding her back from having the future she so deserved.

I didn't want to let go. She had been my heart teacher, and her enduring love and forgiveness had enveloped me for nine years. She had been a constant companion asking little but my total attention.

Alia had woven herself into every aspect of family life, yet the time had come when I needed to send her away. I felt the tug of wanting to leave everything behind to find a new life but also wanting to hold on to the heart center of my old life. I knew what I had to do, and it ripped me into pieces.

I let go of the packing I had planned for the afternoon and made prayer ties, a practice taught to me years before by my beloved teacher Maria. I found a pouch of colored cloth squares a couple of inches on each side. Into each piece of fabric, I placed cornmeal or tobacco and a prayer.

"Thank you," I prayed into one of the packets, "that Alia has a home.

"Thank you," I prayed into another, "that Alia has people to love her.

"Thank you that she has woods to run in.

"Thank you that she has four-legged friends."

After I tied up each square with string, I fastened the packet onto a long cord. After hours of praying, I had what seemed like miles of prayer ties. I took them outside and hung them on tree branches around the house, where they waved in the wind sending my intentions out to the universe.

I had already looked at all the options I could imagine. I had sent emails to old students, friends, and even friends of friends. We had begged and pleaded, all to no avail, but I had finally stepped out of the way, letting my heart offer Alia up to love that would no longer include me. I could only trust that my love for her would open the way.

I woke up the following day with an uneasy feeling in my stomach. We had to leave, and we couldn't go if Alia didn't have a home. I saw no answer in sight. What would we do if nothing showed up? How could we squeeze her into a car already filled to the roof? How could an elderly dog be included on a trip into the unknown? What would we do?

Chris and I were having breakfast when the phone rang. It was my friend Peter who lived in Wendell, Massachusetts. He and his wife, Pam, had been my students years ago, and we had become fast friends. He had heard my pleas about finding a home for Alia but had not heard my desperation before.

"Well, I don't know if my idea will work," he began, "but there is a guy named Adrian here in Wendell who takes care of our dog when we travel. You might have to give him some money for food, but he is a reliable person, and I think it might be a good solution."

It seemed like a miracle. I had no idea who Adrian was or even if he would want to take Alia, but Peter's recommendation was the only ray of light in a very dark night, so I took the number and called Adrian immediately.

Adrian answered and listened to my request. I told him of my dilemma, and he seemed willing to help.

"I don't see any reason why taking Alia shouldn't work," he said. "By the way, what kind of dog is she?"

"She's a purebred Akita. She is beautiful, gentle, and exceptionally bright."

"An Akita? I'm afraid that isn't going to work. I just signed a new home insurance policy, and they explicitly excluded Akitas. I'm sorry, but I can't do it."

"That's impossible," I exclaimed. I knew that Akitas had a reputation for being aggressive, but Alia wasn't like that. I wasn't willing to let Alia's future be determined by rules that didn't apply to her.

"I know you are the perfect person. Can't you just meet her? If you still think that taking her won't work, we'll come and get her."

I could feel him beginning to soften, and in that moment of indecision, I asked, "How about Wednesday? We can bring her to Wendell. I'm sure you'll love her."

Miraculously, he agreed, and worried as I was that we needed to be out of the house in just a week, we finally had a real possibility. I held on tight to its perfect unfolding. I trusted the power of the prayer ties and went back to packing with relief and sadness in my heart. Loving is not easy, and having to leave Alia made my heart hurt. Assuming that she would stay if all went well, we drove Alia the hundred and ten miles up to Wendell for a trial run on the appointed day.

Adrian met us at the door of a sprawling house in the woods. Short and scrappy with a curly mop of salt and pepper hair, Adrian looked like a spring about to be sprung. His dark eyes showed bright under bushy eyebrows, and his energetic spirit captivated me immediately.

As we got to know Adrian, we found him a man filled with love, experience, and deep intuition into the inner life of dogs and especially dogs of a certain age. He already had a sixteen-year-old dog named Bumper, the house was surrounded by woods, and an herbalist lived in the house and tailor made tonics for dogs. Everything was perfect!

In those first moments, we saw Adrian falling in love with Alia, and we knew she would be in good hands. He agreed that she could stay, and before leaving, I wanted to share the warning we got from Alia's long-distance therapist.

About six months before we planned to go on the road, one of my students convinced us that Alia needed therapy to deal with her anxiety about our leaving. Having a telephone therapist for a dog seemed absurd, but I had a lot of guilt about abandoning our beloved dog, so I was willing to give it a try. I called Annie, the dog therapist, and we chatted as I explained the situation. Alia had started to chew her magnificent curly tail, and I guessed that indicated her anxiety about the changes happening in the house. When I finished giving Annie the background information, she told me I should hang up the phone and call back in forty minutes. Meanwhile, she would talk to Alia.

I walked into the living room where Alia had been running around. In minutes, she settled down into her usual resting posture with her head on the floor between her front paws. She closed her eyes and looked as if she were sleeping. Forty minutes later, she stood up and started running around the living room, seemingly complete with her session.

I called Annie, who told me sternly that Alia was heartbroken that we were leaving and that, as an older dog, she might not be able to make the transition after we were gone.

"So, that is the situation," I said to Adrian. "If anything should happen to her, I want you to know that we won't blame you. It won't be your fault. We are the ones responsible since we are leaving her behind."

"Don't even think of it," he said, obviously insulted. "I have taken care of dogs for years, and nothing has ever happened to a dog in my care. Alia is safe with me. Don't worry."

I still had concerns, but he had accepted Alia into his home, and it was time for us to leave her with him.

The goodbye was excruciating. Just as we drove away from Alia's new home with tears in our eyes, the heavens opened up in grief and poured down a torrent of rain. As we headed back to Connecticut, we tried to comfort ourselves, knowing that Alia would be loved and well cared for in her new home, but we were bereft at losing our beloved friend. Trusting that all was well, we were surprised to get a call from Adrian the following day.

"She's gone!" His words streamed out. "I don't know how it happened. The door must have been open. I'm so sorry, but I'll find her. I know all the dogcatchers around here, and she'll be found. Don't worry."

I tried to comfort him, saying that she had always followed her own will and that he was not at fault. He refused to listen.

"I'll find her," he declared, and with that, he hung up the phone.

I spent an agonizing day saying goodbye to Alia. I thought I had let her go when we left her with Adrian, but my grief showed my continued attachment to her. In preparing to leave our home, we were letting go of every shred of our old life. Yet in the most heartrending way, our beloved dog Alia had forced us to face more concretely all that we were leaving behind.

At about 8:30 that night, after a day of wrestling with love and loss, we got another call from Adrian. He had sent out the alarm all over the countryside. Two little girls found Alia ten miles away from his house. She was following our route to New Haven, trying to get back to us. Adrian brought her back to his home, and their glorious love affair began.

With Alia safely situated, Chris and I finished the last of our packing. Two days later, we cleansed the finally empty house with the smoke of burning sage and left our home to the new owners. Sitting in our driveway for the last time in our Volvo station wagon, lovingly named Black Mystery Rider, we looked at each other. "Now what?" I asked, and the new story began to unfold.

On the Road

The journey of a thousand miles begins with one step.
—Lao Tzu

We made the leap and entered the world of "I don't know." A new life spread out before us, an abundant menu inviting us to make choices and commit to next steps even though we were clueless about where we were headed. Fear lurked beneath my consciousness, along with the dubious idea that I had to understand where we were going and do it right even though I had no idea what that meant.

"What were we thinking?" I asked Chris as we sat in the car in the driveway before taking off on our journey.

I knew it was far too late for such concerns, but as my thoughts swirled around, I recalled being in the desert just months before with our teacher Carlos, under the loving gaze of the stone outcropping we called Grandfather in the Utah desert. Deep in the medicine, I was filled with extraordinary power and energy. I felt confident that I could do anything, be anything, or go anywhere. The world lay open to me.

However, instead of feeling happy and excited about the possibilities, I felt immobilized and clueless. Overwhelmed by not knowing what to choose in the face of infinite choices, I left that journey unsatisfied, thinking I had failed miserably to take the opportunity to be as creative and imaginative as I should have been.

A week after returning home from the desert, I realized I had misunderstood. I thought I had to decide and control my life through my will and ego. Instead, I began to understand that by aligning myself with the natural flow of the universe, experiences materialized that I could never have dreamed. When I went to the desert with Carlos, I surrendered to the flow, and not knowing what would emerge, I ended up in the perfect place. I was just beginning to learn that lesson of surrender, and I suspected I would be learning it for the rest of my life.

As we drove out of the driveway and watched our home disappear in the distance, I remembered that Chris and I were entering a grand experiment of surrendering and trusting that Spirit was leading us into the unknown, informed by our own deepest desires.

We started our journey with a quick visit to our friends Peter and Pam in Wendell. Only two hours from our now deserted home, it offered a safe and familiar beginning. We made the heartrending choice not to see our beloved Alia because we didn't want to confuse her, but our friends gave us a loving send-off as we set our course westward.

On our second day of travel, we stopped for lunch along the Huron River, a meandering waterway in Ohio, where we met a couple quietly fishing.

"Did you catch anything?" we asked.

"Yup, we caught six beauties," they said proudly. "But we threw them back. We're just fishing for fun."

An older African American man sat peacefully nearby. As we passed, he looked up and, with a broad smile, looked deeply into our eyes. "Bless your family and blessings to you," he said as if talking to old friends.

"Thank you and to you," we said, feeling the man's heart and generosity to two passing strangers.

We felt the depth of those brief meetings. The people we met were teachers who knew the ordinary and could embrace it. I was so tangled up in needing to be exceptional that I often missed the simple. I was plagued with fears that my journey wouldn't be significant enough, that I wouldn't grow enough or learn enough, that people wouldn't be impressed enough, or that I wouldn't be productive enough. I was terrified that I would fail.

Exhausted after the flurry of activity required to empty the house and prepare for our travels, Chris and I were thrilled to find Warren Dunes State Park, with its impeccable sandy beaches on Lake Michigan, high mountains of sand rising to 260 feet, hiking trails, and expansive views of the lake. Far away from everything and everyone, we finally had a chance to take a breath and soak up the July sun.

I started meditating, intending to visualize the Mother Goddess at the top of my head, pouring light through my body. I assumed that the Hindu goddess Kali would appear since I had been closely connected with her powers of creation and destruction since my mother's death. Surprisingly, it was Mary, mother of Jesus, who came into view. When I explored to see if I had made a mistake, Mary seemed very clear that she was staying.

Perhaps it was time for me to sink into the experience of a mother who could hold me tenderly, look for me when I was lost, and even wait for me. As I lay on the beach, the sand held me, the sun warmed me, the breeze gently caressed my skin.

The sound of waves calmed my spirit with a perpetual cycle that didn't require my effort. I felt lovingly held by the Mother.

I wondered what it would mean for me not to have to strive. What if my actions came out of flow rather than will? Who would I be? What would I do? Would I go anywhere, or would I just be still and meditate on the wonder of it all? I came to no conclusions.

We stayed at a nearby hotel for three nights and rested until ready to move onward. I had recently reconnected with two old Shalom friends, Jim and Sally, and we gladly accepted their invitation to visit for a few days. They had joined forces with three other couples to restore a large tract of land in Wisconsin to its original prairie habitat, which they wanted to share with us.

We called Sally to say we would arrive the next day, and she asked if we had heard about the London bombings. We hadn't heard any news for several days while we recuperated at the beach. As we drove to their home, we listened to the radio and heard that there had been a series of coordinated terrorist attacks in the London transportation system. Fifty-two people had been killed, and more than seven hundred injured.

The violence and apparent meaninglessness of the attack shook me. I wanted to meditate and connect to all the people, perpetrators and victims, involved in such a violent ordeal. Needing to find a place where we could be still, we looked for somewhere to stop. Off the road, we saw a trailhead that led down to a small rushing river. I found a flat rock where I could sit at the edge of the water, and Chris left me to meditate alone. By quieting my racing thoughts, I hoped to sort out my feelings about the troubling event that had invaded our peaceful retreat.

I practiced tonglen, a Buddhist method of transformation. I watched my breath and then began visualizing that I was taking the grief and fear of the victims into my heart. In my vision, I let their pain burn and then let the cleansed smoke of their transformed pain out as clear fresh air, sending healing to those suffering. I repeated the tonglen process of taking in the anger of the attackers and transmuting it to love. It seemed like a small thing, but I had to feel like I was doing something. I realized I couldn't change what had happened, but I could practice compassion for all suffering humans and open my heart. It was all I could do at the moment, and it had to be enough. Taking in such grief would help me train my heart to live love more deeply in our complex and confused world.

When I finished the tonglen ritual, I considered the possibility that we humans move constantly through an evolutionary birth canal. The natural birth process is often filled with blood and guts and brings the baby violently from the familiarity of the womb to a totally new world. Perhaps the growing violence was a sign of a new birthing. If true, I wondered what role I would play in the unfolding evolution of love on the planet.

In my life in New Haven, I knew who I was, what my work was, and who my family was. I was too busy to explore options outside of that. Now I had infinite options, and having left my work behind, I no longer knew who I was nor what I *should* be doing.

Contemplating the events in London, I chose to believe that the recent violence amounted to a call to humanity and to me personally to remember my connection with all beings. I needed to remember, not for the first time, that love surrounds me and all beings and that love is embedded in all that is. Love is the glue that holds everything together, from the smallest atoms to the orbits of stars and planets. On the road, I no longer had a clear purpose defined by my work. I began to see that my new vocation was to learn to be a lover, not just when it was easy but under all circumstances. In the face of such chaos, such a calling was challenging.

I finished my meditation and left my quiet perch by the water. Still feeling unsettled about the disturbing news, Chris and I continued our drive to Jim and Sally.

They called their home Manitoumie, which means Land Where the Spirit Dwells. When we arrived, fields of wildflowers met us in blues, greens, yellows, and reds. A variety of grasses clung close to the ground, and taller ones waved gently in the wind. Majestic trees surrounded a lovely pond. The beauty of the land reflected the years of hard work Jim, Sally, and the other owners had spent restoring the prairie to its original vegetation.

When we gathered for dinner in the large open-spaced living room/dining room, we were introduced to Fred and Karen, two co-owners of the land. They told us that they were both Sun Dancers. We were intrigued. We had read about the Sun Dance, but we had never heard stories from people who had experienced the ritual for themselves.

Fred began by telling us, "The Sun Dance is an intense form of prayer practiced by Native Americans of the Great Plains. It is a ceremony of death and renewal for the individual and for the community. It is a way of connecting to the Earth's power. Suffering is part of the ritual as the dancers are pierced by having two slits cut into the skin above each breast. Thin pieces of wood are placed under the cuts in the skin and tied to rawhide thongs, which are then attached to a tree specially cut for the occasion."

"The tree is called the Tree of Life," Karen broke in excitedly. "It is ritually cut and erected in the center of a large circle which holds the dancers and the drummers. For three days, the dancers fast and do a shuffle for many arduous hours under the blazing sun. Perhaps surprisingly, human skin does not easily tear, making it almost impossible to willfully break through the tough human skin holding rawhide thongs connecting dancers to the tree. They trust that eventually and at the perfect moment, Spirit will enter their bodies and allow them to break through.

"Each dancer will perceive the appropriate time to tear the skin and release from the tether, often after hours or days of dancing. While the dancers carry out the ritual, the observers stand around the edges of the circle, under an arbor made of pine boughs, offering their support."

"The powerful Sun Dance ceremony had been criminalized under federal law in 1883 and was not allowed until 1978 when Congress passed the American Indian Religious Freedom Act," Fred said. "Now it is having a resurgence as elders are beginning to teach the young men the old ways."

Chris and I were both fascinated and hoped that someday we would have the opportunity to participate in such a ceremony.

We spent several days at Manitoumie enjoying the quiet of the prairie and then continued our journey westward until we reached Minnesota. We crossed the Mississippi and found a city park on the river's shore, where we pitched our tent in our first ever attempt at camping. We realized that we were woefully unprepared. We had nothing to cook with and little food except a box of crackers and jars of peanut butter and jelly. It had never occurred to us that there might be some skill attached to camping, and it was evident that we were innocents in a new world.

We got into our tent just as a spectacular rainstorm started pelting huge globs of water on the roof of our fragile dwelling. Wild light danced violently over the river while the land rumbled with crackling bursts of thunder. Mesmerized and frightened, we huddled in our tent. The rain fly on the tent whipped in the wind as we peeked at the grand show before us. The power of lightning, thunder, and rain aroused us, and Chris and I made passionate love, feeling the wild energy of the Thunderbeings, powerful Native American storm spirits often visualized in the form of eagles, coursing through us.

We intended to leave Minnesota in the morning, but something kept us there for almost a week. Every day, we woke up and said to ourselves, "Ah, today is the day that we'll finally move forward," but every day, some task required us to stay—a tire needing to be fixed, a medicine that had to be picked up, a call one of us had to make. It began to feel like a magnet prevented us from leaving.

After a week, we were finally released from what seemed like prison in Minnesota. Relieved, we drove for about an hour and found a lovely campground surrounding a small lake in South Dakota. It was a family place filled with young children happily playing in the water and surrounding woods. Chris and I watched a stunning sunset in pink-and-orange-sherbet colors dance across the sky. The clouds and colors felt so intimate that we felt shy and inadequate in the face of such glorious beauty. We could do nothing but bow down in adoration at the mystery.

We woke up the following day thinking hard about what we wanted to do. Although we had found a lovely campsite, we had no privacy. We wanted to find another place but had had no preference beyond knowing that we wanted to leave. Nothing called us north or south or east or west.

We consulted our oracles. We watched the clouds and saw where they headed. No message came to us. We threw sticks, hoping to receive some direction. Nothing. We laid out the tarot cards. Again, nothing presented us with a preference for one course over another. It puzzled us to be stuck because we had no specific desire.

We walked to the ranger station and asked the man behind the desk where we should go.

"There's a beautiful spot in Nebraska," he said. "That would be a great destination."

I had no desire to go to Nebraska with its monotonous rows of endless cornfields. But we had asked, and the ranger provided the only answer we had gotten. So we agreed.

"You better hurry, though," he said. "It's Friday. The place is small and will fill up quickly. You won't find a place if you wait too long."

We got into our car and started rushing to the campsite in Nebraska, a place several hours away where neither Chris nor I wanted to go. Speeding down the highway, we started laughing at our foolishness. Why were we so eager to get to a place where we didn't want to be? Still, we couldn't think of a good alternative, so we continued until we saw a big green sign that read, "Sioux County Headquarters." I had no idea what that meant, but we made a split-second decision to turn off the road to investigate.

We followed the signs and found ourselves at nine in the morning at the only building in town—a casino, a sad setting dark and smoky, filled with lost and desperate-looking souls. A middle-aged white woman guard saw us hovering near the door. Seeing us very much out of our element, she came over to offer assistance.

Embarrassed to state our real need—admitting that we couldn't figure out where to go—we instead began a casual conversation. The woman told us she was married to a farmer who grew corn not for food but for ethanol. She continued telling us that it was a hard life and that she needed the job as a guard at the casino to make ends meet.

After half an hour of hearing the small details of her life, she asked, "What are you doing here?"

"We're on the road, just traveling, but we can't figure out where we want to go next."

"Well, what are you interested in?"

My mind drew a blank as Chris said, "We're interested in Native Americans."

"What about Native Americans do you find interesting?" she probed.

Chris surprised me by announcing, "Pipes. I am interested in getting a pipe."

"Well," she said, "You need to go to Pipestone. It's eighteen miles back into Minnesota."

Oh, no! We had just spent a week trying to get out of Minnesota, and now we were being called back. What was going on?

"There is a museum with a gift shop, and that would be the best place for you to buy a pipe."

Neither of us was eager to return to Minnesota, but you need to listen when you ask, so we thanked our guide and got into the car to head back to Minnesota.

We found the museum, and the first thing we saw on the outside wall was a poster announcing a Sun Dance starting that very day. What a remarkable unfolding. After hearing about the Sun Dance at Manitoumie, we had hoped we would someday find a ceremony to attend, and now Spirit had brought us to the perfect place. All we had to do was listen and trust.

We spent a week with the Sun Dance community. Immediately put to work, we helped set up the ceremonial area and kitchens to support the 125 people for the week. Then we watched the ritual raising of the Tree of Life. The event was an important gathering of the Lakota Sioux and Plains tribes, and people had come from as far as South America to dance.

The drum provides the heartbeat for the Sun Dance ceremony. That time, eight drummers sat on a platform and began the rhythmic cadence that would continue throughout four days of the ceremony. From our position in the shade of the arbor encircling the outer perimeters, we watched tribal chiefs enter in full regalia. The ceremony opened with lengthy prayers to Wakan Tanka, the Great Spirit, followed by an elaborate ritual of exchanging gifts of blankets and drums. Amidst all the abundance, the most esteemed offering was a small bag of heirloom corn seeds brought from a Mexican tribe.

Once the opening rituals had completed, the mostly young male dancers prepared to be tied to the tree by having slits cut into their skin to secure the leather thongs that bound them to the Tree of Life.

All week we supported the dancers as they shuffled under hot sun sending their prayers to Great Spirit. They directed many prayers toward the Red Lake Indian Reservation where a sixteen-year-old boy had gone on a recent spree of killings. Seven people had died, and five more were wounded, making it then the deadliest school shooting since Columbine in 1999.

Because of the severity of the situation and need for powerful prayers, several older chiefs who might otherwise have attended as observers took an active part in the Sun Dance. They piled heavy sleds with buffalo skulls and pipestone, the sacred red clay stone that some Native Americans use for making prayer and ceremonial pipes. Then they each dragged a sled around the circle until Spirit released them from the thong's hold on their skin.

In the evenings, we shared meals, were invited to share sweat lodges, and were graciously welcomed as family. Chris and I were moved by the dancers' commitment to putting their bodies on the line in the brutally hot sun as they brought their prayers to Great Spirit. We felt honored to do our part as we shuffled hour after hour under the arbor to encourage them. Their devotion humbled us.

After helping to pack everything that had supported the ceremonies for the week, we left the Sun Dance and returned to the museum, where we bought the prayer pipes that had called us to the sacred gathering. Spirit had taken us exactly where we needed to go, and we had followed. Our journey had begun.

Flitting Butterflies

The wind, my mirror, rushes through me. I am empty.

—Kai Carol Jud

Since we left in June, our basic shelter was a comfy blue two-person tent gifted to us by Chris's daughter Hope as a going-away present. Blue Moon was printed on the side, a perfect name for our home. With pockets on the side where we could store our phone, flashlight, keys, and glasses, it had just enough room to sit up and move around a little. We brought an oversized white down comforter as a luxury to cover our sleeping bags. Netting on the top and sides of Blue Moon gave splendid views of stars, fireflies, and the leafy canopy of trees as we drifted off to sleep. If it rained, we covered the tent with a fly but could still peek out the front flap to avoid missing the show. When I fell asleep, I loved feeling close to the earth and close to Chris.

Every day, we had to determine the place we would call home. Shall we stay? Shall we move on? We stayed in state parks most of the time and occasionally in a motel when we needed a shower or soft bed, but there were many possibilities and no way to know the best place.

Our lack of experience showed in our paucity of equipment for cooking. I loved to cook for my family and retreatants in our old life. The kitchen at Knollwood was well stocked with everything a gourmet cook could want, including a professional stove with two ovens, a grill, and bright red knobs.

But with all of my past experience, we had no idea what camp cooking would require. We had brought a cooler just big enough to hold a block of ice, a pint of half and half, and not much more. We had no pots and pans, and it hadn't occurred to us that we would need a fuel source.

With no stove on our first night of camping, we ate raw corn on the cob from a farm stand, topped off with peanut butter and jelly on multigrain crackers. We felt ourselves at the most magnificent feast with simple food as we ate under the starry sky, the moon lighting up our table.

We talked together about what we sought on the journey we had just begun. The idea that we had left everything behind and were homeless was just beginning to sink in. We comforted ourselves by saying that Spirit was teaching us to practice action without attachment, although there seemed little left to be attached to.

In the month we had been on the road, I felt like we were on a lovely vacation and would eventually return home. But there was no longer a home to return to and no way to see into the future.

Mystery engulfed us, and we knew so little that we barely knew the questions to ask. We could only do our best to be awake with curiosity and awe at everything going on, trusting that we didn't have to understand.

It was new to be away from the world of work, consumerism, and demands of the everyday world. We had the luxury of not having to make money for the moment and weren't spending much. We rarely saw a newspaper or heard the news on the radio, and except for short visits with friends, our only interactions were casual meetings with rangers or with people we met on the road.

We made up for what we lacked in social relationships by connecting to nature. One day during a hike, Chris noticed a butterfly floating in an icy stream. We looked around and saw hundreds of blue and white butterflies sprinkling the air around us. Chris gently lifted the floating butterfly out and warmed it in his hand. We watched as it gradually came back to life and took off from his hand.

There were birds of all kinds to see, insects, fish, clouds, stars, spiders spinning their webs, and fireflies lighting up the night. We swam in lakes, prairie ponds, trout streams, and icy springs, and at night, we slept under the star-filled sky.

We met challenging teachers, including a fat, brazen, albino raccoon who invaded our campsite to gnaw on the bones of fried chicken left by previous careless campers. He refused to be frightened by our urgent demands that he depart, and we ended up retreating from our campfire to the safety of our tent, leaving him to his chomping. In the morning, our car was covered with his tiny paw prints.

Our days always started with yoga and meditation. We had plenty of time for the little things. In fact, those things were the focus of our days. We watched animals come to greet us, the clouds and sun, stars, and moon as the chatter of our thoughts began to quiet. We made an unwavering resolve to remember the perfection in all things even when not apparent and be grateful for the infinite abundance surrounding us.

Isolated from familiar patterns, we observed our thoughts and emotions in new ways as we started relating to each other in an unfamiliar environment.

In our old life, we each knew our jobs and our roles. Because I led retreats in our home, I saw myself as the leader and Chris as my support. Now we met on an even playing field, neither of us knowing much at all. In this new and unknown territory, and with our lack of experience, we saw how much we needed to depend on each other.

We often thought about friends and family we had left behind. When we went on the road, we assured them they would be traveling with us. At the time, we barely understood the words. As we drove further from all that was familiar, we found ourselves telling such vivid stories about our beloveds that we felt their physical presence.

Over and over, we experienced no separation in the vast and complex world, not between us and the butterflies, the brilliant sky, nor the people who had touched us so profoundly.

In the Utah desert, we met our teachers Carlos and Maria around the sacred fire where they guided us in medicine work. They suggested that our purpose in the journey we had taken on so innocently was to become flitting butterflies and carry a message of love everywhere we went. We had no idea what the task required, but we found it comforting to have definition for our amorphous adventure.

We felt newly hatched as if in a dream state. A new space had opened from which everything looked different—more beautiful, more connected, and more mysterious. We were grateful.

After our ceremonies with Carlos and Maria, they suggested that we go to Silver Lake at sunset to watch the moose. We arrived at a beautiful, wooded area and walked around the lake for about an hour, catching sight of only a distant silhouette of one moose. Disappointed, we began our trek back to the car.

Then we saw him. Impressive antlers topped his massive bulk set on slender legs. He ambled a mere ten feet ahead of us on the path and then paused for just an instant, letting us take in his magnificent presence. He walked ahead of us for a few brief moments, then crossed the path in front of us and disappeared into the brush.

When we got back to our campsite, I referred to Ted Andrews's book *Animal Speak*, which describes the spiritual meaning of animals. Moose had appeared as a timely teacher. It represented primal feminine energies and the magic of life, death, and sexual energy. Moose invited exploration of new depths of inner awareness. We felt blessed that he had come to greet us.

We left Silver Lake and stopped in a tiny town in southeastern Utah where we discovered a small lake with a private spot to camp. We set up the tent near the shore and settled in. Carlos and Maria had given us medicine to practice with, and we decided that the night would be perfect for a journey. We lit a ceremonial fire, made the medicine into a tea, drank, and quietly waited for it to take effect.

The medicine kicked in for me quickly. I rested my head on the damp earth and felt my mind lock into adoration of the stars, the fire, and Chris. Not yet affected by the tea, Chris lay down beside me. He gently held space as I journeyed far away.

Cold began to penetrate my body, and I wanted to go back into the tent and the warmth of our sleeping bags. We fell into each other's arms. Chris gently caressed my body so lightly that it was barely a touch, but it opened me to intense ecstasy.

As I returned his touch, the medicine activated Chris. Adoration for me and everything in creation overtook him, and tears came to his eyes. He started to cry, calling me deeper into my own journey.

I held him close, and the intensity rose in us both as our bodies came together. The sky above was clear and filled with stars while lightning lit up the darkness in wild flashes of brilliant luminescence. As we made love, I noticed that I was peeling away layers of protection and letting Chris into me without boundaries, perhaps for the first time. It felt sweet, ecstatic, and, paradoxically, I felt almost free of my body.

The spectacular light show went on all night as we fell deeper into making love with each other and all that surrounded us. We met not merely in sexual experience. We instead experienced the disappearance of our boundaries as we became one skin. We delighted in adoring each other through the night as we watched the stars and lightning-filled sky. It wasn't until dawn that thunder burst out and rain finally fell.

When the sky began to clear in the morning, we packed up our campsite and headed for Mud Canyon Ruin, a place where the Anasazi, ancient American people of the southwest, flourished between 100 BCE and 1500 AD. They lived high up in the cliffs in homes carved into the stone before some mysterious cataclysmic event forced them to flee their homes and homeland.

We thrilled at seeing remnants of actual dwellings and imagined the life that must have centered around the steep precipices.

At the base of the ruins, I found a spot to meditate. I started by asking the Ancient Ones to speak to me. As soon as I asked, it began to drizzle, and I heard a distant voice tell me that the rain was a sign of grieving.

"Everything is always changing," it said. "If you insist on trying to stop change, then you will only cause yourself great suffering. We are the holders of the wisdom," they continued, "but we are not invested in what you choose to do. You can come to us and find the truth."

As I looked at the desert canyon in my mind's eye, I saw that—with no investment in how that would manifest—it had allowed itself to be shaped by Spirit.

The voice continued, "How can you control what has not yet taken shape? You can't know what Spirit has in mind for you. You have to trust that by allowing yourselves to be shaped, you will find the way into your purpose."

The words comforted me, but I still longed to know what I would become though my shape had not fully formed. I realized that, even at the stage of letting go, my ego remained invested in doing a consummate job of trusting the unfolding while simultaneously fighting desperately to stay in control.

I laughed watching my ego's manipulations and story-making in the course of my inner battle. "I am the best, I am the worst, I'll never learn to let go. Look at the great job I am doing." The stories tumbled out in a wild mishmash. I was grateful that I could just observe and watch the show without falling into collapse.

We had already let go of a lot merely by leaving our life in New Haven. I suspected my flailing represented my ego's attempt to control what it had already lost. I had to remember the message from the canyon. I had to let Spirit shape me like the air, water, and sand that shaped the canyon. The form I would become would result not from my will but from Spirit's.

Still feeling the presence of the disembodied voice, I asked, "Who are you?"

After some moments of quiet, I heard, "I am Red Hawk Woman, a woman past my moon times. I've lost all my children and my land. My father was a medicine man, and now I am a medicine woman. You can always see me in the sky and listen, or you can call me if you need me."

And her voice dissolved into the wind.

The Voice at Estes Park

May we all grow in grace and peace, and not neglect
the silence that is printed in the center of our being. It will not fail us.
—Thomas Merton

Jack and Marlena Kochner were old friends of my father's. I had met them almost fifteen years before on the trip to the Grand Canyon but hadn't seen them since. Just months before Chris and I planned to go on the road, we met them with thirty other people at a gathering of Shalom friends at Timshel, my father's home in Lawton, Pennsylvania. I was surprised that they had made the long trip from Colorado to Timshel for the weekend gathering. I hadn't expected ever to see them again after our river trip and barely remembered them when they arrived.

Jack, a bear-like guy of about seventy with a close-cut salt and pepper beard and mustache, had piercing eyes that quietly took in everything around him. His wife, Marlena, whose wiry body appeared tightly strung for action, sported a ready smile.

During the Apollo 17 Mission Jack worked in human resources at NASA. Although soft-spoken and seemingly conservative, Jack had a highly developed and vivid dream life. He had never taken any psychedelic drugs, but his night dreams and meditations were as wild as my medicine journeys.

We quickly started sharing stories about our spiritual journeys and felt the spark of friendship growing. I loved talking with them about life, love, presence, illusion, reality, and God, even though we came from different perspectives. By the end of the weekend, we four had become fast friends, and they made the generous offer that we come and stay at their guest house in Estes Park, Colorado, if we should ever be in the area.

It was September, and we had been on the road for more than three months. We had gotten the knack of camp cooking and learned how to make our campsites comfortable and efficient. Although we loved being in the beauty of nature, the promise of a roof over our heads for a few weeks was appealing. I called Jack, and he said that we would be welcome to come at the end of the week.

On our way to Estes Park, we stopped at Sulphur Hot Springs, Colorado, for two nights. Falling into my usual worries about finances, I squirmed at the idea of spending money on a fancy spa instead of the cheaper campground. Despite Chris's unstable finances before our marriage, he rarely worried about such mundane matters as money, so I often ended up taking the role of the financially responsible partner. My anxiety was more about fear than lack of funds, but my habit of wanting to control our spending kept popping up, especially since we had left our jobs.

My distress evaporated when we discovered that, for ninety-eight dollars, we could enjoy the luxury of a private cottage for two nights with unlimited access to more than twenty hot spring tubs. I let go of any lingering resistance and surrendered to the pleasure of soaking in hot water.

We settled into a sweet, private log cabin with a double bed, bathroom, and an Ansel Adams poster of a waterfall on the wall. We ran over to the springs, surrounded by a crazy jumble of stairs, pools, and platforms with lounge chairs. The steamy water provided a balm for our aching bodies, and we spent the day going in and out of the pools, soaking up the sun, and meeting new friends.

In the evening, we were guided to a restaurant in a restored 1890s hotel. Abe, the owner, was a Jewish man from Spanish Harlem, and almost everyone else who worked there shared Puerto Rican heritage. I was delighted to find in the Colorado Mountains a surprising reminder of my beloved New York City.

Abe seated us and told us brusquely that we would have to wait. When he appeared again, he said we couldn't ask any questions. We were simply to order. I asked for a Tanqueray and tonic, and he said, "Okay, one gin and tonic." He wouldn't even discuss brands of Scotch with Chris. He simply said that he would bring a good one. With all the bluster, his tenderness came through. We tried to compliment him, but he pushed it off and went back to his intricate dance from table to table.

Somehow, food appeared, and we enjoyed fresh caught trout and the best and juiciest pork chops I had ever eaten. The rest of the food was pedestrian, but our hearts began to melt in the magic of the setting.

As people drifted out of the dining room, the strains of gorgeous Italian arias reached our ears and transported us into bliss that opened our hearts. Dancing between laughter and tears, we fell deeper and deeper into the moment. When most of the people had left, Abe sat down at a table across from us and dove into telling us about himself

He described how as a hormone-stressed teenager he learned to love classical music after buying a victrola and some cracked records. He listened to the Shostakovich *Piano Concerto #2* and felt he had found home. At that moment, he got hooked for life.

Hearing him talk about his love of music, Chris and I felt as if we were joining him in making love to his beloved.

We got up to leave, wanting to soak in the moonlight before the baths closed at ten. When we reached the door, Chris stopped Abe and told him to put down his drink. He opened his arms into a big bear hug with Abe; amazingly, Abe received it fully. I took my turn and hugged Abe, touched that this stranger had received us so generously.

We raced to the hot springs and got bathed in moonlight as well as water. Returning to our room and bursting with joy, we made love out of a place of overflowing rather than mere desire. There were no boundaries, no agendas, no thought— simply love flowing through us for each other and every living thing.

From Sulphur Springs, we headed to Grand Lake, where we got on the Trail Ridge Road, which would take us to Estes Park. The surrounding peaks up to twelve thousand feet high, alpine tundra, and valleys far below were stunning. Chris drove the narrow road steadily, but I was terrified as we skated the edge of the world with no guard rails to keep us from falling into the abyss. I did my best to trust that we would stay on the road, but I didn't relax until we drove through the canyon and finally reached the town of Estes Park.

We turned off the highway onto a dirt road that took us up to Jack and Marlena's house perched at 9,500 feet. We arrived exhausted and hungry. Jack welcomed us with a green chili dinner, and we began to relax. Since another guest remained ensconced in the guest house, we spent the night in their home and didn't see our new lodgings until the morning.

After our deep sleep in a comfy bed and breakfast peppered with more lively conversation, Jack and Marlena took us over to the guest house, which they called the Green House. It was a steep, rocky five-minute walk up from their home, so we were close but not living under the same roof.

It had been Jack's parents' home, and when they died a few years before, Jack built an addition large enough to house his grown children and grandchildren when they visited. When family was not staying in the house, which was most of the year, they offered it freely to friends who needed a place to stay for short periods of rest and recuperation. We were more than ready to have a roof over our heads and the conveniences of home and were grateful to receive their generosity.

Windows offered views of the vast peaks of the Rocky Mountains on two sides, which made me feel like I was in an eagle's aerie looking out over the landscape. Our new home comprised four bedrooms, a living room with a fireplace, a dining room, a fully equipped kitchen, and downstairs in the addition, a big family room.

The house was abundantly equipped with everything from a coffee grinder to a hairdryer. The simple amenities of life—flush toilets, running water, and electricity—which had not been available in our camping life, felt luxurious. We felt like we were living in utter abundance.

I cooked my first meal in a kitchen since we had gone on the road. It was a feast of chicken with lime, chili, and garlic, fresh corn on the cob, and salad with avocado and tomatoes. After so much outdoor living, we welcomed the chance to sink into the luxury of the Kochners' house, especially in the wake of stories we had heard about Hurricane Katrina, Hurricane Rita, and the War in Iraq. Still, we found it difficult to justify such abundance.

Chris and I had expected that we would be the ones offering gifts on our journey, so accepting a place to live for more than a month required a good deal of surrender and humility. We were more used to being givers than receivers. In receiving the generous hospitality, we could only trust that we could learn to be more skillful at giving by receiving. Since givers need receivers, we held the possibility that we provided a blessing to our benefactors by saying yes to their largesse.

As we settled into our new home, I wondered if leaving Knollwood had been a practice for a more significant surrender that we couldn't yet imagine. In the Kochner guest house, letting go of our home and old life didn't feel like a sacrifice. I understood more clearly that we hadn't really needed the large house, work, and structure of our old life. We were fine just as we were. We were more than fine—abundantly surrounded by love, luxury, and beauty.

Our days were full and sweet. Our home was less than half a mile from the entrance to Rocky Mountain National Park, and we got to know the trails that led to mountaintops, lakes, waterfalls, and stunning views. We were welcomed into a Course in Miracles group that met twice a week for study, potlucks, and weekly ping pong tournaments. I enjoyed inviting our new friends for coffee and lavish dinners, and Chris and I enjoyed having a temporary place that we could call home.

As much as I enjoyed our life, I yearned for quiet, solitary time away from everyone, including my beloved. Chris couldn't understand why I had such a longing for seclusion since he had lovingly given me space to do anything I wanted to do. Still, I longed for quiet space to feel who I was, not just as Chris's wife but as myself. Chris may not have understood my longing, but he was willing to support me, and I was grateful.

I started to search unsuccessfully for a meditation retreat nearby. Finally, I realized that I didn't have to go anywhere. The downstairs family room had a bathroom and separate entrance and provided the perfect place for my five-day retreat. Since I planned to fast with the addition of a lemon juice, honey, and chili pepper drink three times a day, I wouldn't need a kitchen, and Chris could continue his life in the central part of the house while I had solitude.

A couple of days before going into my retreat, we surfed the net on our laptop and saw that in December, Ram Dass would lead a retreat in Maui. We were excited that we might spend time with this legendary spiritual teacher who had researched the therapeutic effects of psychedelic drugs in the sixties with Timothy Leary before becoming a disciple of the Hindu guru Neem Karoli Baba, also known as Maharaji. His book written in 1971, *Be Here Now*, outlined his spiritual journey and became a New Age classic influencing diverse people including Steve Jobs, the Beatles, and Wayne Dyer as well as Chris and me.

We immediately began the application process online and were shocked to read that the workshop cost an extravagant fifteen hundred dollars each for only five days not including airfare, food, or accommodations. My anxiety about finances kicked in, and I announced that it was far too much to spend given that we were not making any money while on the road. Chris agreed, and regretfully, we decided that we would have to forego the experience.

I was filled with anxiety on the night before my retreat. Even though I was the one who wanted to leave, I wondered how I would manage without Chris or if he would be angry because I was going. Would my time away be beneficial? Would challenging issues come up or, even worse, would nothing emerge?

I put aside my unwelcome thoughts and decided to enjoy my last night with Chris. I made a fancy dinner of trout, garlic potatoes, creamed spinach, and white wine. Then knowing that we wouldn't share our bodies for five nights, we fell into bed and made delicious love. Waves of intense release surged through me. As I rested on top of Chris in a quiet moment, powerful energy again flooded through me in a billowing torrent. The pulsations continued as we looked at each other in wonder.

"My darling, we have just created a baby," Chris said in hushed tones.

At fifty-eight, I had long passed my child-bearing years, but we chose to believe that a seed had been planted. Something new and mysterious. Something to look forward to.

Bubbling with the new energy Chris and I had generated, I went down the stairs into the family room and began my retreat.

My days unfolded gently. I woke up every morning on the mattress I had placed on the floor in front of the gas heater that simulated a wood-burning stove. After yoga, I sipped my lemon-honey-chili drink for the first of three times a day. After the first day, I no longer felt hungry.

I spent the next five days practicing yoga, listening to a CD course in Vipassana meditation, and reading Rumi poems and Ram Dass's book *Paths to God*, focused on the *Bhagavad Gita*. I loved listening to recordings of Hindu devotional chants and Native American music introduced by Carlos and Maria that brought back the energy of my past journeys. I drew pictures with my inner child, healing her and listening to her needs. Sometimes I just rested.

Each day provided me with much needed bountiful and sacred time. Occasionally I heard Chris working with Jack or got a peek of him outside my window. I was happy that he was engaged and having fun. Sometimes I smelled something Chris cooked when a powerful aroma entered my space. I smiled to think that Chris was taking good care of himself. Being separate from Chris did not diminish my love for him.

I took care of my body by practicing walking meditations up and down the steep driveway. The first time I walked, I took small, measured steps, saying on each one, "Lift, move, place." Initially, the hill looked huge, and my gait was so small and slow that I thought I would never get to the bottom. Feeling the presence of each step, I understood that the more I want to get somewhere, whether to the bottom of the hill or to spiritual wisdom, the longer it takes. I realized I needed to slow down and concentrate on the journey, not the goal, if I wanted to learn to live in the present moment. Coming back up the hill, I barely noticed the steepness when I stayed present with each step.

Every evening at dusk, I sat on a rock and watched the sun go down behind the mountains. On the last night of my retreat, I watched as the whole scene shimmered with radiance. The sun illuminated needles on the surrounding pine trees and hundreds of slender spider-web strands on every tree and rock. Rays of light danced and glistened, creating a web that seemed to hold all creation together.

I left the magical moment of oneness and began my walking meditation down the driveway. I focused on each step, until a strident sound from above jolted me out of stillness.

"Hawaii, Hawaii," it repeated. I knew the voice referred to the retreat Chris and I had decided we wouldn't attend. Searching for the source of the voice, I looked up at the cloudless sky. Finding nothing, I shouted "No" into the void.

The voice was relentless. The more I said "No," the more it repeated, "Hawaii, Hawaii, Hawaii."

Finally, I gave up. "Okay, I get it. We'll find a way to go." I continued meditating and wondered about the strange visitation as I walked back to the house.

The following morning, having completed my five-day retreat, I restored the space to its original state and said my gratitudes.

Even though I had needed time alone, I had missed Chris and couldn't wait to see him. Going up the stairs and entering through the door that connected the two sides of the house didn't feel dramatic enough. I returned to him via the front walk and knocked on the door.

Chris opened the door, and we fell into each other's arms. We hugged and lingered and hugged some more, happily melting into each other's energy. I was overjoyed to be home.

"Chris," I bubbled over excitedly, "I've got big news."

"Tell me. What's been going on with you over these past five days?"

"We're going to Hawaii," I blurted.

"I know," he said.

"What do you mean, you know?"

"Well," he began slowly, "I was walking in the woods, and I heard a deep voice. It kept repeating the words 'Hawaii, Hawaii, Hawaii.' So, I knew we had to go."

I shared my own story and wondered what kind of flying creatures traveled around the top of the mountain, offering travel suggestions to the two of us. We never solved the mystery, but eager for the time we would spend with Ram Dass in Hawaii, we bought our plane tickets.

We accepted that money wasn't really an obstacle. Spirit had called, and we were ready to follow.

Becoming Elders

Youth and elder meet where the pressure of the future meets the
presence of the past. Old and young are opposites
that secretly identify with each other,
for neither fits well into the mainstreeam of life.

—Michael Meade
The Genius Myth

We arranged to leave Colorado at the end of November and go to Hawaii for three or four weeks that would include the five-day retreat with Ram Dass. We wanted to return east for Christmas with Jerry and Georgeanne at Timshel.

As we started planning our trip, I remembered that, in the desert with our teachers, Carlos had said seemingly out of the blue, "You must go to Hawaii and meet the Indigo kids in the jungle of Kauai."

Some New Agers believed the Indigo children, special kids born after 1970 with exceptional and sometimes supernatural traits or abilities, were destined to make changes that would transform the world. Some of the out-of-the-box kids found it challenging to fit into schools or other authoritarian situations.

About a dozen Indigo kids, young men by the early 2000s of our trip, lived off the grid at the end of the Kalalau Trail in

Kauai, away from the world's demands. They were the ones my teacher Carlos wanted me to meet.

I felt a strong resistance to his instruction. I couldn't imagine what I could say to a young man living in the jungle who had left the ordinary world behind. Despite my teacher's urgings, I had no interest in going to Kauai.

One morning, I woke up with a fragment of a dream I shared with Chris. I remembered only that I was supposed to find a free place to stay in Maui before meeting Ram Dass.

"Great idea," Chris said as I described my dream. "Let's see what happens."

Just a few hours later, my father called. After we both established that we were doing well, he said, "I have a timeshare coupon that can be used anywhere in the world, but it needs to be used by the end of the month, and I can't get away. Do you want it?"

I couldn't believe that my dream had manifested so quickly.

"Of course," I said. "I'll call the company right away."

I dialed the number, and a cheerful woman answered.

"I need a timeshare for the first week of December on Maui," I told her.

The woman put me on hold, and when she returned, she said, "I only have one place, but it's not on Maui. It's on Kauai."

I immediately thought about the Indigo kids and felt as if my teachers were setting the stage so that we had to meet them.

Chris and I talked it over and decided there was no reason not to accept a free timeshare even if it wasn't on the island of Ram Dass's retreat. We booked the site and then started thinking about the trip to India we would take after the holidays.

I had always wanted to go to India. Although I had been raised a Christian with the idea of a monotheistic god, the panoply of Hindu gods and goddesses fascinated me even before we met our medicine teachers, who often called those deities into ceremonies. I wanted to experience the foundation where the Hindu religion had sprung and feel its vibrancy on its home ground.

As we thought about our trip to India, we got a call from our friend Mike, a colleague of Chris's at Hopkins and a Buddhist meditator. He said that the Dali Lama would be in India giving a Kalachakra initiation at the beginning of January, and he thought we might be interested. We weren't sure what a Kalachakra was, but we found the site on the internet and read that the Kalachakra was an initiation that Buddhists strive to achieve twenty-four times in their many reincarnations. Given the strong call to take the ceremony, we told ourselves that we must have taken the initiation in a previous lifetime. We knew little more at the time as we signed up for the eleven-day ceremony.

Going early to attend Kalachakra meant we would have to leave the family right after New Year's, earlier than expected, but both Chris and I were convinced without knowing why that we should be there even though we weren't Buddhists.

Neither of us knew anything about India, so we needed to find someone who could advise us about money, where to stay, and local customs. Since we planned to depart soon after our return from Hawaii, it was not too early to start preparing.

When we first began shamanic work with our desert teachers, Carlos and Maria talked enigmatically about a man named Mac. It seemed clear that there was an inner circle that did not include us, but at the same time, we felt they had enticed us into wanting to meet Mac.

We hardly knew anything about him except that he had apparently given Carlos and Maria the clear, life-sized quartz-crystal skull called Jesus that they carried with them. We also heard that Mac offered personal meetings in his home with Max, the famous, life-sized crystal skull rumored to be one of thirteen ancient crystal skulls that would one day be reunited to share their collective wisdom throughout the globe. Discovered in Guatemala, Max may have been used by Mayan priests for healing, rituals, and prayers. New to the shamanic world, Chris and I found the mystique dancing around Mac enticing.

When we told our teachers we were headed to India, they gave us Mac's phone number and said to call him to see what information he could share. They mentioned that he would tell us about a guru named Nagananda, although they didn't explain why.

Mac graciously agreed to speak with us, and as our teachers had warned, he quickly turned to the subject of his guru. "You have to meet my guru, Swami Nagananda. He's a priest dedicated to Kali, the goddess of creation and destruction, and his ashram is just outside Puttaparthi, where Sai Baba has his ashram.

"You may have heard of Sai Baba. He's the one with the Michael Jackson afro haircut who has been hailed by some to be a living god. But it isn't Sai Baba that you must meet. It's Nagananda. Meeting him is essential."

Mac didn't explain the importance of meeting Nagananda, but he asked us to report to him when we returned.

He seemed pleased when we assured him that we would add Nagananda to our itinerary. He ended the conversation by saying that we should call his friend Parvati if we wanted more practical information about India. We thanked him, and I called Parvati.

Parvati was happy to talk and generously shared her bountiful knowledge of India. She emphasized that we should stay at Sai Towers in Puttaparthi near Swami Nagananda's ashram and contact Aslan, a driver and close friend of Swami. After several trips to India, Parvati had become close to Aslan's family and because of that, she said he would want to treat any friend of hers royally. Without understanding why, we continued to feel the urgency of meeting Nagananda.

Parvati offered practical details about changing money, finding healthy food, local customs, and getting around India with a modicum of grace and ease. We felt lovingly sent off on our journey to India by two people we had never met.

On the fifteenth of November 2005, we flew from LAX to Honolulu and then took a quick inter-island flight to Kauai. When we landed, I took my first breath and was in love with Hawaii. I could feel my aching body start to relax as soon as I took in the soft and fragrant air.

We picked up the rental car and were shocked that the $121 per week rate had suddenly grown to more than $600 with added taxes and extras. I kept having to remember not to hold on to my old relationship with money. I needed to learn to trust abundance and know that we would be fine no matter what. I knew that I worried needlessly about money, but my analytic mind still tried to stay in control.

We started our adventure in Kauai at the Kapa Hostel, a simple establishment filled with love, beauty, flowers, and a diverse group of predominantly young travelers. Our room consisted of a double bed and nothing else, with the bathroom right across the hall. The ocean was only a block away, and on our first night in Hawaii, we watched the full moon peeking in and out of clouds over breaking waves.

We spent a glorious week in the timeshare gifted by my father. We enjoyed luxurious days in the sun at the near-by beach, feasted on sumptuous fresh fish dinners, and luxuriated in long hot tub soaks under the stars on our back deck.

One late afternoon when we had gone to watch the sun set over the ocean, we met a shining young couple, Tobey and Amanda, at Ke'e Beach. They showed us the trailhead at one end of the beach for the Kalalau Trail, the eleven-mile footpath along the Nā Pali Coast, and told us they had visited the Indigo kids living at the end of the trail.

Listening to our new friends talk, I found my curiosity growing stronger than my resistance to meeting the young men. Our new friends bragged that they had reached the end of the trail in one day. Not to be outdone by kids half our age, we decided that we, too, would make the trip in a single day.

Two days later, we parked our car near Ke'e Beach and, with backpacks stuffed with our tent, sleeping bags, and food for several days, we found our way to the trailhead. Early morning sun shone brightly as we set out, but the steep, rocky trail remained dangerously muddy from recent rains. After a challenging half-mile climb through brush and small trees, we saw glorious azure waters spreading five hundred feet below us. The trail had eroded over the years, and sometimes as I walked on the narrow footpath, I could feel the ground under my foot give way just slightly, each step warning me of the danger of falling into the abyss.

We hiked through five lush valleys filled with tropical plants, waterfalls, clear pools, rocky outcroppings, mud puddles, and occasional desert-like areas with dry, crumbly rock.

My legs ached, and I could feel blisters forming as sand found its way into my sandals during the arduous walk. Finally after many hours, the path opened out into a large, sandy beach where waves roared.

We had arrived.

A jungle arose behind the beach, and from inside the foliage, we heard a voice calling, "Hello, come on in."

We made our way through a path thick with vegetation and found eight healthy-looking, tanned young men, the Indigo kids, sitting around a campfire. They welcomed us into their circle and invited us to sit and share a joint with them as we made our introductions. They eagerly told us about living together in the jungle, growing coffee and fruits effortlessly in the gentle Hawaiian climate, eating communally, and supporting each other in tender ways.

As we met more of the young men, the brightness of their eyes struck us as well as a look of clarity and depth.

They told their stories, and we learned that our new friends had followed their hearts and left everything behind to learn from living close to the earth. They moved with the flow, and if the flow was not apparent, they waited until it was. Being away from women seemed to help them develop their feminine energies as they took care of themselves and each other. We appreciated their willingness to share their happiness with us.

The joint kept making its way around the circle, and in the building camaraderie, they invited us to join them for dinner. The day before, Tobey and Amanda had told us that the kids had a practice of making spiritual pizza, the pizza version of stone soup. In the old folk tale, people in a starving village didn't have enough food to eat, but there was enough for everyone when they brought the little they had and put it together.

Since we knew ahead of time, we had filled our backpacks with sausage, tomato sauce, mozzarella, and chocolate. The boys happily received our gifts and asked us to come back later in the evening when preparations for dinner would begin.

We set up our tent, and after a quick dip in the ocean, we walked the short distance back to the campfire where our new friends had started the mysterious process of spiritual pizza.

Not a fancy yeast creation, its crust consisted simply of flour and water mixed, kneaded, and then gently patted into an industrial-sized skillet and covered with the offerings brought by hopeful diners.

Because of our many offerings, the pizza was a master-work. One of the guys poured sauce onto the crust followed by sausage, cheese, more sauce, pineapple, and a sprinkling of onions. Then our chef covered the pan with another cast-iron skillet of equal size placed upside-down to create a sealed unit. He put the double skillet over the campfire and set a small fire on top of the upper skillet. Half an hour later, the pizza emerged perfectly cooked, aromatic, and ready for all of us to devour.

We settled into our new beach home at the edge of the jungle as those kids in their early twenties warmly received us, welcomed us as elders, and trusted us with their stories, pizza, and Mother.

Chris and I woke up after a good night's sleep and started to explore our new home. One of the guys had mentioned a hot pot of coffee always brewing down one of the paths into the jungle, and we wanted to investigate. We found an opening that looked promising, and as we entered the clearing, we came upon Dolphin, one of the young men we had met the previous night. Lounging stark naked in a hammock stretched between two slender trees, his tanned, lean body, and tousled blond hair made a beautiful sight to behold.

Seeing us, he apologized profusely, even though we were the ones who had intruded upon his space. We assured him that all was well, and Dolphin invited us to sit down by the hammock on two rickety beach chairs. He offered us coffee from a pot brewing over his campfire along with some Mother in a fat joint.

We sat close to his hammock while he regaled us with stories. After passing his bar exam, he wandered accidentally onto Niihau, the Forbidden Island, illegal for anyone other than a native Hawaiian. He was arrested and worried that his arrest would put his law license at risk. He told us about his girlfriend, the book he hoped to write, and his love of the land. His tenderness and willingness to share so intimately touched me. We listened as he spilled out his heart. After an hour or two, he got quiet and said, "I know why you two came to Kauai."

"Really?" I asked. "Why do you think that we came?"

"Because I needed someone to hear my story, and you were the ones. You were just what I needed. Thank you."

Later that day, we met Alikai, a scraggly, toothless man of about fifty working on his boat's motor on the beach. We stopped to talk with him, and he told us he was native Hawaiian, one of fifteen children, a world-class surfer, and an elder for the kids at Kalalau.

We had wondered how we could avoid the long hike back to Ke'e Beach since my blisters were still raw. We asked Alikai if he would take us back on his boat when we were ready to leave.

"So, how much would you charge to take us back?" Chris asked.

"A hundred dollars apiece," he said with his toothless grin. "Cheaper if you are willing to swim out to the boat from the shore."

"We only have $150 with us," Chris said.

"Okay. I'll watch the tide, and we'll see," Alikai said as he turned his back and walked away.

We spent our days with the kids, eating with them and listening to their stories, hiking, swimming, and soaking up the sun. It felt like paradise, and I thought I could stay forever.

We heard nothing more from Alikai, but his voice outside our tent awakened us on the fifth morning.

"Now is the time," he said in his booming voice. "The surf is low, the day is clear, and all signs are pointing to today being a good day for our departure."

I wasn't ready to leave our jungle paradise, but my blisters hurt, and I didn't want to walk eleven miles again. Reluctantly, we packed up and began our goodbyes, leaving our leftover crackers, cheese, and chocolate behind for our friends.

The guidebook said that high surf and treacherous currents made the ocean ride to Ke'e Beach dangerous for most of the year, and in the fall and winter months, it was illegal to take passengers. To make matters worse, one of the guys warned us that riding with Alikai would put our lives at risk. He described the dangers of Alikai's boat and regaled us with dark tales of sharks climbing into the boat and biting our legs off.

As I listened to those tales of doom, I remembered that my father had told me that the island of Kauai was the last place he and my mother had visited before she died in the boating accident several months later.

I considered the potential danger of getting on a boat of dubious lineage without life jackets and nothing to hold onto but a thin rope tied to the boat's side. I took a deep breath and wondered if I was bringing my story full circle. Either I would die and my mother's story would repeat, or I would face into my fears and release myself from a story that still shaped me.

We agreed to the trip and gave our money to Alikai.

Chris and I stood on the beach and thanked the seven directions—East, South, West, North, Below, Above, and Within. As our young friends pushed Alikai's small boat into the surf, we felt picked up and crashed down as the little craft made its way through powerful waves.

Our first attempt hit a wall of waves, and we headed back to shore almost as soon as we left. I was terrified and wondered if we would ever make it through, but Alikai was a master and would not be defeated. On the second try, we cleared the surf and were on our way.

We enjoyed breathtaking views from the boat, including of the dangerous path we had hiked days earlier towering high above our little vessel. We passed luxuriant green cliffs, dark caves, and cascading waterfalls. Exuberant flying fish danced around the boat all along the way. I felt love and gratitude for the beauty of the Napali Coast and its inhabitants and wished we could stay longer.

The ride took less than half an hour, quick compared to our long hike. To our relief and surprising people on the sand, our boat shot up safely onto Ke'e Beach as we suddenly appeared from out of nowhere.

We stayed on Kauai for another week camping on the beaches under extravagantly star-filled skies and falling asleep to the roar of the waves. We hiked, ate sumptuous meals cooked over our campfire, and met delightful new friends.

Chris and I found it sad to leave the beauty of Kauai.

We had forged a sweet relationship with the land and its people. With the Indigo kids in the jungle, we had found a new role as elders. Yet after two weeks, we were ready to see what our time with Ram Dass would bring.

Ram Dass

We are the mirror as well as the face in it.
We are tasting the taste of eternity.

—Rumi

We flew to Maui, picked up another rental car, and settled into our room in a luxurious retreat center filled with fruit trees, fragrant blossoms, and a hot tub that held half a dozen bathers. Fifty people had gathered for the workshop with Ram Dass.

In 1997, Ram Dass suffered a near-fatal stroke that paralyzed his right side and limited his capacity to speak. He could no longer travel, so he led retreats on Maui, where he made his home. Since his speech was limited, he co-led the retreat with a charismatic young rabbi named Marc Gafni.

Each day, the group met under a tent for a communal breakfast and then gathered in the main indoor meeting hall. Gafni lectured on the profound and provocative ways that sex, eros, love, and the sacred were entangled in the mysteries of the Temple of Jerusalem. It was heady and complex, although a disappointment to many people who had come to hear Ram Dass tell the familiar and beloved stories they had heard many times before.

Still, I found Gafni's careful delineation intriguing in its consideration of how the erotic had been lost when the Temple of Jerusalem fell. I was content to see Ram Dass radiating like a fountain of light while Gafni lectured at his side.

Krishna Das, the well-known devotional singer, led us daily in kirtan, a form of call and response chanting of mantras or hymns. Along with Gafni's teaching, the guru brothers regaled us with stories about Maharaji. The guru brothers, eight men, including the father of one of them, and Krishna Das had traveled to India with Ram Dass to be with his guru Maharaji in the late sixties.

We had plenty of time between morning and afternoon lectures to enjoy the sun, meet new friends, and luxuriate in the hot tub.

We had no lecture on the third afternoon because we were all invited to a kirtan concert given by Krishna Das at a local school auditorium. After lunch, one of our friends told us he had some outstanding Mother to share. There was only one problem. We had all flown into Maui, and airport regulations did not allow lighters or matches on planes. We had no way to light the Mother.

Our group of three kept growing as we asked one person after the other if they had a lighter. Finally, we found someone who had the necessary device. Eventually, we were eight people, all ready to enjoy the Mother's gift.

I had rarely smoked anything so powerful. The first puff transported me far away from the place we had gathered into distant cosmic realms of love and harmony. Chris scooped me up and found a hammock where we curled up together in mutual bliss for much of the afternoon. Our friend saw our pleasure and gifted us with a generous packet of the dazzling medicine we had shared.

Hours later, when we arrived at the Krishna Das concert, I still felt altered and lost myself in the transcendental music he offered. I danced ecstatically and with gratitude, feeling divine energy moving through me.

At the end of our retreat in Maui, four women asked us to take them to the airport in our rental car. We all felt the afterglow of our time together. Out of the blue, one of the women asked if we planned to have an audience with Ram Dass. An audience with Ram Dass? We didn't even know that was possible. But the idea landed, and we had to figure out how to make it happen.

During our retreat, Chris had made friends with Ram Dass's social secretary, Stephanie, and before I knew it, he had pulled over to the side of the road and called her. When she answered, Chris asked if Ram Dass would meet with us. Without skipping a beat, she said she would check it out and get back to us as soon as possible. We dropped our friends at the airport and waited.

Stephanie called a couple hours later to say that Ram Dass would be happy to meet with us at his home on the beach at three the next afternoon. We were thrilled and wanted to bring him a present. We asked people who knew him about an appropriate gift and learned that Ram Dass loved his cats.

We found a pet store and bought a bag of catnip for the kitties. Then, realizing that we couldn't take the Mother we had on the plane when we boarded in a few days, we decided we would bring the catnip for the kitties and the Mother as catnip for Ram Dass. We were all set.

We arrived at his comfortable home on the beach, where two guru brothers ushered us in. We found Ram Dass sitting quietly in his living room. He motioned to us to sit down, and we offered our small gifts, which he graciously received.

"What can I do for you?" he asked.

"We're heading to India for three months and want to visit the places sacred to Maharaji," we explained.

He smiled, and we felt taken warmly into his heart.

"Just a moment," he said gently.

We waited as he closed his eyes and sank into meditation. He sat in stillness for about five minutes and then gradually opened his eyes, looking straight at us.

"I asked Maharaji if he would look out for you during your travels, and he said he would be happy to do that. He said you'll be fine."

The guru brothers were curious about the gifts we had brought and the purpose of our visit. Five of them pulled chairs up around Chris, Ram Dass, and me. We told them about our upcoming trip, and they clamored to share ideas with us. They told us about half a dozen temples sacred to Neem Karoli Baba and dedicated to Hanuman, the monkey god of devotion, and told us to be sure to visit them all. They also gave us names and phone numbers of people we could call if we had an emergency, and they urged us to ride the Indian trains.

"And," one of them said urgently, "you must meet Maharaji's consort, who is very old but still very much alive. Her name is Siddhi-Ma, and she is considered a saint."

"Where will we find her?" Chris asked.

"She's in India."

"North, south, east, west? Do you know which city?" I asked, looking for some clarity.

The guru brothers conferred with each other until one of them said optimistically, "I have no idea, but I am sure that you'll find her."

We took copious notes from all they shared and left happy that we had been so well supported in planning our journey.

The next day, we boarded the plane, which took us back to Los Angeles, where we had left our car with friends. After catching up with them about our adventures, we began our mad drive across the country to get to Timshel in time for Christmas.

We wanted to cover as many miles as possible on each day of our four-day drive. We had set a goal of twelve hours on our third day and met it, but some force compelled me to keep driving. It was dark, and we were both tired. There were only a few more towns before a long stretch of nothing, yet I passed each exit without turning off.

After another hour, exhausted and starving, we got off the highway and entered a town that wasn't clearly marked on the map. The few fast-food outlets we found did not appeal. We stopped at a gas station that advertised sandwiches, but they were all out. The owners saw our desperation and gave us directions to a restaurant called Jake's, which we would never have found on our own at eight o'clock in the evening.

We settled into a booth in the dining room and dug into rare, juicy hamburgers and fries. After so many hours of driving, we sat happily enjoying each other's company without any distractions. Throughout the meal, we talked about our time with Ram Dass.

Ram Dass had said that getting old wasn't easy, but neither was living and neither was dying. He had described his stroke as a gift that had brought him to a higher level of spirituality, and he was grateful. He had thought that he had to give up his body to be spiritual but learned after his stroke that he was more than his body. Although Chris and I were younger than Ram Dass, we found it helpful to hear him talk about accepting the challenges of aging as part of life while emphasizing that we are "unchangeable, beautiful, completely aware, and eternal no matter what."

Still deep in our conversation, we heard a voice from the booth behind ours. I turned around and saw a young man who began anxiously apologizing for listening to our conversation. He said he needed someone to talk to and wasn't sure where to turn. He thought we might be the ones he was looking for

Chris said, "Of course, we'd be happy to talk."

He took a deep breath and told us his name was Jeffrey and that in eleven months he would be twenty-one. Once he saw he had our attention, his story tumbled out. His dad had just committed suicide, seemingly out of the blue. He said he had gone to a medium, hoping to understand what had happened with his father, but that hadn't helped. Given that we had been talking about death, he hoped we might help him find some comfort.

We gently listened to him talk about his guilt for not preventing his father's death, his ambivalence about their past relationship, and his hopes that his father had found a better place. He talked about his search for meaning in life and his fears of failure. A sweet intimacy developed among the three of us as we listened to his stories.

Suddenly, he got quiet and looked deep into Chris's eyes and then into mine.

"I know you," he repeated as he took us in.

We knew we had never met before, but Jeffrey kept repeating, "I know you." His words sounded like a mantra, continually punctuating the conversation as the minutes moved into hours.

His girlfriend was a waitress in the restaurant. When her shift ended, she came over, snuggled up next to him in his booth, and joined the conversation. The four of us talked like old friends until the lights started to flicker, letting us know that closing time was upon us.

We walked to the parking lot and had a sweet farewell filled with gratitude and hugs. We didn't bother to exchange contact information. We had experienced a meeting of souls that did not need an internet address. Jeffrey's "I know you" had sung into our ears and hearts all night.

When I fell asleep, I couldn't stop thinking about Jeffrey's intense experience of knowing us.

Chris and I talked about the previous night's meeting when we woke up, and gradually I understood. When we were in the jungle with the Indigo kids in Kauai, I realized that we had been called to be clear mirrors reflecting the young men so they could see themselves.

When Jeffrey looked at us and said he recognized us, he saw not only us but the God in us. And seeing God in us, he saw God in himself. In that reflection, Jeffrey remembered that he was held in the One. He belonged and was not separate. It had been a sacred meeting and a much-needed time of healing for his grieving heart.

We continued our three-and-a-half-day journey to Timshel and arrived just in time for the Christmas celebrations. I enjoyed being with the family after our months of traveling, and as we settled in, the adventures of the past six months began to feel like misty dreams.

With the barest idea of what might be required in our three-month stay in India, we packed our bags. We trusted in the support of our *Fodor's Guide*, the list of helpful hints from Mac and Parvati, and the itinerary of Hanuman temples we received from Ram Dass and his friends. We were as ready as we would ever be.

Initiation

Whatever is dependently co-arisen, that is explained to be emptiness.
That, being a dependent designation is itself the middle way.
—Nagarjuna, the Mulamadhyamikakarika

My father, Jerry, and Georgeanne drove us to Scranton, where we rented a car to drive to JFK. Ready for the next adventure, we boarded our plane for Chennai, Tamil Nadu, on India's southeast coast.

The flight went smoothly, albeit for far too many hours. After an endlessly long layover in the Paris airport, we landed in Chennai at 2:30 a.m. after almost twenty hours of travel.

The barrage of people wanting to offer something to us or get something from us was overwhelming, especially given our exhaustion. We arbitrarily chose a driver to take us to our hotel and followed him to his three-wheeled scooter called a tuk-tuk. Draped with a mishmash of statues and pictures of Hindu gods and goddesses in wild and garish colors, it seemed more like a toy than a vehicle. Later, we discovered that most Indian cars and trucks were decked with the driver's religious symbols, whether Hindu, Muslim, Jain, or Christian.

Our driver drove for what seemed like forever until it became clear that he had no idea where he was going. We had no choice but to trust that he would eventually get us to our hotel. After a crazily circuitous route, he found it, and we could finally get some sleep after our long journey. We were only beginning. We still had far to go before reaching Amaravathi, where the Dalai Lama would preside over the Kalachakra Initiation.

We took an eleven-hour overnight train and another three-hour tuk-tuk ride to reach Amaravathi, once a holy site of Mahāyāna Buddhism. We drove through fields of bananas, papayas, sugar cane, cotton, and coconut. People in the fields worked in small groups or alone, and others herded cows. Sharing the same road with goats, chickens, camels, donkeys, people, scooters, bikes, and cars was frightening. There was considerable horn honking and close calls, but someone always swerved the right way at the last minute, averting disaster. We saw no westerners but were struck by the women who wore brightly colored saris that fluttered spellbindingly in the wind.

We arrived in the tiny town of Amaravathi, which had been transformed into a tent city accommodating a hundred thousand people, ninety thousand of whom were Tibetans. Depending on one's budget, tents ranged from two-person pup tents to large canvas structures partitioned into ten separate living spaces or individual Swiss luxury tents boasting electric lights, flush toilets, and air conditioning.

Our sparsely furnished lodging in one divided tent had two twin cots, two chairs, and a table with a dim, flickering light. We used western-style toilets in canvas enclosures behind our tent. Plastic curtains enclosed showers with porcelain bases atop substantial dirt. I found getting clean challenging with a hose for cold water, a spray, a small stool for soap and clothing, and mud all around. Neighborhood restaurants and local people who had turned their homes into impromptu eateries provided food, so we didn't need a kitchen.

As we wandered around our new surroundings, we found ourselves in an endless stream of humanity. Tibetans had taken over the town. Men, women, and children in red robes filled the streets. Music blasted, and the sound of prayers and monks chanting filled the air in a constant kaleidoscope of colors and motion. Strangely enough, there was something peaceful about it.

Only two thousand westerners attended the event, and we gravitated toward each other in the streets, restaurants, and our tent city. A primary meeting place was a Tibetan restaurant called Chonor, set up in a massive tent that served hundreds of people. It had a bounteous vegetarian buffet for five dollars, and even better, it provided real coffee.

On our first night, we enjoyed eating at large round tables where we gradually got to know people who would become friends in the next eleven days.

The following day, Chris and I woke at 5:00 to the sounds of our neighbor snoring beyond the partition and crows cawing, monks chanting, people talking, and cars revving their motors. We met some of our new friends at the Tibetan restaurant, had coffee and a banana, and headed to the meeting place at about 6:30 a.m.

The enormous canvas tent where the Kalachakra initiation took place already bustled with tens of thousands of people. A large stage faced the vast space. A curtain in the center of the stage hid the area where monks would construct complex patterns in a sand mandala under the watchful eye of the Dalai Lama.

A special section of the tent close to the front of the stage had been set apart for the westerners. Chris and I placed our mats on the ground close to friends we had met the night before. We felt we already had the beginnings of an intimate community.

A sea of red-robed monks and nuns, mainly Tibetans, filled the space behind us. Local people were assigned to seats in the back. The white canvas fabric of the tent waved in the wind like flowing water. Monks in front of the stage chanted in low, deep tones. The chanting spoke directly to my body, and its vibrations danced inside me.

The Dalai Lama arrived at the tent later in the morning in a car with bodyguards. Security officials searched everyone before we entered the hall, which felt incongruous for a spiritual gathering but seemingly necessary. When His Holiness entered, we all rose in prayerful attention. He then disappeared quickly behind the curtain to supervise creation of the sand mandala.

The monks' rich chanting continued until a complicated form of dialogue in Tibetan replaced it. We heard loud and intense voices going back and forth, punctuated at intervals by clapping or the sharp slapping of a stick. Although a friend told me that the monks were engaged in a high degree of Buddhist debate that involved underlying spiritual complexity beyond my understanding, the sounds felt violent to my ears. I much preferred the chanting.

The first morning ended with prayers. When His Holiness left the tent and was ushered into his car, I was only about ten feet away as he passed. I found myself exuberantly waving to him. Instead of going into the requisite prayer position, I greeted him as if he were an old friend. He smiled, and I told myself that he had recognized me, too.

The Dalai Lama did not teach during the first three days. We just sat for hours listening to the chanting and debates while His Holiness supervised creation of the sand mandala behind the curtain. The heat was so intense in the tent that I thought I would melt, and my bones ached from sitting for hours on my small cushion on the hard ground. Still, I felt invited into an ancient spiritual tradition activating something essential in me.

With ceremonies paused daily for the lunch break, we explored the town. On the long walk through the crowded main street filled with people, I experienced feelings of pity, sadness, and impotence in the face of the terrible suffering, poverty, and sickness we saw.

Some people simply wanted a smile or a friendly word from us. That was easy to give. Others wanted money, and it was hard to say no in the face of such destitution. Still, we knew the need would not end once we started giving. Our small offering of rupees would not make any tangible difference in anyone's circumstances.

The entreaties persisted relentlessly, sometimes accompanied by endless tugs on our clothing and bodies. The poverty and hardship were heartrending. Chris said he felt his skin was being peeled away. Yet our guilt couldn't solve the problems any more than the few coins we might offer.

Turning away from those suffering humans didn't work either. Instead of offering money, we committed to looking into the eyes of each person and seeing them with our hearts. Then we put our hands together in prayer position and said, "I bless you. Namaste. I see the God in you. Namaste." Only a few people responded to our greeting with hostility. Most offered Namaste in return and moved on, often with a smile.

Feeling overwhelmed with the unfamiliarity of our situation, I wished I could talk to my teachers Carlos and Maria. I knew they were far away, but I trusted that I could meet them in my imagination.

I needed help deciding. Even though I had traveled thousands of miles to meet the Dalai Lama, I wasn't sure I should take Kalachakra initiation vows. Since I was not a Buddhist, I wondered if I should simply observe. That felt good and clean, yet the call to the ceremony had been clear. Perhaps it didn't matter whether I was Buddhist. Maybe I was being asked to be clear about my commitment to my own life's path.

I sorted through my thoughts with the help of my inner teacher, my Wise Woman. Clearly, the path Chris and I were taking in our travels and our inner lives was an intentional one, but what did I need to know at this moment?

I asked the inner teacher, "What do I need to pay attention to?"

The answer came back, "Everything."

"How does one pay attention to everything?" I asked.

"Gratitude and adoration are channels for attention. They keep us focused and then become portals to the One."

As I sat with the words, I understood better what Chris and I sought in our travels. When people asked about our intentions in going on the road, I didn't know what to say. Sometimes I wondered if we fooled ourselves into thinking anything worthwhile would come from traveling from place to place. The whole idea seemed crazy.

Then I realized that focusing on what we might accomplish missed the point. Chris and I had sought a spiritual path, and being on the road had become our spiritual path. Spirit had called us to be present with the "isness" of the moment. We didn't need to strive to get somewhere. We were already there.

A spiritual path is like a boat. There are big boats, small ones, private ones, and public ones, but the point of the spiritual journey is not about the craft. That is just the vehicle. What it is really about is the ocean upon which it floats. And there is only one ocean.

For the mystic, focusing on a spiritual path allows structure and the possibility, not the guarantee, that we will fall through the boat's floor into the ocean of Oneness. More than anything, the spiritual journeyer longs for union with the One. Ultimately, it doesn't matter how we get there. We will drop into the same place of Oneness no matter our theological beliefs. In union all differences dissolve.

As a mystic, I saw the Kalachakra Initiation as a valuable tool on my journey to union with God. We were not Buddhists, but Chris and I needed all the mastery we could get, and we were determined to sharpen our tools so we could be even more awake. My mind had settled, and I felt ready to take Kalachakra Initiation, offering myself while letting Spirit decide what to empower.

I began better to understand my relationship with our teachers. Their job was to point the way by continually posing unanswerable questions—"How can I be on a path without being attached? What does it mean to become flitting butter-flies? How do I let go of the need to know?"

The point was not to find answers but to practice paying attention. We always needed to go deeper no matter how much clarity we might reach. We always had more to learn.

With completion of the sand mandala, the teaching began. For the next three days, His Holiness taught in morning and afternoon sessions from the Mulamadhyamikakarika, written by Nagarjuna, the Indian Mahāyāna Buddhist thinker, scholar, and saint, considered one of Buddhism's most influential philosophers. The Mulamadhyamikakarika is the foundational text of the Madhyamaka school of Mahāyāna Buddhist philos-ophy. The eighteenth verse of the twenty-fourth chapter offers a rigorously logical and religious vision of emptiness and the Middle Way. The verse says,

> Whatever is dependently co-arisen
> That is explained to be emptiness.
> That, being a dependent designation
> Is itself the Middle Way.

The Dalai Lama spoke loudly through the PA system as he taught about Nagarjuna's understanding of the Middle Way. We heard the teachings through a crisp English translation coming through our earphones connected to FM radios we had brought.

I had trouble deciding if I wanted to listen to the vibrations of His Holiness or the meaning of the words through the translator. I often missed the meaning of the words because I focused on the sound of the Dalai Lama's voice rather than the translation. The careful analytical logic made me a little tired, but His Holiness's presence was so beautiful that I struggled to stay attentive.

He spoke of emptiness and said that emptiness doesn't mean that nothing exists. It means that something arises because it depends on something else.

He said love binds us together, and we need love to survive. Independence decreases the power of love, and the more loving we are, the happier we are. Understanding dependent origination, the idea that we are constantly shaped and shaping all that is, increases love. The interconnectedness of everything gives rise to compassion and respect. Although I had not studied Buddhism in any depth, his words resonated with me.

After the three days of teaching, we had a day off. All the two thousand westerners could have a private meeting with the Dalai Lama. A monk in saffron robes organized us alphabetically into our countries of origin, and we waited patiently to enter the smaller tent where the Dalai Lama would greet us. Surprisingly, they called the United States first, which seemed like an undeserved privilege.

Chris and I were fortunate to be right in front of the gate that led to the room, and we found ourselves in the center of the fourth row, about ten feet from where His Holiness would stand.

Crammed into the stifling hot, smaller tent, we waited an hour while the other countries were called in one by one. As more people pushed their way in, we had to keep adjusting ourselves to find new and creative ways to fit together. I wondered if our jostling was an intentional teaching of His Holiness, giving practice to how people of many different countries could learn to join together, like pieces of a jigsaw puzzle.

Finally, we were all settled. His Holiness entered and immediately started joking with us. His light humor captivated us, and he put us all at ease.

"I am so grateful to Nagarjuna," he said in his clipped English, shaking his finger vigorously as he spoke, "for thinking through these teachings so brilliantly. He saved me all the trouble of having to think them through for myself. I recommend that you read lots of Nagarjuna and be compassionate toward all sentient beings." With his final offering, he bowed to us, flashed his gentle smile, and departed.

After His Holiness left, I noticed a dark-haired woman sitting close to me. I soon learned her name was Lisa and that she was from California. We began talking immediately about our teachers. She worked with a master teacher named Tian Gong who prepared his students for cultural upheavals he saw coming with cleansings, protections, and channeled prophesies.

Her sharing resonated with what Carlos and Maria were teaching Chris and me, and I felt I had found a long lost sister. Meeting her made me happy as I discovered that I had a much bigger family than I had thought.

Lisa talked about celestial language and asked if I wanted to learn how to speak it. I wasn't sure what I was saying yes to, but we went off to a quiet corner of the tent for privacy. She started by asking me to repeat word sounds after her.

"Oh sah."

"Oh sah," I repeated.

"Janamah."

"Janamah."

"Oh sah, Janamah."

"Oh sah, Janamah."

As she started stringing the sounds together, I realized that the language she called celestial was the language I express spontaneously when I am in mystic states. Some call it speaking in tongues, and some call it glossolalia. My father told me that my grandfather, minister of a church in a tiny Texas town, spoke in tongues, which made me feel connected to him even though he died long before I was born.

Lisa and I had a long intimate conversation in the celestial language. I would have loved to continue, but we had to go to the tent for the first day of the initiation. When she left me, I was surprised that I started to cry even as I continued my mystic channeling.

Chris found me sobbing and asked, "What are all the tears about?"

I had to breathe deeply before I found words. "It's a lot. It is partly the gratitude of meeting someone who knows my language," I said, "and partly letting some of the pain and suffering of my ancestors come through. I am seeing that serious disruption in our culture's foundation is about to happen and perhaps is already happening, and we need to prepare."

With my tears still streaming, I said, "I'm afraid for those of us who live on Planet Earth. It's going to be very hard if we don't do necessary work."

Grief for the pain of the earth's inhabitants often came to me when I was in the medicine. And here in India I felt it.

Chris and another new friend Juliet held me lovingly while I wept and continued to speak in tongues. They listened as I shared my concerns, and by the time we arrived back at our tent, I felt more grounded but still on the edge of a spontaneous altered state.

We had to hurry back to the main tent because the three days of initiations were about to begin. The Dalai Lama spoke in Tibetan during the teaching days, and I had appreciated hearing his words in English. However, when the initiatory rituals started, his voice took on a shamanic, sing-song quality that took me further into my already altered state. I wanted to hear him directly without an intermediary, and I turned off the translation on my radio. Although I no longer understood the words, I resonated deeply with the sonorous vibrations that felt ancient and of the earth.

In the first rite, the water ritual, we received red strings for protection and kusha grass to put under our beds and pillows to bring dreams. Later, the initiation included vows of compassion toward all living beings.

Some of the higher vows posed difficulty for a non-Buddhist to understand, so I did my own version. I committed to my path of adoration, gratitude, presence, love, and truth. I turned myself over to the alleviation of suffering in the world and asked that whatever strength and empowerment I might receive would be for the relief of the suffering of all beings.

I sat in the position of Quan Yin, goddess of compassion, with my right knee bent on the floor and my right hand resting on my knee. A yellow butterfly landed on my thigh. It stayed motionless for almost half an hour until completion of the morning vows. I took its appearance as support for my becoming a flitting butterfly and a sign that I was waking up to a new level of consciousness.

After the closing of the initiation ritual, a friend told us that the sand mandala was on view. Unfortunately, by the time we heard about it, we had missed the opportunity given to foreigners to be first. When we arrived, massive lines of people had filled the tent.

It was hilarious to see the old Tibetan women, small in stature but large in energy, trying to press forward. Standing and waiting in an orderly procession made no sense to many of them, particularly when the line snaked around, seemingly going in the wrong direction.

Chris and I weren't invested in getting to the mandala quickly and simply enjoyed the show as we watched the women sneak under the stanchions only to be gently herded back by the young male guards. Then, as soon as the guards turned their backs, the women returned to what they considered their rightful place.

After over two hours of waiting in line, we entered the curtained area with the six-foot mandala on view. Brightly colored sand shimmered seemingly alive in the light. Complex blue, green, red, orange, and yellow patterns formed the outer concentric rings. Inside the circles nested smaller squares that could be seen as a blueprint of the celestial palace.

I wished I could have stayed and taken in the detail of the mandala's superb construction, but the crowd behind us quickly pushed us along. Not a Buddhist practitioner, I missed much of the mandala's meaning. However, the care and precision the monks had invested to create a beautiful, symbolic representation of the teachings impressed me.

At the ceremony's end, monks would sweep the sand into an urn and empty it into flowing water, a reminder of the impermanence of life and all things.

Long formal closing ceremonies, a long-life empowerment for the Dalai Lama, gratitude to the people who had helped, and an endless and thorough accounting of finances filled the next day. The ceremony ended with crackers, juice, candy, and fruit thrown to the excited crowd.

As our time with the Dali Lama came to an end, we started to worry about how we would get out of town at the same time as a hundred thousand other people. Then I remembered Aslan, the driver Parvati had recommended.

We found an internet cafe with half a dozen barely working computers and with difficulty succeeded in sending an email to Aslan. He wrote back immediately, saying that he would drive the eleven hours to pick us up and take us back to Puttaparthi. We arranged for him to meet us in the morning at the crossroads outside the tent area.

We were uneasy about leaving the only home we had known in India. We appreciated the support we had gotten from the structure and people at the Kalachakra but feared heading into the unknown alone with little to guide us but Spirit. We had no choice but to take the leap.

Meeting the Gurus

O, Mother, you are at once the Destruction, Flood of Concern,
Light and Compassion, Ocean for our heart's aspiration, Flame.

—Sri Chinmoy

Chris and I stood at the appointed place, but we were two people among a hundred thousand. People milled all around us, and we had little hope of finding Aslan. Yet, after less than ten minutes, a tall, dark, slender Indian man about forty years old approached us and kindly inquired if we were Chris and Carol.

We were filled with gratitude when he introduced himself as Aslan. We couldn't believe that he had found us in the crowd and that we could relax into having a trusted guide who would care for us and bring us to our next destination. Chatting nonstop about India, its history, and the places we were passing through, Aslan drove us safely through the wild Indian traffic. He treated us like deities simply because we knew Parvati, who had been sending money and gifts to his family for several years.

We arrived late at night at the Sai Towers, a modern six-story hotel near the town center in Puttaparthi. Aslan helped us get settled in our room and left us to rest. As Chris and I finally got into bed exhausted, we planned to sleep late and take it easy the next day. We had barely had any rest since we left JFK in New York City two weeks before. Our meeting with Nagananda would have to wait.

Early the following day, a loud knocking on the door awakened us from deep sleep. We hastily dressed and opened the door. Aslan stood waiting resolutely to tell us that Swami Nagananda was sick and needed to go to the hospital soon. He said we had to hurry to meet him before he left the ashram.

We had hoped to rest but didn't want to miss meeting Nagananda, so we quickly went down to the hotel's lobby for breakfast. A waiter approached our table as we enjoyed huge, crispy crepes called dhosas with three delicious sauces. Pointing to his cell phone, he mimed a phone call for me. I thought he had to be mistaken. Who even knew I was here? But he insisted it was for me and handed me the phone.

It was Parvati calling from Salt Lake City to tell me she had had a dream. I didn't yet know that Parvati often had dreams, and frequently those dreams were prophetic.

I found a place in a dark stairwell in the back of the hotel where I strained to hear over the scratchy phone connection. Parvati's voice crackled as she shared that she had dreamed that Swami Nagananda had died the night before. When she awoke from her dream, she concluded that Chris and I should acquire one of Swami's robes before he died so that Mac, whom she believed to be Swami's heir, would have it. I had no idea what it all meant, but I assured her we would do our best and keep her posted.

I bid Parvati farewell and returned to my breakfast in the lobby. I felt ungrounded and confused. The fact that I had just spoken to a woman in Utah while having breakfast in India seemed hard to fathom. Chris and I were caught in a story we didn't understand, and it was unclear how we fit in.

We finished our breakfast, and Aslan appeared, ready to take us on the forty-five-minute ride out to Nagananda's ashram. Trying to ground myself, I meditated on the way.

We went up a rough driveway where a multitude of cats of all sizes and colors met us. They walked around the patio surrounding the small Kali temple as if they were local deities. The main temple was a well-cared-for white marble structure, sparkling with light. However, the outer buildings surrounded by overgrown trees and bushes looked neglected with peeling paint, broken windows, crumbling masonry.

Aslan told us that thugs connected with another guru had come the previous year and blown up some of the buildings, which explained the sad state of most of the structures. We never understood what initiated the conflict, but we discovered that gurus did not always have smooth personal interactions.

Nagananda, a beautiful, dark-skinned man with white teeth and a brilliant smile, sat serenely in an orange robe on the patio. Apparently, Aslan had told him we were coming. Nagananda greeted us warmly in strongly accented English and invited us to enter the temple. Inside, we found a large, airy structure with walls covered in colorful murals of Ganesha, Krishna, and other divinities, rising above a black and white marble floor.

Slightly ajar, a black gate stood at the far side of the temple housing a life-sized statue of Kali, goddess of creation and destruction, of death, time, and change. She conveyed an untamed ferocity with her dark blue, almost black skin, shining eyes, and red tongue sticking out of her wide-open mouth. Wearing a skirt made of human arms and a garland of human skulls around her neck, she reached out her two right arms in blessing, while her two left arms held a severed head and a blood-covered sword. She was wild and beautiful. I stood entranced in front of her.

A woman approached and placed a spoonful of spiced rice into our hands. We were familiar with the practice of prasad, consecrated food offered to the deity in a Hindu temple and then distributed and eaten by the devotees who attend. We ate not knowing whether eating the prasad was safe, but it seemed the right thing to do. Never having met a guru before, we felt clueless about what to do. Nagananda had seated himself by an open window on a wooden chair, the only piece of furniture in the room, with us seemingly left to our own devices. Not knowing what else to do, we sat down to meditate with Kali.

After about half an hour, he called us over to him. Unsure of what to expect, we knelt at his feet. He kindly asked us to tell him about ourselves. We said that we had left our jobs as therapist and teacher to go on the road and learn about trusting Spirit. We imparted the love messages from Mac, Parvati, and our teachers, and Nagananda expressed his appreciation for his connection with them.

Mac had told me to watch Nagananda carefully, as he might manifest something. I watched Swami's smooth dark hands, and seemingly out of nowhere he produced between his fingers a white powder. He sprinkled the powder into my open hand and told me to eat it. Then he did the same for Chris. The fine grains melted like snow in my mouth.

He placed his fingers in the palm of my hand and then put his hand in the middle of my forehead on my third eye. A tremendous rush coursed through my body. Every part of me felt stretched and electric. I watched his hand again, and with the slightest movement, he manifested out of thin air a rudrashka, the tough, round seed with spikes traditionally used as a meditation bead.

Not knowing what else to do, I closed my eyes and started meditating. I felt as if I were falling into a vast empty space. I heard a resounding quiet, even amidst the noises in the temple.

When I opened my eyes, I asked Swami how to meditate with Kali.

"Come back tomorrow morning at eight," he said, "and I will teach you."

I was surprised by the invitation, since we had been told that he was going to the hospital. He mentioned nothing about his illness or the hospital. As I watched him throughout our visit, he seemed to shift in moments from radiant good health to fragile exhaustion. Chris and I gratefully accepted his invitation to return in the morning, and then he dismissed us. I took the chance to ask if we could stay in the temple and meditate, and he agreed.

I found a spot close to Kali's gate and sat for an hour meditating as I shifted my gaze from Kali to Nagananda. I was peaceful and felt I could stay in that position forever. Aslan arrived, and after speaking with Nagananda, he came to where we sat and told us it was time to go back to the hotel. I felt reluctant to leave but happy we could return the next day.

Aslan brought us back to our hotel and explained that the guru Sai Baba dominated the municipality of Puttaparthi. The big shot in town, Sai Baba, had unlimited funds. The walls of every business featured pictures of him with his wild Michael Jackson Afro hairdo, and he presided over a massive, marble temple seating a hundred thousand worshippers. Our new friend Nagananda embodied significantly different values, Aslan explained. Nagananda was poverty-stricken and humble, rather than ostentatious. We had been called to the simple clarity of Nagananda.

Chris and I returned to the ashram the next day, and Nagananda taught us the promised Kali meditation. As we sat on cushions at his feet, he asked us to close our eyes and allow blackness to fill the space. Then he asked us to let the black turn into a deep blue and see two white circles each with a black dot. He asked us to let the two circles of light merge into one as the circle turned bright as the sun. All sounds on the outside disappeared as we continued separating and combining the circles.

He sat with us for about an hour as we meditated. He said, "It is easy to teach but hard to practice."

I found that to be true. I could focus on a single white light, but seeing two distinct circles was beyond me. Later, when I asked Swami about it, he answered, "Practice."

Aslan drove us to the ashram every day for the next five days. Each day we expected it to be our last, since we understood Swami was ill and needed to be in the hospital. Each day at the temple was different. Sometimes we meditated with Nagananda. Sometimes we simply sat with him as he perched on his chair and looked out the open window where local villagers came with requests for help. We joined him for kirtan and sang sacred chants. We talked with him, and we laughed with him. We saw him manifest vibhuti, the sacred ash, and rudrakshas out of thin air, and we watched the light of candles fall on Kali's statue making her appear to dance in her holy shrine.

On the night of our last visit, Aslan told us that Nagananda would enter the hospital the following day. We arrived at his temple after dark. While we meditated, a dozen Indian people gathered in the temple. Nagananda said something that we could not understand, and they started to leave one by one. Chris and I weren't sure what was happening and whether we were expected to go as well. Nagananda turned to Chris and me and told us to stay.

We sat on the floor at his feet, and he said he had seen a shape appear in the ceiling that looked like a man with a beard. He said that he thought the man was Chris and that Chris was his brother. He said no more, but Chris was touched by the acknowledgment of kinship with that holy man.

We took the chance to ask about the robe Parvati wanted for Mac. We didn't get a direct answer. Instead, we got an invitation to stay for evening puja, devotions. We gratefully accepted, and soon another group of about half a dozen Indian people, a German couple, and a young English woman joined us.

Evening puja was Bhajan, a ritual of devotional song. We noticed that Swami often got breathless and taken over by fits of coughing during the singing. He had a helper who sang several lovely songs.

With singing complete, we were served prasad of sweet rice and nuts as we bowed to candles lit in front of Kali, beautiful in candlelight. We had bought an armload of flowers from a woman for ten rupees, and I left them on the altar as a gratitude offering along with a generous offering of money for the ashram.

As we were leaving, Swami told us that we should return in March and stay with him. We felt honored that we had made it into the inner sanctum. However, as it turned out, our journeys led us elsewhere, and regretfully, we never returned. Later we heard that Parvati had secured the robes for Mac.

We stayed in Puttaparthi for another week. After our unpretentious but intimate meeting with Nagananda, we had a very different experience of darshan, or receiving the blessing, with Sai Baba. His marble temple was enormous with wide aisles and open spaces where followers sat on the floor with separate sides of the temple for men and women.

Sai Baba could no longer walk comfortably after a fall earlier in the year, so he was driven through the massive temple in his car. He gazed out the open window, giving his blessing to those seated on the side of his path. I was fortunate to have arbitrarily chosen a seat where I could view him directly as he passed. When I caught a glimpse of his shining face and felt his gaze in return, I felt a warm shock in my body and chose to believe I received his blessing.

We continued our travels in India. We visited the Taj Mahal and were heart-struck by the perfect beauty of the architecture, which brought tears to my eyes. We stayed in Rajasthan, where we went on a camel journey for three days. We took a rickety train high into the Himalayan foothills and celebrated Holi, a holiday in honor of Krishna when people throw colored water on each other. We spent two weeks with a guru in Rishikesh, where we sat under a holy tree learning from nature and writing poetry. We explored the sacred erotic temples of Khajuraho and sat by the burning ghats for hours in Varanasi where we observed the fragility of the human body.

After being sent by the guru brothers and Ram Dass on the seemingly impossible quest to find Siddhi-Ma, Maharaji's consort, we miraculously found her. After a month and a half of making inquiries wherever we landed, we started hearing rumors of her presence when we arrived in Rishikesh. We took a chance and hired a three-wheeled tuk-tuk taxi for the forty-five-minute drive to the Neem Karoli Baba Ashram, where she had been seen.

Of the four ashram temples, one held a larger-than-life-sized, colorful sculpture of the late Neem Karoli Baba. A statue of Hanuman towered almost forty feet above the temple. Alongside the building stood a massive marble lingam, or phallus, symbol of divine generative energy worshiped as a manifestation of Shiva.

There was also an imposing marble temple almost empty of ornament and people. In a practice that is a form of prayer, a lone young woman circumambulated a square block that stood in the center of the shrine. A dapper middle-aged man and an elderly woman stood in the corner of the temple quietly talking.

We suspected that we had found Siddhi-Ma.

I noticed that the man had stepped away from the woman, and I asked Chris to ask him if she were Siddhi-Ma. Chris returned minutes later saying the man had affirmed that it was, indeed, she. I felt shy, so I begged Chris to go back and request a meeting with her. Reluctantly, Chris went and came back with the message that the man would ask her if she would be willing to speak with us.

We stood quietly and waited as we watched him approach her. He returned soon after with her at his side. She was a slight woman in Indian dress. Her eyes shone brightly. She had a quick smile and a bounce in her step, belying her advanced age.

She greeted us in English. We told her that we were honored to meet her and brought greetings from Ram Dass. She lit up when she heard his name and asked about his health after his stroke.

We told her that he was doing well under the circumstances, and she chatted lightheartedly about times they had shared together. She gave us her blessing and then was gone. It was a quick meeting, but we felt the power of intricate threads connecting us in that short time with all that is.

While Chris and I processed the chances of meeting Siddhi-Ma, given that we had no idea where to look on the whole continent of India, we noticed the man heading back toward us, cups of tea in his hand.

He offered us the tea, and in a low voice, he said, "I hope you know what a blessing this meeting was."

We assured him that we understood, and he disappeared. It was hard to say whether it was the power of the blessing Siddhi-Ma bestowed upon us or the astonishing fact that we had found her at all with only our clear intention that made the meeting so inspiring. Finding Siddhi-Ma reassured us that, although we felt clueless about what we were doing on our travels, Spirit guided and safely held us in her arms. In three months, we had barely scratched the surface of the ancient civilization of India, but as we got on the plane back to the States, we knew that we were being led on a journey that was changing us forever.

Losing My Brother

If you would indeed behold the spirit of death,
open your heart wide unto the body of life.
For life and death are one, even as the river and sea are one.

—Kahlil Gibran

We boarded a plane in Chennai to take us back to JFK and returned to Timshel, where we had left our car. We found the transition back home challenging.

When we got back to Timshel, I wondered where the Christmas tree had gone and then realized we had been gone for three months and Christmas was long over. The equinox had passed, and it was already spring. It felt like India had been a dream, and we suddenly woke up.

The amount of stuff in western life shocked us. For the past months, we had lived out of backpacks, but after experiencing India, even the limited belongings we carried in our car seemed lavish.

The first time I entered a supermarket, the abundance of goods overwhelmed me. Various cereal brands on shelves in one aisle covered more space than the entirety of some Indian stores. However, I was happy to return to the blessings of hot water and flush toilets.

We spent five weeks at the cottage, where we shared meals with the family, took short jaunts to visit friends, and slowly digested our Indian adventure. The time at Timshel had been nourishing, but Chris and I were ready to get back on the road by the beginning of May.

We packed up the car, said goodbye to the family, and headed west. As we passed through Salt Lake City, we called Parvati. We wanted to thank her in person for helping arrange our trip to India and were eager to share some of our adventures with her. She was happy to hear from us, and we made a date to meet at a restaurant in a local mall.

We found Parvati, a brassy blonde with enormous energy waiting for us. We settled into a booth inside, and as our stories about Swami started to spill out, we felt like we had known each other forever. She told us that she and Mac believed that Nagananda had stayed out of the hospital just so we could meet. Still, we couldn't figure out our part in the ongoing drama.

Excited to hear news about her guru, Parvati asked question after question. She was determined that we meet Mac as soon as possible. As she pressed the importance of a meeting, we looked out the window and noticed a giant red neon sign on a pole posted high above the parking lot, advertising a clothing store. In bold letters, it spelled out, Mr. Mac.

The unexpected synchronicity caught our attention, and we asked Parvati to make the necessary arrangements for a meeting. She said that Mac lived in Florida but was in the process of moving to Marin County, California, not far from where we planned to stay for six weeks. Clearly, destiny wanted us to meet.

A few weeks later, Chris and I started house-sitting in Watsonville, California, near Santa Cruz, at the home of Lisa, my celestial-language-speaking friend from the Kalachakra, with whom I had maintained contact. We agreed to stay for seven weeks while she visited family in Pennsylvania. Lisa was relieved to have someone to watch over her house, and we were grateful to have a place to stay. The mutual benefit pleased all of us.

Three days after we arrived, Parvati called to tell us that Nagananda had died. He was only fifty-five and had died from complications of diabetes. Even though I doubted I would ever return to India, it made me sad to think I would never again see that beautiful human being.

A week later, Parvati called again and said that Mac had arrived at his new home in Muir Beach, California, and wanted us to visit. Although eager to meet Mac, we kept postponing our meeting during three weeks because of a visit from Chris's daughter and because Mac had other obligations. Finally, we made a date.

Traveling north from Watsonville, Route 1 skirts dangerously close to the edge, high above the Pacific Ocean. I trembled as I looked down into the watery abyss far below, fearing we could fly off the road at any moment. Thankfully, Chris brought us safely to Mac's home situated at the end of a road among several other luxurious residences.

Mac's red wooden house was a wild mishmash of angled roof lines. It perched over a ravine and looked out on spectacular views of the Golden Gate Bridge with its blue waters and the scrubby vegetation of Mount Tamalpais. We parked our car on the side of the road and knocked on the door. Mac, a tall, slightly stooped man in his fifties with greying hair, a short beard, and a soft southern accent, welcomed us. He brought us into the living room where we saw a circle of over a dozen life-sized carved crystal skulls. That novel medicine wheel filled most of the room and overflowed with ritual objects in the north, south, east, and west. Candles, crystals, cards, and even a movie script Mac was working on were carefully placed in each quadrant.

Mac's desk, covered with papers, took up one corner of the room, and three easy chairs circled the edge. As we settled into our seats, two cats greeted us and jumped into our laps, making us feel at home.

Deep in grief from the recent death of his guru, Mac eagerly waited to hear stories of our visit to the ashram. In appreciation, he gave us each a small rose quartz crystal egg. He told us that whenever he traveled, he spread crystals as symbols of unconditional love. We gratefully accepted his generosity.

Parvati had identified Mac as her teacher, but we didn't know what that meant. Chris and I weren't looking for a teacher, but I felt a resonance with Mac and wanted to share something of my own spiritual journey. I told him I longed to become a dreamer able to more fully live in the world of form and no form and asked him to read a story called *Moon Dreams* that I wrote after a meditation in Watsonville.

The story concerns a Native American girl who wanted to learn to dream. She enters a mystical world where she meets a mother bear, walks in a stream, and feels her roots in Mother Earth. She falls into her reflection and becomes one with the light of the moon. She dissolves and lets go into death and rebirth as a tree in the forest where she began her dreaming. It was a tale of life, death, and the cycles of rebirth.

Mac read the story on the spot, taking about ten minutes to take it in its entirety. "Don't worry about becoming a dreamer," he said. "You're already there." Mac then replaced the little eggs he had given us with two three-inch rose quartz crystal skulls. I felt I had allowed him to know me and that he had generously received me. We had recognized each other, and I knew we would become friends.

Later in the evening, we drove the nearly two hours back to Watsonville. On the following morning, Chris and I prepared for an all-night medicine journey. We created sacred space with altars filled with candles, flowers, crystals, and sacred statues. We intoned prayers and called in the seven directions. At noon we brewed the mushroom tea we would share.

We started the journey with one capsule of Syrian Rue, and after an hour, we drank the tea. The medicine came on very gently.

Soon, however, Chris quickly began to bellow, which I recognized as his typical response to entering the ecstatic state. Since we were in a residential area and not out in the wild, I was concerned that someone would hear the noise and call the police. Still, I didn't want to interfere with his journey. For the first couple of hours, I stayed grounded enough to tend him, putting my own journey aside.

Over and over, I whispered in his ear, "You are tired. It is time to rest. It is time to dream a new dream." Often that would be enough to quiet him. Sometimes I put my hand gently over his mouth so that he would be still.

While I tended to Chris, voices in my head gave me messages to carry out particular rituals with candles and other objects on the altars in my mind. A voice asked me to pour holy water from Ammaji, the hugging guru, on objects on the altar. One voice asked me to move things closer to each other or to different places on the altar. Voices told me to keep watch over the candles so they didn't go out, and I heard a voice that said each candle represented a particular person.

One candle represented my sister Ginger, who had struggled with bipolar disease since she was twenty-seven. The very dim flame of that candle kept going out. I relit it, telling Ginger it was time to be strong. Eventually, I noticed that two metal pieces in the candle interfered with the flame. When I removed them, I had the feeling that Ginger would no longer have any difficulties.

A voice told me to bring a mirror from the other bedroom and place it on the altar with the Shiva lingam, flowers, and a skull. I looked at the reflection of my face, and it morphed into dozens of different people. Eventually, it rested on one, clearly the face of my niece Amira. When her face appeared, transposed on my reflection, red dots spread down the left side of her cheek as an eagle feather cupped the right side.

I found it strange to look at myself in the mirror and see Amira's face, yet I was delighted to feel our ongoing connection in present and past lifetimes.

By the time I finished with the mirror, Chris for the first time began to move into a new stage of his journey. His bellowing had ended, and he no longer needed my attention. In fact, he seemed available to hold space for me.

I put my mat down near the door where I intended to do yoga moon salutations. When I got there, I no longer felt that was the right thing to do. I had worn a purple bandana all evening, and I found myself joining the ends of the bandana so that it made a circle at my side. I repeatedly reached in and out, feeling as if I dipped into a never-ending source of energy and manifestation. When I did so, it seemed possible for me to manifest anything that I wanted.

I was fascinated by the idea that we are God playing hide and seek with Him/Her/Them. I played a game of hiding the skulls Mac had given us in the bedding where I lay and then forgetting about them. The game then had me go looking for them.

As the night went on, I kept finding the skulls. Eventually, one disappeared, and I invented a ritual in hopes of finding it. I took each piece of bedding, cradled it in my arms, said goodbye, and placed it to the side in an imaginary graveyard. Eventually, I had used up all the bedding, but I still hadn't found the skull. I did, however, experience the connection between grief, loss, and looking for God.

The Native American music we played all night carried me through my journey. During the pause between each track, I fell into the void. I rested in stillness until music started up again, and I imagined that I was reborn over and over into new lifetimes. After sixteen hours of journeying, I was exhausted and understood for the first time why the Buddha wanted to get off the wheel of life. I knew there was more to learn, but I was running out of energy. In our journeys with Carlos and Maria, a finite amount of wood was cut, which created a built-in endpoint. Since I constantly replaced the candles, we had no natural ending point.

At 4:30 in the morning, still significantly altered, I couldn't do any more and thought it would help if I pulled the plug on the music. Thankfully, it brought me out of the medicine so that I could sleep, which I gratefully did until eight in the morning.

When Chris and I got up after our brief rest, I went outside to pick up the newspaper. Wind blew with wild and eerie energy. Leaves rustled in a sinister dance, and the world felt unsettled. My head ached from the night's ritual, yet the wind told me that the work had not finished. Something remained open and waiting.

As I listened to the wind, fear threaded its way through my body as if a foreboding presence lurked nearby. I couldn't connect it with anything from the previous night's journey, but the darkness stayed in my mind. I checked the voice mail on my phone for messages, but for some reason, I couldn't connect.

After breakfast, I rechecked the phone and saw I had received an unusual number of messages in the night. I watched the wind move in the trees as I finally connected to voice mail.

The first message was from my brother Dan's partner, Anna. The voice sounded urgent and said only, "Please call. I need to talk to you."

The second message from my father made everything clear. "Dan died."

That was all he said. "Dan died. Call me."

I was stunned. No tears came to my eyes and barely a thought. I struggled to assimilate something so far beyond my mind's capacity for understanding. Died? Died? What do you mean he died? He's my brother. How could my little brother die? How could a light as bright as Dan's be snuffed out?

My sweet, beautiful brother, dead.

His death came as a shock, although perhaps it shouldn't have. Dan was a childhood diabetic, first diagnosed when he was nine. Even then, so many years ago, we were warned that he would not live into old age. Insulin, the magic medicine that allows the diabetic body to function, also destroys internal organs even as it supports life. By the age of fifty-five, the organs of most childhood diabetics have been damaged beyond repair.

Our family, well aware of that reality, managed to find a way to forget. We chose to believe that, because we loved Dan profoundly, his body would be hardy and he would somehow escape or postpone his destiny. My brother was active, seemingly healthy, and full of life. Most of his friends didn't even know about his diabetes.

Dan left home right after he graduated from Columbia University. Although I missed him once he was gone, I understood why he had to go. Our father was a powerful and charismatic being, a force of nature. I had the advantage that I had been born a girl and not a boy, so I didn't have to compete with my father's fierce, masculine drive. My brother, far more like his grandfather, a minister and a mystic, had no interest in striving or competing.

After college, Dan moved three thousand miles away to California where he could live a quieter life. He found Sufism, worked for the American Red Cross, and eventually became a Sufi sheik. He followed the Jud tradition of being a spiritual leader and teacher, but he did it out from under the shadow of his father's striving and conventional success.

With Dan's death, a part of my world, family, and my own being vanished. Something in me had died as well. I was no longer the person I was just days before when I shared the earth plane home with the only brother I had known.

We had had a future. We had had stories to tell and triumphs to celebrate. With Dan's death, I had to live in a world empty of his energy, voice, and dreams.

When he was initiated as a Sufi, his teacher gave him the name Ishaq, which became his preferred name. As a wise spiritual teacher and Sufi sheik, a loving father of three bright and creative human beings, and a gentle man, he was a gift to the earth. I didn't want to accept that Ishaq, the simple presence that made my heart happy, was no longer on the earth plane.

First came the anger. I didn't want to learn a new way of being in the world without Ishaq. I wanted my old life back. And yet there was nothing to take back. That story had ended. It was over, dead. If I insisted that things remain the way they were, I would be left with nothing but dry memories. Living in the past would keep me separate from the mystery and the new form and gifts it would provide.

I knew the reality that my brother had died, but I still wanted to hold on to him. If only I could have him just a little longer. Even in my longing, I knew I'd never be ready to let him go. I felt angry that I had to surrender to the uncompromising truth of his death and the necessity of stretching myself to make room for the change that I had never wanted to happen.

Then I was filled with grief. Remembering the fleeting beauty of Ishaq's life, I saw its preciousness and tenderness. I thought of him playing his guitar, singing, leading Sufi rituals. I remembered him talking about the adventurous hikes he took with his three kids or the last gig when he played his guitar and sang with his long-term partner, Anna. I saw his light shining, sometimes flickering, sometimes burning strong. I saw him showing up when it was hard, giving his heart and soul to his work with the Red Cross, his students, and his life.

I remembered his last trip to Timshel when he and I cut down an outrageously tall fourteen-foot tree to celebrate our inflated memories of the Christmas trees of our childhood.

Ishaq had a remarkable capacity to celebrate the small things in life, holding the ordinary and making it extraordinary. He lived a simple life with barely enough money to pay the bills, but he always felt singularly blessed. His Sufi students appreciated his generosity and integrity as he breathed beauty and spirit into everything he did. How could he be gone? I wanted him back.

The world needs the kind of simplicity he brought. I grieved for the loss of his physical form that had graced our world. I knew I felt the kind of grief born of the abundant joy he had brought me. It was a grief deeply touched by his presence, and I was filled with gratitude that I had had the privilege of being with him in my life. Like the cherry blossoms in spring, my brother's short life awakened my spirit. But also like the pleasures of spring, I could receive the blessing. I couldn't hold on to the fleeting moment.

In shock and pain, I took care of all the necessary communications with family and, surprisingly, found myself calling Mac to tell him of Ishaq's death and share my grief. Even though we had met only the day before, I knew he was someone who could understand what I was going through.

"When can you come?" he asked, needing no further explanation."

I explained that we were coming to the end of our seven-week commitment to house sit for Lisa and that it would take two days to move out of our temporary home, but we would get to him as soon as we could.

"I'll be waiting for you," he said.

When I got off the phone, I finally broke down and cried deeply for the first time. Sobs came from places I barely knew, deep inside of me. I kept saying, "Oh," over and over. Trying to find a way to digest it, I felt I had repeatedly to remind myself that Ishaq had died. Gradually, I slipped into speaking in tongues. I was conversing with my brother in a language we had never spoken together.

Chris covered me with essential oils called gratitude and joy. Even with all my grief, I was celebrating Ishaq. As Alan Watts says of one who has died, "Now he has graduated." Sad as I was, I was grateful that Ishaq was flying free with the angels and no longer bound by a body ravaged by diabetes.

The Wedding and the Funeral

*Tender words we spoke to one another are stored in the
secret heart of heaven. One day like rain, they will fall and spread, and
our mystery will grow green all over the world.*

—Rumi

We took the next two days to pack up our belongings from our Watsonville home, where we had been house-sitting, and drove to Mac's house. I could hardly wait to see him. It didn't make sense that I longed to see a person I had met only once, but I felt as if I were lost in the desert and heading toward an oasis.

When we arrived, Mac hugged me and ushered me into his healing room, where he began the many hours of bodywork he would provide. The table where I lay had a heated cover filled with amethyst crystals delivering healing negative ions. Moving his hands expertly over my body, he knew just where to probe to create the release I needed. I trusted him implicitly and allowed my feelings and body to go where they needed to go. I screamed, cried, and retched. I clawed, and I groaned. Mac relentlessly and effectively followed the energy through my body.

Even lost in my own sorrow, I realized I grieved not only for my brother. I was also giving voice to Mac's unexpressed grief for his beloved Nagananda. Both he and Ishaq were beloveds who had died at fifty-five of complications from diabetes. We grieved together, each in our own way, for two much-loved spiritual teachers who had left us too soon.

Mac finished working on me and told me to go out to the hot tub to ground myself. Then he started to work on Chris. When I walked onto the deck, the world felt transformed. The branches of trees danced, the sky filled with sparkle, the hills seemed to dance. Spirit energy was so thick it almost looked like it was snowing.

It seemed as if my connection with Ishaq had blessed the land and healing work that Mac would do in his new home. I had a vision of Ishaq no longer constrained by the limitations of a body and saw him flying around the world blessing, healing, and teaching.

Over the next three days, Mac helped me release more pain in my body and heart. He held Chris and me in tender love as we began to heal. Our healing was not only for ourselves. Dan's oldest son, Shems, was getting married the very next weekend, and we wanted to arrive as a strong presence holding space for the grief of other family members.

It was a harsh reality that my brother died one week before Shems's marriage to his beloved Crystal. Having been swept into the shock of Ishaq's unexpected death, holding both grief for having lost him in the present life and joy for his son's upcoming marriage presented a formidable task.

We all did our best to meet the challenge as we gathered for the wedding in the small California beach community of Sea Ranch. On Friday, August 4, just one week after Ishaq's death, my family gathered at a spectacular rental house near the edge of the cliff going down to the Pacific Ocean. The house provided everything we might need during the wedding weekend, and we felt surrounded by luxury.

In the evening, Chris and I joined friends and family for the rehearsal dinner at a close-by winery. Despite my desire to honor Shems and Crystal joyfully, the boisterous energy of the gathering felt unbearable. Without a container to hold our feelings, we were a family grieving with raw emotion. No one talked about the inescapable fact that the groom's father had just died. Trying to support the bride and groom, we simply conducted ourselves as if all was well.

Yet with our family's grief so heavy, I imagined that—afraid our suffering was contagious—other guests shied away from us. Shems and Crystal did their best to look happy, but the strain was evident as the celebration unfolded.

As the sun went down, bitter cold invaded the outside dining tables. My body's physical discomfort added to my desire to run away. The bride and groom had thoughtfully gifted each woman with a pashmina shawl to protect us from cold winds, but that brought little comfort. We ate, danced, and celebrated, yet the shadow of death hovered.

Chris and I left the winery and sat alone on a cliff. We looked down at waves crashing on rocks. The power of the waves and their continuously changing form comforted me. We knew that death was part of life, that nothing stays the same for very long, and that all was well, but it didn't feel that way. My tears fell for my beautiful brother as I watched the reflection of the almost full moon dance on the waves.

My father and Georgeanne, my sister Ginger, my stepmother Elisabeth (who had stayed close to the family after her divorce from my father), Ishaq's partner, Anna, and Chris and I returned that night to the rental house provided to accommodate us.

I found one bit of good news in the darkness. My sister Ginger appeared to be far more grounded and balanced than we had expected given the challenging circumstances. Perhaps the healing in my journey the week before had actually made a difference.

The following day, we had breakfast at the rental house and dressed in our wedding finery. We looked the part, but I felt like I was preparing more for a funeral than a wedding. My father seemed calm when we arrived at the wedding site. He put on his blue clerical robe and asked Chris and me to sit in a place where he could see us while he officiated.

Dressed in white sundresses, the bridesmaids processed to their places next to the flower-adorned arbor. Shems stood bravely with his groomsmen as he waited for his beloved to join him at the altar. Watching him, I saw the enormous effort he needed to keep from breaking down. He reminded me so much of his father, Ishaq. Even in his happy and relaxed moments, Ishaq seemed to have a shadow of grief, and I remembered his trembling lower lip when he felt hurt as a child.

Radiant in a strapless, red silk gown and short white veil, Crystal walked down the aisle. She and Shems stood before the trellis, and my father moved to begin the ceremony with the invocation. Instead of words, however, only sobs emerged. I saw his shock at the uninvited rush of emotion.

He steadied himself and continued, stopping several times during the ceremony to weep and compose himself. Chris whispered to me that we should go up to support Jerry, but we both knew that he had to get through the moment by himself.

As Crystal and Shems made vows to bring their separate lives together, my father's tears presaged the full range of life experiences that a couple commits to when they marry. The stark truth that joy and sadness are inexplicably linked in a marriage is rarely expressed so explicitly in a wedding celebration. My father's honest emotions invited the couple and congregation to enter the reality that life is a dance of light and shadow held by love.

After my father said the requisite "I now pronounce you man and wife," the bride and groom kissed, and the receiving line began. Chris and I scooped my father up, took him to an out-of-the-way bench, and quietly held him. He continued to feel out of control and embarrassed. He insisted that his emotions had shown a shameful lack of professionalism.

Nothing we said broke through his wall of defense. He could not accept the possibility that he had gifted us all by sharing his love and his own grief. We tried to help, but he had to experience his sorrow in his own way, so we left him to sit with his thoughts.

As we waited for the celebratory dinner, I had no energy to start a conversation with anyone. I began to drift further and further away from everyone in the room. I felt surrounded by strangers who seemed to care so little that a precious life had ended. Fortunately, through the efforts of friends and family, dinner proceeded, eventually with toasts, stories, and dance music that raised the energy. When things started to wind down, Chris and I gratefully returned to the quiet of our rental house.

The following day, we awoke to preparations for a different ceremony. Since the family had already come together for the wedding, Shems rented a tiny chapel in Sea Ranch to celebrate Ishaq's life. The small gathering included my father, Georgeanne, Ginger, Elisabeth, Anna, Ishaq's kids Amira, Dan, and Shems, Shems's new wife, Crystal, half a dozen Sufi friends, and Chris and me.

Driving to the chapel, we saw something moving in the woods at the edge of the parking lot. A young stag with antlers stood very still for almost a minute. We watched as he abruptly turned his head and stared directly at us. After our brief meeting, he turned and leaped off into the woods.

The stag widely symbolizes the god who dies and is reborn again. How powerful that the beautiful creature greeted us in our grief. I felt that Ishaq had sent the stag to remind us that his spirit was and always would be present with us.

A beautiful jewel in the shape of a shell, the Sea Ranch chapel features a roof covered in flowing patterns of cedar shingles. Three stained glass windows create a rich and warm light on the stone floor inside. Seashells and sea urchins from the ocean nearby are embedded in the ceiling. I rearranged the movable redwood pews into a circle to create a sense of unbroken wholeness.

With the room ready, a dozen friends and family arrived for Ishaq's celebration of life, which I would lead. His partner, Anna, began by singing *Tender Words*, a song she and Ishaq had set to a Rumi poem.

Tender words we spoke to one another
are sealed in the secret heart of heaven.
One day, like rain,
they will fall and spread,
and our mystery will grow green
all over the world.

The words and music vibrated in our hearts, and we moved into the quiet of a Quaker service where people sit in silence and speak from the stillness when they have something they want to share.

Our stepmother, Elisabeth, shared her regret for not showing her love more expressively when Ishaq was alive. As much as she spoke of disappointment, it was her love that shined through. Ishaq's friend Kahlil led us in a Sufi practice of sacred breath, and one person after the other shared funny, touching, and sad stories. We laughed and cried together in the intimacy of the chapel.

Shems brought a recording of his father telling a favorite story from Sufi camp. It began:

> A sheik arrived in town and was purported to have been leading strange and suspect practices. News of this holy man worried the local priests, and they came to investigate. The sheik asked his accusers if they wanted to hear what was real or only what they wanted to hear.
>
> They asked for the truth. Suddenly, the holy man made himself disappear, and then just as suddenly, he reappeared. As if that wasn't enough, he proceeded to make all of the priests disappear and reappear. In his final act, he made everybody disappear and reappear.
>
> After the unsettling demonstration, the local priests decided they didn't want to see anything else and that it would be best not to bother the strange holy man anymore.

The story ends there, but perhaps for those of us grieving, the story offered something prophetic, something about shifting form, disappearing and reappearing, and knowing that it could all be real. My brother loved to tell the story, and with Shems's offering, we heard it again.

How eerie to hear Ishaq's voice sounding so alive and wise. It made me wish I had been awake enough to have received more of his spiritual life. I could have learned a lot. More than regret, however, I felt gratitude that I had shared as much as I had of his inner world. I felt grateful that his spirit would always be alive in me as I continued on my own spiritual path.

The two hours of our allotted time in the chapel sped by, and I realized that I had to bring things to a close. I had asked Anna to bring a jug of tap water from their home in Eugene, Oregon— water sourced from the McKenzie River, where Ishaq had died. I poured the water into a red pottery earth grail Chris had made, and sharing the water, we carried out a variation on the communion ritual. I asked everyone to bless each other with the words "the water of life" and to add whatever personal blessing they wished. We passed the grail around with prayers, tears, and laughter. We ended with three Oms. Just as my mouth began to take the shape of the first of three final Oms, I saw a hawk, messenger of the gods, fly by the window. We completed our ritual and filed out of the little church.

Days later, I learned more about what led up to my brother's death. One of Ishaq's friends, Jamilla, an emergency room nurse, told me he had gone to the doctor for a periodic checkup in early July. The doctor had not given him a clear understanding of his medical report, so Ishaq asked Jamilla to translate it for him. He told her that he wanted the truth, not a comfortable story.

She told him honestly that his kidneys were likely to fail within six months and that dialysis would be necessary. One of Ishaq's teachers had been on dialysis for many years, and Ishaq had told me he never wanted to live that way. He hadn't shared what he learned from Jamilla with the family, and I heard the story from her only after his death.

A week before Ishaq died, he called me. He sounded almost ecstatic. He told me that he had spent a gorgeous day visiting seven bodies of water—the ocean, a lake, three rivers, a pond, and a hot spring. He talked as if he had been initiated into a new level of consciousness. He said he was ready to cut back his work at the American Red Cross and perhaps even stop work entirely. I heard him getting ready to fly free, and I was happy for him. A week later, he was indeed set free.

Late in September when his Sufi friends held another Celebration of Life, I heard the details of my brother's death. Every summer, Ishaq's colleagues at the Red Cross made an expedition down the McKenzie River. A week after the visitation to the seven waters, Ishaq joined his friends at the river early on a glorious, sunny morning, and they traveled lightheartedly down the river deep into the wilderness.

At noon, they stopped for lunch at a place called Jump Off Point. While the others prepared the meal, Ishaq swam out alone to the middle of the river and raised his arms to the heavens. Letting out an ecstatic laugh, he left his body. At the precise time, two geese flew over his head and tipped their wings as if sending him wishes for a joyous journey.

His friends on shore noticed that Ishaq's laugh had quieted and saw his body sinking. They rushed to bring him back to the beach where they spent hours trying to revive him to no avail. His soul had already left his body, probably due to a heart attack. His earth plane story had ended.

For me, even in my grief, Ishaq's death gave me hope that when my time came to die I might do it with such grace and ease. With failing kidneys, Ishaq understood that his life as he knew it was over. In a matter of months, he would no longer have had the freedom to live life in ways he had found so satisfying. Feeling complete, he could gently let go gracefully and with a laugh that echoes in the hearts of all who knew him. What a gift to live life full out yet lightly enough to let go when the time is right.

After his death, I dreamed of Ishaq. I saw him trudging laboriously in a heavy, black wool coat that almost reached the ground. As he moved forward, it started to slip off his body, and with each step, its weight hindered him less and less. Gradually, the coat fell totally away, and his form dissolved.

Ishaq was free, free from this world, and free to move lightly into next adventures awaiting him. His spirit took flight.

Preparations

Be here now. Don't anticipate, don't yearn for things of the past.
Let the past go with forgiveness, and
let the future go with no anticipation.

—Ram Dass

I spent nights that followed Ishaq's death wandering in my dreams. I tried to understand who I was with my brother gone. His death affected my life in the same way that a slight turn of a kaleidoscope radically changes the former pattern.

His dying shook my understanding of who I was as a living being and what it means to die. When Ishaq was alive, he had a sense of who he was. Those of us who knew him experienced him in our own similar and different ways. All those Ishaqs floated around simultaneously in a shifting field. My connection to Ishaq didn't come primarily from being physically present with him. Since he had moved to California after graduating from Columbia University, I hardly saw him. My relationship with him connected to his voice on the telephone several times a year. He was most often a thought in my mind.

So how could a thought die?

Or, for that matter, how could a thought live?

With my brother no longer living in a body, I began to think of him not just as the little brother I had known and loved, but as a portal to the One. He was still alive in my thoughts in spirit form even though he no longer inhabited a body. I wondered if I could meditate on him as I often meditated on the ninety-nine Sufi names of God. The quality of each name of God is only one aspect of God, but by connecting deeply with any given element, we can connect with the whole. By meditating on Ishaq and practicing the name Ishaq, I hoped to find a channel into the One. But nothing was moving inside of me. My thoughts were a tangle, and I couldn't make sense of Ishaq's sudden departure. I barely knew what I was feeling. I was sad, but what was I grieving? Had my life changed that much with Ishaq's death?

Nothing had changed in any literal sense, yet the way I saw my place on the planet had changed. I knew people died all the time, but if my brother could die, I could die. My own eventual death had grown into a more concrete reality.

Experiencing Ishaq's death didn't make me fear my death. It made dying look easy. It also made me realize the fragility of my beloveds. It wasn't death I feared but the enormity of facing their loss. I kept wondering where Ishaq was and what he was feeling. The fact that I couldn't find answers to where he was and how he was feeling made me wonder even more.

As I processed my grief, Chris and I prepared for a trip to work with shamans in the jungle of Peru. When we started studying with our teachers, we looked forward to experiencing other medicines, especially Ayahuasca, a hallucinatory plant-based tea taken under the guidance of a shaman.

Before we left to go on the road, we heard from a friend and student of Carlos and Maria about an Ayahuasca circle in the

Los Angeles area. We wrote to the facilitator, Oskar, asking if we could join the ceremony. We got a polite response saying that he was not interested in our participation. Not dissuaded, we wrote, asked again, and received the same answer. Audaciously, we asked our friend Steve to speak directly to the facilitator and finally received our longed-for invitation. However, the invitation pertained to a ceremony not in Los Angeles but in the rainforest of Peru.

We read every book and article we could find about the process. We learned that ingesting Ayahuasca was a widespread practice within the Indigenous tribes of the Amazon.

The books described a vast array of healing visions and wild hallucinations of jaguars and crystal castles, but they warned us to keep our expectations modest since responses varied widely. The experts assured us that the tea, respectfully called Mother Ayahuasca or Mother Vine, would provide the unique emotional, mental, physical, and spiritual healing we needed.

In October, two and a half months after my brother died, Chris and I packed two large duffel bags with everything we needed for living in the jungle for two weeks with Oskar and a dozen others.

Two days before our departure from Los Angeles International Airport, we began *dieta*, the required preparatory fast that eliminated almost every food I enjoyed—salt, citrus, dairy, sugar, acid, pork, and iced drinks. The forbidden list also included sex and alcohol. The *dieta* was not pleasurable, but we wanted to honor Mother Ayahuasca by observing all the necessary protocols.

We left our car at my friend Marilee's house, and she dropped us at the bus station to get the shuttle to the airport where we would meet Oskar and the other participants.

As soon as we stepped out of her door, the universe started playing tricks on us. We missed our bus by three minutes, which wouldn't have been a big deal, but the next bus was more than twenty minutes late. Although we hadn't met, I imagined Oskar, our facilitator, a stickler for promptness, and I didn't want to begin on the wrong foot. All the others on the trip had experienced at least one Ayahuasca ceremony. They all knew Oskar, and most people knew each other. Chris and I alone had never tasted Ayahuasca and didn't know any of the others. We worried about our possible lack of preparation for the new adventure but took comfort in knowing we would be facing it together.

Despite our delay, the bus got us to the airport with plenty of time, and we began the long process of checking our bags. Finally, we joined the line to get our boarding passes. As the endlessly long line snaked around to the check-in desk, we enjoyed chatting with three men in front of us who were also heading to Peru with Oskar. I got my boarding pass with no problem, but the check-in person kept looking at Chris's passport. "Do you have another passport, sir?" she inquired politely.

"No, do I need one?" Chris asked.

"Well, this passport has expired," she answered. Looking at me, she said, "You can go," and to Chris, she continued, "and you can't. You have ten minutes to make up your mind about what you want to do."

We looked at her in disbelief, but there was no doubt. We knew we had no way to get around the indisputable reality that Chris did not have a valid passport. The plane would board shortly, and we had to decide how to proceed.

We found a quiet spot in the waiting area and sat together in dazed silence. Finally, Chris broke the stillness.

Looking at me tenderly, he said, "It would be fine if you go or if you stay. Either way, I'll be okay."

Touched by his generosity, I took a deep breath, and with tears in my eyes, I answered, "I will miss you, but I've been waiting for this opportunity for a lifetime, and I have to go."

I felt selfish and unloving, but I sensed that the trip was my destiny, and I had to show up.

We talked a little more and agreed that I would go to the jungle, and Chris would stay behind. I was in awe of the grace with which Chris accepted his fate. I didn't think I could have acted as unselfishly in his place. His love for me touched me, and it seemed so easy for him. It was one of the many reasons why I loved him.

I left Chris sitting in the waiting area and went to find Oskar to tell him that Chris would not be joining us. On the way, I heard an announcement that the plane was delayed by five hours, so there was no great rush. At the security area, I found the three men we had met in the check-in line, and after hearing my story, they graciously brought me to meet Oskar, a dapper man in his seventies. Kind and sympathetic, he did his best to offer helpful solutions, but the truth was that there was nothing we could do. It was midafternoon on a Friday, and even if we could have found a passport office, we could never get back in time.

Giving up on finding a way for Chris to join us, I fell into conversation with Oskar and, after a few minutes, remembered I had promised Chris I would come back to say goodbye. I left my new friends and found my way back to the waiting room. I got back to where I expected Chris to be, and he was gone. I was terrified that I'd lost him. I waited for five minutes and paced and finally, since I didn't have a cell phone, decided to look for a telephone booth to call him. I felt desperate as if I had passed through a time warp where Chris no longer existed.

I found a phone and called Chris, who had our cell phone. He said he hadn't moved. How could I have missed him? I felt crazy, sure that I'd looked everywhere.

I walked back and still couldn't find him. I felt more and more deranged, thinking he had picked up and left in anger without saying goodbye, even though I knew that wasn't like Chris. Finally, I realized I was in the wrong area and found him waiting patiently, exactly where I had left him.

I started to cry when I saw his face, but Chris seemed calm and even a little excited about the possibilities ahead of him. He walked me back to the security gate, and we had a tearful farewell. I didn't know whether it was the prospect of leaving or the sweetness of his loving me, but fat tears rolled down my cheeks. We said goodbye, and I kept looking back, seeing his loving face until I had to turn a corner.

As he disappeared, I walked into a new world. I felt grounded and steadily on course, yet I felt as if I were walking through dream space. Still emotional, I returned to Oskar and the guys. They welcomed me warmly, and I knew I would be okay. One other woman would join us when we reached Lima, but for the time being, I was the only woman among a dozen men who took me in lovingly.

Finally, I began to settle.

Into the Rainforest

The ocean pours through a jar and swims inside the fish.

—Rumi

As I waited to board the plane with my new friends, I remembered that I had been thinking about going on an adventure without Chris when we returned from Peru. Traveling alone, I realized the universe had answered my request but not in the way I expected. I learned that I had to be more careful about what I asked for.

We didn't take off until 2:30 in the morning, which meant we would miss our connecting flight from Lima to the city of Pucallpa. Because of the delay, when we finally arrived in Lima, the airline put us up for the night at a fancy hotel with an elaborate buffet. The food looked mouthwatering with savory dishes and luscious, colorful desserts we couldn't eat because of the *dieta*.

I walked past the food just to get a whiff, which only made me crave the food more, but with difficulty, I kept to the *dieta*.

In the morning, we flew to Pucallpa to meet the shaman. The fourteen of us, by then including Nikki, the only other woman, divided into three cars for the three-hour drive to the river where our boats into the rainforest waited.

My group piled our bags into a beat-up, rusted car that looked as if it had been through many wars. As we set out, the wind whipped up, and rain started to fall. The windshield wipers didn't work, so our driver periodically reached out the window with a dirty rag to create some modicum of visibility in the pounding deluge. I sat in the back praying for our safe arrival.

We stopped at a river just as the sun started to peek out of the dark storm clouds that had been accompanying us. The other two cars were waiting, and we all climbed into a flat boat. A second, smaller boat carried our baggage in black plastic bags. We moved lazily through the chocolate brown water. The land on both sides of the river rose lush and outrageously flamboyant with giant plants in reds, greens, oranges, and yellows. I felt at home and happy.

A fish jumped out of the water and into the boat. I picked it up and playfully passed it to the front, where with much laughter, the others threw it back into the river. Colors in the sky emerged—deep orange, red, and purple as the sun set over the river. We all quieted in the presence of such glorious beauty. Soon the sky darkened into inky blackness, and the stars came out in full force. It was disorienting to see no familiar constellations. The ones we saw seemed curved rather than angular like those in the western northern hemisphere. It felt as if we had entered a strange and magical land.

After a couple of hours of travel, we reached the smaller river that led to camp. We had hoped to keep going in our boats, but the low water level prevented it. Porters waited to unload the boats at the beginning of a trail into the jungle, and we prepared to walk.

I loved being in the rainforest with its thick canopies of leafy branches, curvy vines, and the raucous sound of insects serenading us. The half-hour hike was fun and just challenging enough as we climbed up and down steep slopes, through some little creeks, over roots, and under fallen trees. On the way, we met a gigantic frog the size of a soccer ball who just watched us go by. It made me think of the frog Chris had given me when he came to my birthday party ten years ago.

When we got to the camp, a strip of land alongside the river, dinner was ready. A feast of potatoes, rice, chicken, and spicy corn balls made a surprising break from our *dieta*. Tired and hungry from our long journey, we all overate, knowing that soon the real *dieta* of bland grains and roasted plantain would begin. While we ate, porters carried in the bags from the boat, and I was relieved to see that mine had made the journey safely.

More than sufficiently fed, I undertook my next task of choosing the place I would call home during the following week of ceremonies. Michael, who had befriended me at the beginning of the trip, gave me a tour of the compound where our dwellings bordered the river. We would each stay in a tambo, a simple wooden hut on legs set a few feet off the ground and open on four sides with slanted tin roofs held by posts in the corners. Each tambo had a bed, desk, stool, hammock, a large jar of water, candles, a lighter, and toilet paper.

Across the path from my new home and behind some bushes I found my personal jungle toilet. Nothing but an oval seat held up by metal rods over a hole in the ground, it was simple but much cleaner than the ones I used in India.

For privacy, I chose a tambo a little off the beaten path. I found it luxurious to have a place mine and mine alone. Dense cotton muslin mosquito netting surrounded the platform bed in one corner so that I couldn't look out when I lay in bed. I didn't like not seeing possible dangers lurking outside the net, so I moved to the hammock in the center of the tambo.

During the next day, we splashed in the river, walked around the compound, did divinations with tarot cards, and in the late afternoon, began our preparations for the first ceremony.

Our journeys took place in the maloca, the round, wooden, open-air building about ten minutes down the path from my tambo. Nervous and excited that my long-awaited dream had come to fruition, I walked alone through the gradually darkening skies to meet my new friends at the maloca. As I made my way, the sounds of unfamiliar insects and birds resonated through the rainforest, heightening my anxiety.

The fourteen of us plus Oskar and the shamans Miguel and Pedro sat in a circle around the maloca's perimeter. Each of us had created a nest out of our sleeping bags and pillows and surrounded ourselves with ritual objects, crystals, tissues, and our own personal bucket for purging.

Ayahuasca is a purging medicine, and icaros are specific songs sung by a shaman and designed to help heal wounds while loosening long-held beliefs that no longer serve. As the medicine works, there comes a time when the body is ready to let go into purging, a healing process called getting well. Waiting for the moment when it would be needed, my bucket sat at my side. I didn't like the idea of throwing up, but I had to surrender to the demands of the medicine. I willed myself to allow whatever must happen.

Sharing our intentions, we went around the circle in preparation for the ceremony. I intended to remove obstacles that prevented me from living in love and barriers that prevented me from dreaming and being creative for the good of us all. I wanted to learn about death and find my purpose. And, finally, I hoped to meet God. I was aware that my intentions were grandiose, but I had nothing to lose in asking for what I wanted.

Punctuated by the raucous sounds of insects, dark surrounded us. The light of one small candle cast eerie shadows around the maloca. I watched as each person went up and knelt in front of the shamans. Pedro carefully poured out a thick syrupy substance into a tiny silver cup. I had been told by veterans that Ayahuasca is the most despicable tasting drink imaginable, and I observed as people tipped the cup and struggled to swallow.

When my neighbor returned from the altar to his seat, I could no longer simply observe. I had to commit. I walked to the altar and knelt as the others had done. Pedro poured my cup, and I drank. It tasted of thick molasses, not nearly as horrible as I had expected. I later found out that the body doesn't recognize the foreignness of Ayahuasca the first time. It's like a free pass, a preliminary gift from the Mother. Once the body learns the taste, it never again tastes as sweet. In fact, it leans toward detestable, but that is the price we journeyers must pay.

After we had all been served, we waited in darkness for the medicine to do its work. Out of the stillness, Don Miguel sang an icaro, accompanying himself on the guitar as he sang in a mixture of Spanish and nonsense syllables. Icaros are designed to induce visions and a profound healing state. Shamans often receive songs directly as gifts by the plants or through shamanic lineages. Through vibrations of the icaros, Don Miguel would direct the healing in our ceremony.

I listened. The beautiful icaros pulsated in my body. I grew altered in a way hard to describe. I felt deeply relaxed and profoundly in love as I experienced the vibrations balancing my right brain and left brain and opening my heart. But disappointingly, no visions occurred, and I had come for visions. After an hour, Oskar invited anyone who wanted to drink more to approach the altar. I followed my friend Michael, knelt, and gulped down another cup. The second cup didn't provide the desired visions either, but thoughts buzzed in my altered state.

One icaro made me believe that a planetary shift would happen with much of our familiar way of life destroyed. I saw that great suffering would arrive from those changes, but that in time, we would move into a new consciousness. I felt encouraged as I experienced everyone sitting with me in the maloca representing the whole world, moving through the crisis while holding each other in love. In another moment, while discouraged about not having visions, I saw how we are all a part of one mind. Someone else could see what I could not see. I didn't have to carry out all of the roles, just the ones assigned to me.

I saw Chris as my teacher and realized he easily faced issues challenging for me since he wasn't as wound up in ego. Loving him so dearly, I was willing to learn from him, but sometimes I found it hard to surrender.

Finally, an icaro came that seemed to stir something dark in my belly that had to be removed. It didn't have a name or story, but the slight movement in my body eventually brought violent purging from my depths. Speaking in tongues, I repeated "O-ba-dah" and other sounds over and over during the icaro. The sounds felt like prayer.

I called on God for support to let go of all that required release. I purged and then purged again. I finally felt complete as I sat in meditation position at the foot of my nest. Seeing that I had undergone an intense healing process, Oskar came and kneeled in front of me. He placed sweet perfume under my nose, stroked my head, sprinkled me with water, and blew into my hands. His ministrations were tender, loving, and healing. My body began to relax.

I settled back into my seat and felt the next icaro as snake energy making me want to dance. Jason, another young man who had befriended me at the airport, moved behind me, dancing his fingers on my back. It felt sweet and lighthearted, and I simply received his energy until a new icaro made me want to move back into my own process. After about five hours of feeling the power of the medicine move through me, Oskar said it was time to close the circle. Still lost in a timeless place, I felt so filled with love that I was bursting.

Pedro sang a beautiful prayer thanking the Mother Vine for her healing energy, and my first Ayahuasca journey came to completion. All of us in the circle relaxed and enjoyed the love energy that had been spun. We shared stories and celebrated the courage it took for each of us to enter such radical healing. My friend Michael walked me home when it was time to return to my tambo. Still held by the medicine but without visions, I climbed into my sleeping bag in the hammock.

I tried lighting a candle, but I knew I needed the darkness and extinguished it. Lying in my hammock, I began turning round and round in my jungle bag and blanket, entangling myself in knots and then finding my way out. Hours went by. I had no idea what I was doing, but I seemed compelled to accomplish something that I couldn't name even as I kept twisting and turning. As the night moved on, I understood that I was in the process of reorganizing my DNA.

I intended to let go of the I-me-mine program and the personal dramas that accompany it. The need to purge rose up forcefully, and I wrenched myself out of the hammock and out onto the ground to expel all that I no longer needed. I couldn't complete the purge. Something remained in me that wanted out, but I got back into my sleeping bag and went back to my spinning. I tried to purge again but produced only dry heaves.

I heard cicadas and saw dawn breaking. I put on my headlamp and patiently untied the knots I had made in my bed during the night. With my sleeping bag finally unknotted and properly zipped, I felt satisfied with my night's reprogramming and allowed myself to rest.

I took the morning hours to reflect on my journey as I explored my childhood wounds and other hurts I had accumulated over my lifetime. I saw that everything could call me into a deeper understanding of my connection to God and all that is. Everything, every person, and every action was an invitation to go deeper into the mysteries. I imagined myself inside a solid sphere from which my explorations created a tunnel directly into the light. From there, I could radiate that light back out into the world.

I understood that everything is a reflection of God. There is nothing else. The darkness in me is an invitation for God/Love/Light to penetrate more deeply. To know God, I need to find the light in everything, even in the darkness.

Rumi says, "The ocean pours through a jar and swims inside the fish." I am made of matter, but I must remember that I am also Spirit. I am light hiding in form. The darkness in another, especially a beloved, calls me to look at the wounds in myself. I call it a wound, but it is where I have forgotten that I and we are God and failed to see the light.

What would the world be if we looked at everyone and everything as God? I wondered. There would be no enemy, and there would be only love.

I chose to take the wild leap into trusting love even though I feared that if I surrendered to love, I would die. Yet I knew that without allowing love, I would already be dead, numb, stuck, and lost. Love says that what I think I am needs to die and be reborn into new form that can't even be imagined.

My wounds were like a womb that held me until I could be born into a new remembering. The process can't be rushed, but attention must be paid to avoid staying in the womb wound longer than necessary. Safe as it may seem, the womb can't be a permanent home. Eventually, there's no room, and stifling pressure requires inching toward the unknown but as yet invisible light.

It is a battle of life and death. The old form fighting for its life must die and bring new growth.

Just as the seed must dissolve for the plant to be born, my wounded self must die if I am to remember my true self. Life and death are one. The seed dies, but the plant is born. Life and death are indivisible.

There is no word in English for dying into rebirth. We separate the two and lose the true meaning of the process. There is no such thing as dying without being reborn or being born without dying. We fear death because we've forgotten that its real purpose is transformation.

Could I remember yesterday? It was already a dream. I knew that the one writing these words was not the one who experienced the events. She had already died in the way that the self dies with every breath. The scent, the vibration, the surroundings, and the company made each breath an alchemical process that shaped me in new ways.

With my thoughts still brewing, I readied myself for our second ceremony. I had had a day to reflect on my initiatory journey, and having experienced the power of the medicine, I felt more nervous than previously. Still, I looked forward with excitement to the next journey.

When dark descended, we entered the maloca and settled into our nests.

Pedro lit the candle in the center of the room and prayed to the Mother Vine to begin the ceremony. I blessed each person as they went up to receive the Ayahuasca in the holy and courageous ritual. I was one of the last to approach the altar.

I watched as Pedro filled the little silver cup to the brim with the thick liquid. I struggled to get the contents of the cup down in four arduous slurps instead of the easy sip on my first night. My body had learned to be on guard, making the tea much harder to swallow.

I gagged as I raced back to my seat. As soon as I settled, the medicine came on quickly, producing an almost sedated state as my body surrendered. I let go as I slipped into the void.

Love permeated the room, and light filled my body. I had felt queasy all day after trying to ingest the bland food of the *dieta* and especially roasted plantain that tasted like burnt cardboard. I feared I would have to purge before the medicine settled in, but with care, I contained my nausea by cradling my belly and breathing deeply into my hands. I listened to Pedro sing prayers to Mother Ayahuasca that sounded like the sweet words a lover speaks to his beloved.

A couple of hours into the ceremony, I heard my name called, "Carol, are you high?"

"Yes," I said.

"Can you stand?"

As I attempted to find my balance, I realized that Oskar was calling me for a shaman's healing, though I had no idea what that meant. I slowly found my footing and stumbled awkwardly in the semidarkness to the altar, where I knelt, wondering what would come next. Don Miguel stood above me shaking branches of leaves over my head. They sounded like rustling paper. Singing an icaro, he continued the rattling, striking the sheaves against my body as he chanted.

I had no idea what was being healed or even what was happening. Eventually, I heard an inner voice say that I must love myself. I felt myself take ownership of that familiar thought and realized that the more love I could give to myself, the more love I could bring to everyone and everything.

I assumed that my realization marked the end of my healing, but Don Miguel hadn't finished. My confusion threw me into desperately wondering what he expected me to do next. I realized that my discomfort came from being judgmental and not loving myself. I understood that it was okay to not know all of the answers and that I had to make space for not knowing. I took a deep breath and finally relaxed a little.

The end of the healing was exquisitely loving and tender. Don Miguel stroked my face, arms, hands, and back with perfume, and I felt warmly awakened. He blew a steady stream of air into my crown, an extraordinary wind, gentle yet powerful—the breath that lights a fire.

Enlivened but confused, I returned to my nest. I hadn't achieved the clear "aha" I hoped for. I had to accept as unrealistic my fantasy of a big drama that named me the one who had come to save the world or that led me to enlightenment. I saw the foolishness of that wish and realized I had to surrender to the unfolding. The fantasy of the big blast had to go if I were to find my true calling.

I felt I had made another step toward the surrender into humility. As only a tiny piece of the story, I felt that I personally didn't have to hold the world together as I had felt necessary when I was a child. I had to remember that the grandness of my role didn't matter. I could give only the gift that was mine to give as well as I could. In gratitude and relief, I bowed my head to the ground and offered myself to the will of Spirit.

The ceremony went on for several more hours, and Pedro again closed with loving prayers to the Mother Vine. I knew I could find my way back to my tambo, so feeling embraced by the jungle, I walked up the path. I dropped into the inviting and orderly hammock, and although I didn't fall asleep immediately, I felt pleasantly quiet and peaceful. It was a good night of work, and I was satisfied.

I realized that I might have found answers to some of my intentions, but not in the way I expected. I understood that I hadn't needed to take Ayahuasca to find God. God is everywhere, embedded in everything: the light and the dark, the sacred and the profane. My purpose is to play in the wild game that the universe offers me. It doesn't matter to the universe how I choose to play, but it matters to me, and my play must be directed by love.

Even so, questions didn't go away. I continued to explore, searching to bring more light to my answers. What could I be but a mirror of God reflecting God back into the world? Perhaps I didn't have to worry about what to do. Maybe I really could trust the unfolding and be grateful for the multitudinous ways I had received blessings. I had found my way into the rainforest to take Ayahuasca with people I was learning to love. Before, it was a dream, but my dream had become my present. Soon, it would be a memory.

It rained all morning, and I happily listened to the drops make loud music on the tin roof of my tambo. Gratitude filled me for the glorious sounds, sights, and smells.

We gathered in the maloca at dusk for our third journey. When I went up to the altar to receive the tea, it tasted even worse than before. I had a slight queasiness and caressed my belly with my hands to avoid losing the medicine. But something felt different.

I sat happily in silence during the first hour until Don Miguel began his magic. When he spoke, whistled, or sang, I could feel him calling jungle plants and animals into our circle. I tracked how he led us step by step down into the depths of the earth. I saw a giant firefly with two protruding eyes looking down on me from the ceiling of the maloca. I followed the firefly into the underground into a dark place unfamiliar to me. Don Miguel, however, clearly knew the area intimately. He seemed to light up areas for me to explore. I became a seed and then watched myself dissolve in the earth. Waves of energy started to move through me, and I felt myself begin to grow. I continued growing until I pierced the soil and found myself dancing in the sun.

Even though Don Miguel stood far on the other side of the maloca, I experienced him standing next to me, talking to me personally. He seemed to speak a language that I once knew but barely remembered.

I got caught in the loop of trying to figure out what to do next. I wasn't sure there was a correct answer, although I wanted one. Again I found myself face to face with my issue of having to be right all the time and feeling that I would die if I got it wrong.

The persistent icaro music felt far too harsh for me in my fragile state. I kept wanting to go off into bliss, but the music kept demanding that I stay grounded. As the tension grew, energy moved through my body, and I felt that I had sprouted wings. I couldn't take flight, but the music filled me with love to the point that I almost burst.

A song repeated over and over in my mind. It began, "Surely, the presence of our love is in this place." I knew I was in the presence of love in the maloca, yet I also understood how privileged I was to know love when so many people on the planet felt separated from love. I imagined myself singing wherever there was pain, loss, and hardship. The song was the medicine I wanted to send as a reminder to those suffering that love is present even when it is not visible. Otherwise, there could be no hope.

Meanwhile, the queasiness in my belly continued to grab my attention. I couldn't purge, but I found myself getting tired and impatient between rounds of incredible love and happiness. Toward the end of the journey, I still felt really high and more nauseous than earlier. The circle closed, but I couldn't join the celebration. I felt far too vulnerable. I could only lie back, close my eyes, and listen to my friends in their sweet conversations.

After resting for a while, I headed back to my tambo. I loved walking down the path alone at night. I felt brave, balanced, tender, and grateful as I felt plants, trees, and animals embrace me as I walked in their midst. I felt a living part of the jungle.

Arriving at my tambo, I determined to complete the purge. I knelt on the damp ground and let go of everything that no longer served.

I had learned a challenging but valuable lesson. I hadn't known it was better to purge than hold on when the queasiness came. I thought I should be intentional and ride it through, feeling superior because I didn't have to purge. Once again, I had to pay attention and let go of my need to be exceptional.

I continued feeling gratitude that Chris had given me the opportunity to be in the jungle on my own, allowing me to engage without seeing myself as an extension of him. It had been a long time since I had been thrown back on my own resources, unable to count on him to fill in my gaps, and I appreciated the opportunity to grow.

I obsessed that I hadn't seen crystal castles or jaguars. I thought that was what I had come for. Looking inward, however,

I remembered that I had asked for the work to be about my heart, and I realized that my experience, exactly as it was, had massaged, pierced, held, and polished my heart. It occurred to me that an astounding vision or revelation might have pumped up into an ego triumph I worked so hard to avoid.

I began exploring the idea that I was fine just as I was. I didn't have to have magic powers, an open third eye, or entrance into crystal castles. I could show up, love, and just be me. It was hard to tell if I was avoiding the responsibility of doing the work of fulfilling my destiny or sinking into a deeper understanding of surrender than I had known before. Whichever, the process made me realize how little I knew. I had had many adventures in my lifetime, studied psychology, and called myself a teacher, but there was so much I didn't know. I could only do my best to be open, observing, focused, and loving. I could do no more.

I was glad to be back in my tambo, tucked into my sleeping bag with my stomach settled. I drifted off into a deep sleep, grateful for the night's experience.

On the following night, the fourth ceremony, I went up to receive the cup, and my mouth screwed up with the bitter taste. The cup seemed impossibly even more full than the night before. I drank and drank without getting to the bottom of the small cup. The tea was thicker, and solid particles got stuck in my teeth. Although after the first cup, the shamans invited us to return to the altar as often as we wished, I had decided to content myself with a single dose. The acrid taste confirmed my decision. I returned to my seat to let the medicine settle.

Don Miguel's guitar playing made me think of my brother Ishaq, who loved to share his music, and the pain of missing him washed over me. I could see him in his essence but not in his form. I watched as he became boundary-less, and as

I looked at him, I saw him descend and become one with everything. There was no place where he wasn't.

I understood that we do not have to die to be one with everything. Our body may resist that idea because it needs form to maintain its integrity. As a result, we only get hints of how embedded we are in everything that exists. I wanted to talk with my brother, but he chose simply to be present and let me watch him infuse everything with his essence. I was grateful to meet him that way.

I started feeling a strange kind of altered state anchored in the first, second, and third chakras—energy centers, according to ancient Hindu tradition, located at the base of the spine, belly, and solar plexus. I felt deep presence rather than any feeling of being high. At the same time, the upper chakras— my heart, throat, third eye, and crown—were wide open and awake. I wondered if that might be what a tree feels, totally rooted in the ground yet reaching for the stars.

I slogged around endlessly in the world of duality. I tried not to analyze the experience, whether good or bad, whether I liked it or not, or whether I would come back to another ceremony. I simply wanted to stay receptive to whatever happened.

The session ended, and feeling drunk with love, I walked back to my tambo. The object of my regard didn't matter. I was simply compelled to love.

I tried not to think about leaving the jungle nor about Chris, because I wanted to stay present to the very end, but I had started to miss him.

My time of solitude and retreat brought me a profound experience of Mother energy. I accepted that I was loved and held safely in the arms of the Great Mother, and in meeting the Mother Vine, I acknowledged that I had received generous, abundant, and overflowing gifts of insight and healing. The *dieta*, the jungle, the community and shamans, the medicine, and Chris's absence all flowed together to create a significant change in my consciousness.

I realized that, just as when I bake a cake, specific ingredients are needed. Individually, they are not sufficient, but they transform into something completely different when they come together. I understood that I needed all the elements of my time in the rainforest, not just the medicine, for my own transformation to emerge.

My experience of the Mother Vine had blown me away even though I had just begun to learn her capacities. I knew well that any words I found to describe my jungle experience would diminish its power and mystery. Containing my journey in words felt parallel to describing the Grand Canyon as pretty or a Beethoven symphony melodic. Words could not come close to holding a cupful of the depth and breadth of what I witnessed and experienced.

The Mother Vine had provided a time of dissolving into deep presence and union, yet even to talk of separation missed the point. I had touched the place where I knew myself beyond myself and as part of everything. I was thunder and rain. I was shaman and people being healed. I was a part of the creative process of the universe in all of its diversity and mystery. I could lose my identity while maintaining wide awake consciousness to all that is.

I had all that I needed for my mind and body. I had loving, supportive energy and presence not outside me or anything else but embedded in me. I had been richly blessed and was ready to see where the blessings would take me.

The Journey

For what is it to die but to stand naked in
the wind and to melt into the sun?
And when the earth shall claim your limbs,
then shall you truly dance.

—Kahlil Gibran

My time in the jungle with Mother Ayahuasca had come to an end. Once we arrived at the airport in Lima, our tambos, the maloca, and the river already seemed far away.

We boarded the plane for LAX at close to midnight. I found sleep hard to come by in the cramped seat, and I spent most of the flight processing the ceremonies, retreat, and my time away from Chris. I knew it would take a long time, perhaps lifetimes, before I would make sense of all that I had experienced, yet I was ready to come home, not to a place, but to Chris.

Wide awake at 5:30 in the morning, I journaled until breakfast and soon saw the lights of Los Angeles flickering below us. The flight attendants told us to prepare for landing, and the plane began deepening its descent.

We were just a few feet from the runway, almost touching the ground when, instead of landing, the plane lifted off sharply, and we were high in the sky again. A flight attendant told us that the pilot had attempted to land with visual cues but had unexpectedly hit a dense cloud bank that gave him no visibility. He had no choice but to bring the airplane up again and try the landing again with support.

Fastened securely in our seat belts, we looked out as the plane made endless circles around the airport below—close, yet so inaccessible. I knew Chris waited for me in the terminal, and I longed to be with him after our time apart.

The half-hour we waited for permission to land felt like an eternity. When the pilot finally got permission, he attempted the runway again. Although he had unobstructed visibility when he touched down, a thick cloud obliterated everything around us within seconds of our landing. Fortunately, the pilot had turned on an instrument landing system, and we rolled safely up to the terminal building.

The aborted landing offered a good metaphor for my challenges in finding a way to ground my journeys in the jungle. It reminded me that I would need all the support tools I could find to land safely in my new life after traveling beyond the edges of normal reality.

We deplaned and lined up to go through customs and immigration. My heart leaped when I spotted Chris at the top of the ramp. We got through customs quickly, and I ran up the ramp and happily fell into the warmth of Chris's body.

I introduced Chris to Oskar and the guys who had not yet dispersed. Oskar generously offered Chris and me a place in the ceremonies coming up in six weeks in Los Angeles so that Chris could experience meeting Mother Ayahuasca himself. We enthusiastically accepted.

We gathered up my baggage and headed back to my friend Marilee's home, where we would stay for a few days until we decided where next to go. Tired and hungry, I felt disoriented by the traffic and noise of city life.

As soon as we arrived at Marilee's home, I headed for a bath. I had missed the miracle of hot water while in the jungle. I called Chris into the bathroom with me, and we talked endlessly as I soaked. I couldn't wait to share all that had happened yet felt frustrated that many of my experiences were almost impossible to put into words. Still, Chris listened with interest and a bit of anxiety, knowing that he would soon have his own meeting with the Mother Vine.

Chris told me that he had made good use of the time during my absence. He had enjoyed being alone in the desert with our teachers. Days later, he flew east to attend the christening of his newest grandson and had the opportunity to have healing conversations with his first wife, from whom he had been estranged.

Since taking to the road, we had barely been apart for almost a year and a half. Yet, we both benefited from our time of separation and were grateful for the unexpected and bountiful gifts.

After six weeks of camping, visiting friends, and generally letting the wind take us where it wanted to take us, we arrived at the place in the outskirts of Los Angeles where we would gather with others for the Ayahuasca ceremonies. I loved seeing so many beloveds from the jungle. Meeting them felt very different from a mere six weeks before when I headed off by myself with a group of strangers into an experience I couldn't even imagine. Now Chris was the virgin entering uncharted territory.

We drove up a steep driveway and found two buildings, one the hostel where we would eat and sleep and the other the ceremonial space perched on the third floor of a wooden structure with an outside staircase. Arriving early, Chris and I got a room with a double bed, door, and a bathroom, so we didn't have to share the dormitory room with its cramped bunk beds.

We had entered a new home.

My friend Michael from the jungle had already saved us a place in the large meeting hall that would hold more than two dozen people. Once Chris and I settled, we began setting up our nests for the three ceremonies. We brought mats, sleeping bags, and our fluffy white down comforter to cover the two of us and make us feel as if we floated on a cloud. I had an extensive array of crystals and essential oils to support our journey, along with the requisite bucket and plenty of tissues for cleaning up after a purge.

People began to float into the room. I gave big hugs to beloveds from the jungle and introduced myself to the new people. I discovered in the rainforest that for me to feel safe journeying with people, I had to know who they were before venturing forth with them into the unknown. I circled the room to make my love connections with each person.

Chris seemed calm and relaxed as he prepared for the ceremony. We had carried out the *dieta* of bland foods, and he eagerly started getting to know his fellow journeyers. He appeared confident that he was ready for whatever was to come.

Before we started, Michael told me that Oskar would provide Peruvian whistles and that I should offer to blow one. He called it a transcendent experience not to be missed. I had no idea what a Peruvian whistle was, but I told Michael I would consider it.

The ceremony began with Pedro's beautiful and tender prayers to Mother Ayahuasca. As soon as I saw the bottle containing the brew, my stomach started roiling. My body no longer naive, I readied myself for the impending assault. Chris, on the other hand, seemed blissfully calm in his innocence.

Pedro introduced us to the Peruvian whistling vessels dating to pre-Columbian times. About five inches tall, each was a peculiar pottery jar that looked like a little clay teapot with a face. Each whistle was tuned to a slightly different frequency so that when seven or more played simultaneously, the vibrations created a sound that enhanced the plant medicine and drew one into a deeper, altered state.

I watched as each person went up to the altar, knelt, and swallowed medicine from the small silver cup. My turn came, and I choked down the unpleasant brew.

Just as I began to settle into my seat to wait for the medicine to take effect, I heard Oskar inviting people to play the whistles. Remembering Michael's encouragement, I walked into the center of the dimly lit room and sat next to one of the seven whistling jars.

I heard an eerie sound rising as people blew into the jars, producing the sound of a high screeching wind.

The tuning of the jars created dissonant beats between vibrations that violently upset my body's equilibrium. I had to consciously work to stay grounded enough to blow into my whistle, but I blew and became part of the otherworldly orchestra. As the medicine started coming on, I began to have dim memories of a time lifetimes before when I played the whistles in rituals.

When we finished playing, I was so altered that I could barely get back to my seat. I settled and noticed that the medicine was starting to take Chris, who began making the low mooing sounds I recognized as his entrance into an ecstatic state.

For the comfort of the two dozen journeyers in the room, the group agreed to avoid making disruptive noises. However, we didn't need to feel shame if we couldn't control our sounds or actions in the medicine. In such circumstances, helpers would gently remove the noisy person from the ceremonial space and a sitter would take the person to a room to continue their journey safely without disturbing the others.

Sitting next to Chris, I was hyperaware of the sounds he was making as he fell into the medicine. I knew his sounds could likely disrupt those sitting close by. Although directed not to get involved with another's process, I took it upon myself to shake Chris continually and tell him to be quiet. Over and over, he thanked me for my concern, took another breath, and returned to his blissful love sounds. Like a drunk lover intoxicated beyond any reason, he was quite happy to be exactly as he was. I envied his rapturous state, but I also knew that he would not be allowed to stay in the room if he continued his bleating.

Oskar came and attempted to get Chris to sit up and quiet down. He spoke patiently, but Chris was in another world. Pedro came shaking his rattle, singing and talking to him, but nothing interfered with the celebration of ecstasy that Chris expressed.

I did my best to concentrate on my own journey but got lost in Chris's energy. Unrealistically, I believed Chris was my responsibility and that I needed to control his behavior. Powerless and frustrated, my altered state dissolved, and I was cold sober. I wondered if a person with a terminally ill spouse might feel the same way. I was stuck between wishing that Chris would miraculously move out of his unease and hoping he would just go away.

Meanwhile, Oskar announced that the first hour had passed and invited anyone who wanted another cup to come up. I decided that having more medicine might get me out of my earth-grounded state, and I went up to the altar. I watched as Pedro poured a quantity of the thick brew back and forth from cup to bottle and back until he determined the exact amount he decided I needed. I gagged as I swallowed, recoiling at the taste in my mouth.

I returned to my seat and allowed the medicine to move into my body as Chris's sounds continued to escalate. I was not the only one in the room disturbed by his noises, and soon six men approached our seats to carry Chris out. By then, he was too far gone to notice. Two of the guys took his arms, two took his legs, and two supported his mid-section. I could see that he was dead weight, and as they struggled to remove him from the room, I heard a thud. They had dropped him, and I watched in horror as they picked him up and disappeared into the darkness. His bellowing sounds continued outside the window until he could walk down the three flights of stairs to the quiet room where a sitter would tend him until he was ready to return to the meeting hall.

Meanwhile, Mother Ayahuasca had its way with me. Seeing Chris removed from the room convinced me that he had died and undertakers had taken him away from me forever. I purged briefly, but that didn't alleviate my despair. I fell into intense emotional agony and wailed quietly to myself at the loss of my beloved. I couldn't imagine my life without him. I felt shattered and desperate.

Finding no light and no relief, I spent hours in the darkness of the underworld. The heaviness of my sorrow paralyzed me. I wanted Chris back, but he was nowhere to be found.

Then a shred of light appeared in my consciousness. Wait a minute. I knew Chris was in bliss, but I was sitting in leaden unhappiness. If I wanted to meet Chris, wherever he might be, I couldn't stay locked in darkness. I needed to rise into the light, into the ecstasy that we had known and shared together. We couldn't meet physically at that moment, but I could meet him energetically in the euphoric place that he inhabited.

I began to understand that being with a person doesn't require being in the same physical space. I could be with

Chris in an area of shared energy. I could breathe him in as I breathed in air. There was no way we could be separated entirely. We were more than our bodies. We could meet with or without them.

I began to settle into that new understanding when, seemingly no worse for wear, Chris walked back into the room. We couldn't talk, but with him back at my side, I realized that I had been lost in a dark dream of my own. I could hardly believe that he was back. I was euphoric, and I curled up around his body, holding onto him for dear life.

Though relieved, I knew we would be separated again. No form lasts forever. Life is forever changing, and death is an intrinsic part of what we call life. I knew that the life that Chris and I had together was fleeting and we could not take it for granted.

The ceremony ended, and we both realized how much we had to learn about the medicine, our relationship, and loving ourselves. Mother Vine had given us a shared journey of exploration into the depths of our personal selves and the world beyond where everything is connected. Once again, we saw how our love for each other gave us the courage to surrender to whatever would come.

As we sat in the darkened room, our hearts overflowed with the pleasure of feeling our bodies wrapped around each other, thinking not of future adventures but only of the moment.

My Name Is Kai

Bee to the blossom, moth to the flame—
each to his passion. What's in a name?

—Helen Hunt Jackson

Even though my parents named me Carol for the Christmas carols my father sang when I was born, I never felt that the name belonged to me. Carol sounded like the name of a stranger, a stranger who inhabited my skin but who wasn't really me. People would call me, and I'd wonder who they were talking to. Then I'd remember, "Oh, yes, I'm Carol. They're talking to me."

I had wanted to find a more suitable name for myself for years, but all the names sounded wrong. Nothing sounded right, so I let go of the search and settled into Carol.

I wasn't looking for a name when, in January of 2008, Chris and I attended a holotropic breathwork session as part of our shamanic training. Stan Grof, a Czech psychiatrist who had been a strong proponent of the therapeutic benefits of LSD, created the breathwork process. In the late sixties, the US government made LSD illegal, thus terminating Grof's psychedelic research. He shifted gears and developed a new healing practice that created a non ordinary state through the breath rather than a substance.

255

Chris and I took part in a breathwork session with a group of eight of Carlos and Maria's students who met for the weekend at a lakefront property in New Jersey. We had worked with medicines the day before, but we used no medicine for the breathwork. We gathered in a darkened room with yoga mats spread around on the floor. Our facilitator Christian asked us to lie down and place masks over our eyes to block outside stimuli.

He taught us a simple breath consisting of a sharp intake of air, followed by a comfortable exhale. That was it — just a quick breath in and a gentle letting go, over and over. We continued the breathing as Christian played evocative music that helped us sink deep into our emotions.

At first, I found it difficult and couldn't imagine practicing that tedious breath technique for a full hour. As I settled in, the breathing became more natural, and I relaxed into feeling delicious waves of breath moving in and out of my body.

Ten minutes passed, and an enormous surge of energy moved through, shaking me violently. Strange ecstatic sounds emerged unbidden from my mouth, the mystical speaking in tongues. I writhed on the floor in a powerful twisting motion. I experienced no story, only steady moving energy.

The motion quieted, and layers of white petals came into my mind's eye. The top of my head opened into a patch of dark sky filled with bright stars looking like crystals in a kaleido-scope. They cast a mesmerizing light, sparkling and bright. An image of a crystal head appeared that emitted an even more dazzling radiance while the faces on the head shapeshifted like a slide show. Images of Buddha, Jesus, my teachers, Chris, and countless others flashed before my eyes. A bright, white light sped by at a blinding pace.

As I tried to process the energies, I heard a booming male voice that seemed to come from above.

"*Your name is Kai,*" rumbled the invisible voice.

Trying to find the source of the declaration, I looked around.

The voice roared on, "The time has come to acknowledge your soul's true name. You are Kai. That is who and what you are. How you use this information is your business, but you must know the true name of your soul."

Kai. I had never heard the name Kai before. It rhymed with hi and felt wide and open as I rolled it around in my mind, trying it on. The power of the one who had spoken to me still vibrated throughout my body. I realized the communication didn't concern my earth plane name. Kai was the name of my soul, that part of me that endures eternally, never born, and never dying.

"Kai. Kai." As I quietly spoke the name to myself, I recognized my rightful name.

On completion of the breathwork practice, we shared our experiences. I could hardly wait to tell the group about the voice that had given me my name. For the rest of the weekend, I asked people to call me Kai. I wanted to get used to the sound so I could own my new identity.

I loved hearing the open resonance of Kai. Saying Kai naturally brought a smile to my lips, and my heart vibrated with pleasure. Finally, I had a name that reflected who I thought myself to be.

After the weekend, when Chris and I returned to the cottage, I felt more protective of the name and didn't tell my friends. I asked Chris to call me Kai in our intimate interactions, and Kai became my holy name, the way into my inner sanctum. Still, I didn't feel ready to make a complete break with Carol's name, which I had carried over sixty years. I identified with my name as my connection to my family, friends, and clients. Carol was how people knew me. Could I be ready to let that go? Not yet.

I thought about the many names that I had been given in my life. The name Jud connected me to my family's long line of mystics that went back to the sixteenth century in Switzerland. That was a positive connection, but it also entangled me with my father and the larger-than-life energy he brought to the world.

Before marrying Bernie, I longed to let go of the name Jud, feeling that securing a new name might help me separate from my powerful father. Curiously, taking another man's name when I married didn't diminish my sense of autonomy. For fifteen years, I was proud to be Mrs. Bernard Fromartz. When our marriage ended, however, I was happy to return to my birth name, having worked through some of my father issues.

In 1991, after experiencing a Native American vision quest in the high desert of southern California, I received a Native American name from Bird Brother, the shaman who led the session with his wife, Sedonia. For my three days of solitude, I had chosen a ridge as my temporary desert home looking down on a valley surrounded by distant mountains. The mountains appeared as if made of soft velvet. Sparse vegetation, cacti, and trees the size of small bushes shaped by harsh winds scattered through my campsite.

As I walked with my camping equipment up to my questing spot for the first time, I noticed a snake crossing my path. It stopped and rattled. Fear did not occur to me. I heard the rattle as a friendly hello. I stopped less than three feet away from where it lay still in the middle of the path.

Speaking respectfully to my slithering friend, I said, "I know this is your territory, but I have come to offer prayers and ask for a vision in these next days. I hope you will welcome me into your home. I hold you sacred and want you to know that I have a soapstone snake on my altar. And as you can see, I am

258

wearing snake earrings. Snake, I am your sister. I am honored to meet you."

The snake rattled, which I interpreted as meaning that it had heard me and felt our conversation complete. It slid away, and I continued up to my camping spot on a ridge looking out onto the high desert.

That night, I didn't remove my earrings before going to sleep. When I awoke in the morning, the earring in my left lobe was gone, and I never saw it again. I concluded that my snake friend had come and removed it in the night as a symbol of our bond.

When I returned to the base camp at the end of my vision quest, I told the group my story of meeting the snake. Bird Brother asked me how far away the snake was when we met. When I told him it was less than three feet, he said, "That is striking distance. You were in danger."

"That had never occurred to me. I knew I was safe."

"Then you shall be known as Snake I Am Your Sister."

Along with my Native American name, Sharma, a Tantric guru my father had brought to Shalom Mountain from India, had given me the Hindu name of Gita, which like my birth name, Carol, means song.

After my brother Ishak died, his friend Saladin, a Sufi sheik, gave the me Sufi name of Fatima, the youngest daughter of Mohammed.

All those designations had special meaning to me, but I never invited others to use them.

When I married Chris, I wanted to give him a special gift to express my deep love. I decided that surrendering my maiden name to him would be that gift and that I would take his last name, Boeve, and become Carol Boeve. After our wedding ceremony, Chris and I went to the state department of motor vehicles to apply for my Connecticut license. I happily filled out the forms with my new married name.

Soon, it became evident that I had made a mistake. Chris's friends knew me as Carol Boeve, but in my therapy and retreat practice, people knew me as Carol Jud. When people asked my name, I didn't know what to say. Was I Jud or Boeve? It depended on who asked. Finally, my business name won out, and I reluctantly withdrew my romantic gift to Chris and reverted to my maiden name.

On our seventh anniversary, we met our medicine teachers in the desert, and they blessed us with a spontaneous remarriage ceremony. At the end of the ritual, we each received a rose quartz necklace, and Maria formally pronounced us Mr. and Mrs. Walking Together Lightly in the World. I loved the name because Chris was not Mr. and I was not Mrs. We were both Mr. and Mrs. Walking Together Lightly in the World.

Still, none of the names seemed to express the totality of who I was. I started researching the name Kai and found that it had many meanings. In Hawaiian, Kai means ocean. In Navajo, it means willow tree and friend. In South African, it means beautiful. In Scottish, it means fire. In Welsh and Scandinavian, Kai means keeper of the keys, and that definition most grabbed my attention.

A key is small, but the right one can open something immense. I knew I carried keys that could help people, although I had no idea how anyone might use the keys. I didn't need to know, but I offered myself to the process by accepting the name Kai.

When I heard Chris calling me Kai, I found a sweet intimacy in being acknowledged in that new way. I started to meet long hidden parts of myself coming up from lifetimes before, yet familiar. I began to trust more in my ability to show up in full presence and be open to how the energy of the cosmos came through me with information that might help others. When carrying the keys, I didn't need to be in a teaching relationship. I needed only to allow myself to be a channel for the energy of the universe to come through. I could open doors for people. If they chose, they could then walk through.

Nine months later, Chris and I returned to Peru to work again with the shamans. I was delighted that many of the same people were present and that Chris was at my side. Instead of the rainforest, we met in a small retreat center in the Andes Mountains in an area called the Urabamba Valley, the Sacred Valley of the Incas.

Before the evening Ayahuasca ceremony, our group went on a paragliding adventure. Fourteen of us took a bus to the top of a high mountain. On the way, we passed a lake where local tradition said unidentified flying objects land. It startled me to hear how matter of factly people of the region accepted the possibility of alien visitors.

Stunning scenery and the natural sacredness of the land moved me as we drove high up a mountain on a dirt road to the cliff where we would jump. Surprised that I did not feel crazed with fear, I remained calm and curious. We arranged ourselves in groups, and Chris and I held the fifth place in line to fly.

Arriving at the flat area where the gliders would take off, we laid several blankets on the ground and spread food and drink to occupy us while watching our friends fly. The beauty of the mountains surrounded us, and we felt celebratory.

The glider's wings lay limp on the ground, their rainbow-colored fabrics painted to look like a broad smiling mouth. They stretched out for more than forty feet, rippling lightly in the wind, waiting for the moment of flight.

The pilot strapped Ashley, the first flyer, into the harness seat in front of him. We watched him give her detailed instructions as they waited patiently for the arrival of the perfect wind.

When everything was just right, the pilot directed her to run with him full tilt toward the edge of the cliff, a terrifyingly unintuitive thing to do. She ran, and with each step, the wings filled with air and billowed up behind her. Her legs continued to move back and forth even when she no longer had any ground beneath her. We watched from the blanket below as she flew far above us.

Munching our delicacies, we watched as the gliders took flight, one after the other, filling the sky with their giant wings above our heads. Feeling the surreal quality of the moment, I remarked to Chris, "Ah, so this is how the gods play." And it did seem that our friends had transcended the earth plane as they had taken to the sky.

Without warning, the energy shifted drastically. Bill got suited up and tripped on the ground before he could lift off, partly because he was so big and stocky that the pilot couldn't carry his weight. Then Peter, a smaller man, tried where Bill had not succeeded. They waited for almost half an hour until the right wind appeared, but the glider kept getting pushed back instead of forward when the pilot tried to take off in another failed launch. Linda was next in line, but the wind shifted just as she took to the air, and the wings collapsed briefly, causing the rig to plummet straight down until the pilot got it under control again.

The mood had changed from ecstatic fun to dark and dangerous work. The pilot called for a heavier man, and Gaston offered himself. They landed safely, but when I talked to Gaston later, he said they had experienced heavy crosswinds and a lot of debris flying through the air. He said the scariest moment came when he heard the pilot say, "Oh no, we're in deep shit now."

The paragliding had become too dangerous to continue, leaving those who had not flown grounded. I felt more relieved than not. The night before, I had dreamed I died when the paraglider I flew crashed. Still, I had looked forward to jumping off the mountain carried by the giant rainbow wings. I wanted to feel the freedom of being carried by the wind high above the earth plane. But it was not to be.

Chris and I returned to the retreat center disappointed but grateful to have been part of the experience of watching our friends. I wondered about the meaning of the dream that predicted my death.

After a brief rest, we gathered for the evening ceremony. We made the requisite prayers, and then one by one went up to receive the offering of the Mother Vine.

I choked down the tea, and the medicine started taking effect quickly after I returned to my seat. On the inner stage of my altered state, I found myself sitting inside a small stone chapel with several rows of crude wooden benches facing a rough-hewn wooden altar. A few candles provided the only light, and as they flickered, they created eerie shadows on the walls. My father and I sat close and alone in the chapel. I held his hand.

An open coffin sat atop the altar. In the casket, the body of Carol lay wrapped with white silk and strewn with flowers. Tears flowed down my father's cheeks as he grieved for his daughter Carol just as he had mourned for his drowned wife and infant son. I held his hand and sought unsuccessfully to comfort him with soothing words. He was inconsolable. His daughter Carol was dead, and he was bereft.

I knew, however, that it was not Carol comforting her father but Kai. Carol was gone. Kai had taken her place.

When we returned to the States, I wrote to my friends and family, telling them the story and asking them to support me as I moved into my new identity, free of any of the entanglements and stories that came with the name Carol Elaine for the past sixty years.

In that dark chapel in the jungle, I left a part of myself behind, dying to one life as I moved into a new and unknown future. I was Kai, Keeper of the Keys.

I was reborn, and I was free.

Going Home

Clowns

The appearance of this world is a magus's brilliant trick,
though its affairs are nothing into nothing.
You are a divine elephant with amnesia trying to live in an ant hole.

—Hafiz

Chris and I heard about a plant called Salvia Divino-
rum, related to the lovely plant that grows in many backyard
gardens. Given that it was not an illegal substance at the time
but not knowing what to expect, we sent away for a sample
from an online store. We had heard it offers a brief experience
of less than half an hour that would likely cause hallucinations.

Our mail order shipment arrived, and we were excited to
schedule a day to explore a medicine new to us. In Oregon at
the time, we found a small out-of-the-way lake surrounded by
trees and flat rocks a few feet above the water's edge. Happily,
we saw no other visitors.

We spread our red striped Native American blanket out
on the rock and created an altar with a small wooden statue of
Ganesha, the elephant god, along with a clear quartz crystal
and metal singing bowl.

I opened the small package we had received and found a
dry mound of greyish-green leaves. Friends had told us we

needed to smoke the leaves to get a hallucinatory effect, so we prepared our classic brass pipe. Chris asked me to try the medicine first, and he agreed to hold space while I journeyed.

I sat holding the pipe that had taken us on many cannabis journeys. I had no idea what I was signing up for, but I trusted that Chris would hold space for me no matter what happened. We didn't know how much salvia we should smoke, but we filled the pipe and said our prayers of gratitude. Then I waited for the moment to take the leap.

I breathed in hot smoke and immediately felt my heart do flip-flops. Before I had time to exhale fully, I found myself in an unimaginable new world.

I had landed at the edge of a busy town green surrounded by small shops. It could have been any small town in the 1890s except for one startling difference. All the people walking around were clowns with bushy orange hair, round red noses, white make-up, and brightly colored pajama-like outfits. I saw men and women clowns, clown butchers, clown bakers, clown mothers pushing baby clowns in carriages, and unbelievably, I was a clown, too. Curious about the clowns walking past me around the green, I had no fear of them. But it scared me to be a clown with the good possibility that I would never find my way out of that world and stay a clown forever.

I had barely enough presence of mind to seek out Chris and ask him to remind me that I had taken a medicine, that he held space for me, and that I was and would be okay. I found him through the haze of my consciousness, but seeing him did little to put my mind at rest.

Like a shot, I was back in the clown world. Seeing my reflection in a shop window, I saw not my recognizable form but a white-faced, red-headed clown. Once again, I was a clown among clowns—and terrified that I would be a clown for all eternity. How could I have made such a horrible mistake that might leave me lost in a clown's body for the rest of my life?

Time passed. How long? Minutes or a lifetime? I had no idea. Eventually, I felt myself move back into the more recognizable consciousness I had before taking the medicine. I saw Chris sitting and smiling in the sun on the rock by the lake just as before. I felt my mind grab hold of him, but before I knew it, I was back in the town square with clowns everywhere I looked. *Oh, no,* I thought. *Will this ever end?*

Then I was back with Chris. Hoping for some relief, I looked into his eyes but soon found myself back with the clowns. Back and forth, I swung between worlds with nothing solid to hold on to.

And then I really returned. I looked around and saw not one clown. I looked at my body and saw my skin with no body paint. My nose felt like my nose and not like a round ball. Curious about what I had gone through, Chris gazed at me.

I should have been okay, but I wasn't. I saw myself seemingly unchanged by my strange experience and back at the lake with Chris. But a niggling thought remained. *Am I really back, or am I a clown dreaming that I am Kai?*

How could I answer such a question? Chris could say I was the same as always, but how could he know? No one on the planet could tell me with certainty who or what I was. I would have to find the truth for myself.

At that moment, I realized that we humans can't know anything for sure. Many spiritual paths include the teaching that what seems like reality in the earth plane is a dream. If what we perceive as reality is a dream, how do we know what is real? As a human, I don't know where I came from and don't know where I am supposed to be going. I don't know why I am here nor what I am supposed to do. The culture does its best to give us answers, but given how little I know, the ambiguous stories conflict at best. What can I do?

Right then, I decided. Since I knew I could never be sure of Truth, I could do nothing but make up a story based on the best evidence I had. Given that I was making up a story, I decided to make up a good one that I liked, a story that nourished me, a story that brought me into a context of love and belonging that made my life worthwhile.

And so I did. I created a story that confirmed that I was an adventurer who had journeyed to other realms to learn to love. I had come home safe and sound to my beloved Chris, who had lovingly awaited my return.

My experience allowed me to understand the importance of writing my own stories. I can't always control what unfolds in my life, but I can choose the narrative.

As we sat on the lake's edge, Chris and I wondered what stories we would write in the coming days.

Seeing the Face of God

Try not to resist the changes that come your way.
Instead let life live through you.
And do not worry that your life is turning upside down.
How do you know that the side you are used to is
better than the one to come?

—Rumi

It was our seventh summer on the road, and Chris and I decided to find a place to camp in Crested Butte, Colorado. The official campground was full, but the camp hosts told us we could camp anywhere we wanted off the road. Fortunately, we found a great place left by other off-road campers complete with a big firepit, an abundance of wood, a flat area for the tent, and a meadow for morning sunshine.

Moving into the secluded spot required carting everything down a steep hill. Since the site provided everything we needed, we felt it worth the effort. Lugging our belongings up and down the bank at an elevation of more than ten thousand feet was challenging, but we both worked with good spirits. After an hour and a dozen trips, our new home was ready.

We spent a week hiking in the beauty of the mountains with gloriously colored wildflowers, waterfalls, streams, and spectacular views. We made fabulous campfire meals, sat around our ceremonial fire, and made love under the stars. We woke at dawn's light and then lolled in the tent for endless hours cuddling, laughing, and telling stories.

I loved the laughing part. It felt like a prayer. We opened up to the light for no reason except that it wanted to shine, and we wanted to enjoy it. We laughed and laughed at the silliest things—making faces, saying wacky words, tickling each other, and just riding the energy. I loved allowing my child to play and that Chris willingly accompanied me in my delight.

While we camped, Chris and I both celebrated the surrounding beauty of the mountains and of our life together. We felt happy and filled with gratitude, but soon our wanderings called us back east to help officiate at the marriage of Jeff and Shelly, two of our dear Shalom friends.

We packed up our campsite and made the journey back to Timshel where we would stay for a few days before going to Shalom Mountain for the wedding. Chris slept next to me as I drove. Out of the corner of my eye, I noticed a car coming onto the highway. Without warning, it came speeding in from the entrance ramp toward the left lane, seemingly unaware that I occupied that space. Without thinking and trusting I could get out of the way, I swerved smoothly onto the left shoulder. The driver in the other car must have seen me at the last moment, and he passed by, barely missing us.

Chris jerked awake and asked what happened. The gods had watched over us and kept us safe, but our close call with death shook Chris. Perhaps still in shock, I felt my body calm. I barely registered the danger. I did wonder, however, if we had been killed and existed still alive and well in a parallel universe.

How could one ever really know?

That thought made me strikingly aware of the fragility of life and the mystery of life and death. I looked at Chris, and my heart swelled with gratitude that we could continue to love each other.

We made our way back to the Timshel cottage just in time to meet Hurricane Irene. After several days of rain and flooding, we set out to Shalom Mountain for Jeff and Shelly's wedding. Half an hour from Timshel, a big traffic jam brought us almost to a standstill.

When we got to the shopping center close to the highway entrance, we saw the entire parking lot under water. Though most cars had evacuated before the storm, four or five cars stood in water past the top of their windows. We weren't sure we would find a way around the flooding, but kind local people directed us through back roads to the highway, which was dry, and we arrived safely at Shalom Mountain.

It felt strange to be back at my father's former home and my former place of work. I was a guest—a welcome guest for sure—but no longer one who belonged. Much had changed in the years we had been on the road. Shalom had new leadership, different furnishings, and new energy.

I let go of my feelings about the past and settled in to celebrate our friends.

The bride and groom provided a big barbecue for fifty friends and family. As night fell, the sky painted a magnificent sunset. Shades of red, tangerine, gold, and blue danced on wildly shaped, fluffy clouds. A steely grey sky remained as the color of the sunset dissolved, a stunning punctuation to our gathering. I felt that Jeff and Shelly performed special magic to bring beauty out of many days of rain.

The following day, we helped set up chairs and tables in the high meadow behind the big house. We decorated chairs with flowers and ribbons and then set tables in the pavilion for the wedding feast following the ceremony.

The wedding party gathered at the High Meadow to do a quick run-through of the ceremony, a ritual that drew from many different religious traditions.

Shelly began by processing up the path to the edge of the high meadow, singing "Ong Namo," a Sikh chant. Jeff called in the directions in the Native American way, thanking the energies of the east, south, west, north, the below, the above, and the within. The ceremony continued with a Tantra exercise, some thoughts about the masculine and feminine from Jung, a Hafiz poem, one by D. H. Lawrence, and the congregation singing the round "Dona Nobis Pacem." Chris and I presented a cosmic look at "we-ness." The rehearsal was good, spirited, and efficient, and I was happy to be part of it. With preparations complete, we had the rest of the day to hang out with friends and family.

We came together for lunch, and then all fifty of us gathered on the front lawn to play a game led by the groom's fifteen-year-old son, Moseby. He seemed remarkably comfortable telling the group of his elders what to do and how to do it.

The simple directions required, first, that each of us find a partner. Thinking it would be an excellent way to reconnect, I chose my old Shalom friend Victoria, whom I had not seen since Chris and I went on the road.

Moseby asked one of each pair to join him and, in a group, listen to him tell a story. He gave each of those left behind the task of figuring out the story by asking their partner a series of yes or no questions. Victoria agreed to hear the story while I waited a few minutes for her return.

When she came back, I began my questioning.

"Did it happen on Shalom Mountain?"

"Yes."

"Was it on a Shalom Retreat?"

"No."

"A work weekend?"

"Yes."

Through question after question, I discovered that something happened at a Memorial Day work weekend and that Jeff's kids Phin and Moseby were present, as was Shelly's mother. I understood that something embarrassing had happened to Shelly that had to do with her clothes coming off and that, although her mother knew about it, she didn't judge the matter. I didn't have the whole story, but I felt confident about what I had discovered.

After about twenty minutes, Moseby called us together and invited the questioners to share our interpretations of what our partners had heard. Waiting my turn, I listened in shock as the first person shared a story so different from my own saying that something had happened in the winter when Jeff and Shelly had a fight over plans for the wedding. To make peace, they traced angels in newly fallen snow. The following two people shared similar stories about a fight happening in the winter.

Then another person shared and said the story happened in the spring, although the plot still centered on an argument. I couldn't believe everyone had gotten so far off track and decided I had to share what I heard from Victoria to help them realize the actual facts.

I told the group what I understood from Victoria about Shelly's embarrassing experience of being undressed on that work weekend. My story was followed by other listeners providing even more conflicting reports.

What was going on?

With a mischievous smile, Moseby explained the trick to his puzzled audience. The real story, he said, was that there never had been a story. Instead of telling an actual story to the first group, Moseby asked them to pretend that there was a story. He then directed them to respond to questions from their partners randomly but logically with yes or no answers.

As a questioner, I believed I had gathered genuine evidence from the answers. It shocked and unsettled me that I had devised a story of my own invention, a story I felt deeply attached to and ready to insist upon.

I had always felt that we humans, not God, made up the stories that created civilizations, what we believed, what we longed for, and what constitutes right or wrong. Still, I never really took in the possibility of no underlying truth. Perhaps simply curious about how the drama would unfold, Creator embedded seeds of every possible story in our consciousness, and we gave the stories we made up the substance of truth.

I had seen in real time how we humans can create reality. We make up our stories with limited information and then fall into believing our creations unquestionably. We fight wars against enemies we have never met. We judge other people's religions without taking time to understand. We create fictions that see our fellow humans as less because of the color of their skin, the amount of money in their bank accounts, or the school they went to. We even make up stories about ourselves, our worth, and our abilities. We think that reality is solid and unchanging and forget that we constantly shape it just as it shapes us.

Before Moseby's exercise, I wouldn't have thought a story I had made up would fool me. I have strong, hard-fought-for opinions, but I found it enlightening yet humbling to discover that I could so strongly believe and fight for an imagined, unproven story—a figment of my imagination. I hoped I would remember the game when I fell into forgetting the unimagined complexity of that squishy thing we call reality.

The game ended, and we all dispersed to put on our finery for the wedding ceremony. The sun shined brightly as we made our way to Shalom's High Meadow. Jeff stood eagerly waiting at the altar as Shelly appeared gloriously arrayed in a long, white lace gown. A dozen children, also dressed in white, surrounded her. Her voice rose into the mountain air as she began to sing, "Ong Namo Guru Dev Namo"—"Oh, my beloved, Kindness of the heart, Breath of Life, I bow to you." The sweetness of sound rang through the clear air, bringing us all into sacred space. Slowly she made her way to meet her beloved at the altar.

The bride and groom had asked four couples, including Chris and me, to speak at the ceremony. When it was our turn, we met the couple at the altar and bowed before sharing the piece we had written for them from our own experience of marriage:

> The path of the mystic lover calls us into a world that turns the life we have known upside-down. It is a path that requires courage and the willingness to lose oneself in love, dying to one's old life. It is easy to talk about Oneness—to talk about universal love, forgiveness, and union with God. Yet, there are few places where we are invited to experience what it means to surrender our boundaries and merge with something bigger than ourselves. Mystic lovers follow a path in the world but not of the world. Mystic lovers ask the question, "What does it mean for two whole beings to merge into one larger entity where they offer themselves up into an alchemical vessel to be cooked over and over, dying and being reborn?

We finished our offering, and another of our friends officially pronounced the bride and groom man and wife. After a sumptuous dinner, the tables were pushed aside, and we celebrated long into the night, dancing and loving each other.

After several dances, Chris said he preferred to watch rather than dance because his rib hurt. The pain had started after he had helped Jack move large boulders to clear the road up to the Green House in Estes Park more than a year before. It had caused discomfort for some time, but a chiropractor had told him that he had probably fractured it and that he had to be patient and give it time to heal. I was disappointed that we danced only one more time together, but Chris said he was happy to watch me enjoy myself with other people.

The party went on, and soon after midnight, we decided to return to our room in one of the bungalows. It had been a glorious celebration, and we soaked in the loving energy of the gathering. Before getting into bed, Chris and I found a spot to share Mother under the moonlight. Curling up together, we listened to wedding celebration music filling the night air. We had been married for fifteen years, but that night we felt like we were celebrating our own wedding. We talked, laughed, and made love until we finally fell happily asleep in each other's arms.

After the festivities ended the following day, we returned to the cottage at Timshel, where we planned to stay for the next several weeks until we left for Colorado.

A week before leaving, we celebrated our fifteenth anniversary by making a special dinner in the cottage. I made a shrimp cocktail, and then, with deep gratitude, we sent two giant lobsters to the next world. It was strange to be a part of killing animals we would eat even though without thinking about it, we normally ate animals that others killed. But right after the beautiful celebration, we felt something holy about being a part of that life and death process and doing it in a sacred way.

The lobsters were delicious. I sucked every possible place and didn't miss a morsel. It seemed unnecessary to make a special occasion about our anniversary since we were grateful for each day, but we had a good celebration.

We got into bed and started our Mother ritual. She offered us a special anniversary gift. We flew together way out into the cosmos. With a delightful intensity to our connection, our bodies wrapped around each other in such sweetness that we dissolved and melted into space and tumbled through the universe, immersed in love.

At the same time, I felt as if I had entered another dimension where my body had dissolved into pure consciousness. I experienced orgasms so deep I was sure my body would fall apart from the intensity. Instead of feeling terror, I simply watched and took interest in what would happen next. Feeling overwhelming gratitude, I kept telling myself that the universe needs such love energy and that we had gifted the universe with our pleasure.

Loving in that way, we fell in love with everything—old lovers, family, friends, trees, and mountains, even politicians for whom our rational minds had contempt. As we lay together in each other's arms, I felt flooded with a profound feeling that all was well. We had everything we needed, and we had each other. We had so much to be grateful for, and the day's minor frustrations had no fundamental importance. Whether what Chris and I did mattered to anyone else didn't matter. We had accepted the calling literally to make love and send it into the world. We felt lucky to have been given such glorious work.

The following day, we began our preparations for the trip back to Colorado, where we planned to spend the next six weeks in our beautiful, borrowed mountain home in Estes Park. We had much packing to do, people to see, and many goodbyes.

I felt on edge but didn't know why. I always found transitions stressful. I never loved organizing and packing our belongings into bins and into the car and attempting to plan for unknown circumstances. I often had some anxiety, but the level of concern I had after the wedding didn't feel familiar. No matter what I tried, I couldn't find my center.

I couldn't stop thinking about Moseby's game that accurately demonstrated how we make up stories based on little information. I realized that Chris and I were making up the story that we were spiritual nomads carried by the wind. I wondered what other stories we might create in the coming chapters.

Back in Estes Park after only one day, I had the feeling of something off with Chris. He complained about his sore rib, a strange itch on his eyes and forehead, digestive discomfort, and a general feeling of malaise. The vague symptoms didn't seem to point to anything serious, but something wasn't right.

We tucked ourselves into bed that night and started to drift off. In that mysterious space between waking and dreaming, I heard Chris say, "I just saw the face of God." In the mythologies of many cultures that we had studied, seeing the face of God means that you will die. Such awe-inspiring energy more than our fragile bodies can hold.

Chris became quiet after his declaration and fell into his own private space. I didn't want to intrude with questions, but listening to Chris breathing heavily beside me, I felt that something momentous had happened, something that could change our lives.

Suddenly, I heard a booming male voice from somewhere above the bed. "It is time for a breach to be made, a time to break through the wall between night and day." The voice left as quickly as it came, leaving me to wonder who had spoken and what the words meant. In a dizzying torrent of confusion, thoughts kept tumbling through my mind.

I wondered if the voice referred to the way Chris and I felt that we inhabited two worlds, the day and the night. Our conditioning, egos, and engagement with the culture ruled the domains of the day. In the night, Mother opened up a dimension with a higher vantage point where we could watch the day's events without identifying with them and explore beyond the realms of form. For me, to mix the two states of consciousness had always seemed confusing and even dangerous, yet I couldn't mistake the voice suggesting that I break through the walls of separation. Perhaps a breach in the wall between night and day might allow a new way of seeing both dimensions. Still, I didn't know where the voice might lead me.

I woke Chris and chattered wildly about breaches and breaking through barriers. Because of his low energy, I assumed correctly we would have no lovemaking that night as we had on most nights, and I started to drift off to sleep. Yet I continued to feel uneasy about the messages we had both received.

We woke the following morning and lolled in bed before rising to meet the new day. I noticed that something had changed. Chris didn't bound out of bed as he usually did. He slowly made his way to the breakfast table, and I could see something was not right. I asked him what was going on.

He said he didn't know. All he could say was that he was tired. It was as if all his energy had leaked out the previous night, and he was empty.

Where, I asked myself, was the Chris I had known? I wondered if it had something to do with his seeing the face of God.

I didn't know what I was supposed to do to help him or even if he needed my help. Chris's energy hadn't been quite right for the last couple of months if not longer, I realized, and although nothing seemed desperately wrong, the length of time that had passed with no improvement left me worried. I tried to talk to Chris about it, but he said he didn't know what was going on and took no interest in my probing.

Oddly enough, my body didn't feel right, either. I didn't have any worrisome symptoms but felt dizzy and ungrounded as if a river of fear had risen and then gone underground. I didn't know whether my body spoke to the changes going on in my own life or the life of the outer world. I felt helpless, clueless, and lost.

In the years we'd been on the road, we trusted that Spirit would always guide us to exactly where we were supposed to be. We answered her call even when we didn't understand our purpose. As we sat at the breakfast table that morning, I felt as if everything familiar had fallen away, and I felt lost without an anchor.

In the days and weeks that followed, I had to let go of a lot. Chris's lack of energy brought our lovemaking close to a halt. Much of the time, he sat in his easy chair in the corner of the living room and read magazines or an action novel. I felt alone, forced to create my own pleasures. I enjoyed playing the piano, writing, and talking to friends on the phone, but I struggled as I felt Chris's absence after years of finding happiness together.

I wondered if I had to accept the possibility that we might never make love again. I wanted to be able to love Chris with all of me, and although I knew that our love would endure no matter what, our physical and spiritual relationship had been so central to our life together that its loss, even for a few weeks, caused a deep sadness. I had to work hard not to blame Chris for no longer being the lover and playmate I had grown used to.

Gradually, he talked more willingly, and our conversations went deeper and felt more intimate. We spoke of our beloveds and shared stories of heart meetings. We talked about our travels, the beauty of places we had visited, and our gratitude for being able to love each other and share such grand adventures.

But Chris had no words to explain what was happening to him.

* * *

We saw on the internet that the husband of one of Chris's close colleagues had died suddenly as a result of his contact with Agent Orange in Vietnam. It shocked us to hear of his end so quickly and soon after the death of Chris's cousin, who had struggled with Alzheimer's for many years.

Chris and I spent a lot of time talking about death. We remembered times when we had experienced letting go in our medicine journeys and lovemaking, times that felt as if we were dying. Neither of us had a deep conscious fear of death. In fact, we both confessed to some curiosity. We knew that we would never really know death until it was too late to tell anyone.

Our story appeared to be changing, but our love was solid. We trusted that whatever was going on with Chris was temporary. Yet, as a week became two then three and four, I could feel the desire in Chris, but the energy behind that desire had weakened.

It hurt me as I watched him fall deeper and deeper into lethargy. I couldn't bear to see my beloved nearly unrecognizable in a state so spiritless and fatigued.

I tried to resist making up stories about what was going on. But I wondered. Was Chris going through a physical crisis or a spiritual one? Had I done something to cause it? Had we been on the road too long? I had no idea. I could only accept that we didn't know and take each day as it came.

Because we were on the road, we didn't have personal doctors. We checked with a local doctor and an acupuncturist, and they assured us that Chris was just tired and needed to rest.

I could only trust that that, too, would pass, all as part of the training for something we couldn't even imagine.

Chris was clearly in a radical process of change, which meant I was too. I tried to hold the story lightly and trust that whatever was going on was for our highest good. Yet, the thread of fear moving through my belly did not quiet.

The Right Thing for the Wrong Reason

Life is the glorious moment before the fall when all plans are abandoned,
the love you give as you hang, loving those who hang with you.

—Rebecca del Rio

The following two months felt like riding a roller coaster. I longed for the old, familiar Chris who had been my lover and companion for almost sixteen years. He emerged from the darkness at random times, and we met as in the old days. He stayed long enough for me to relax and believe we had gotten through the passage and without warning disappeared again.

I started to wonder if I had made the whole thing up about being soul mates connected forever and whether I was the one lost. I tried to remember how the old days were different or even when the old days were. When we left Timshel in the beginning of October, I knew something didn't seem right, but we were so busy that it didn't seem like a big deal. When I tried talking with Chris, he didn't seem interested or able to pinpoint anything.

I couldn't distinguish between the physical, psychological, spiritual, or even volitional, and Chris seemed as confused as I. I missed the good old days of easy and joyful living. I missed

Chris's laughter and enthusiasm, our play, and our sense of adventure. Most of all, I missed our nightly Mother rituals not just for the pleasure and ecstasy, but also because we enacted them together as our gift to the universe. Since Jeff and Shelly's wedding, I wondered what constituted our contribution and whether we even had a gift to give.

Perhaps just being present for what developed comprised a gift to the universe as did the times when I held space during medicine journeys. At least I could hold on to that.

In late November, we left the Estes Park Green House to take part in Ayahuasca ceremonies. Chris's energies seemed to rally sufficiently to participate fully, and I felt like the old Chris had returned. We drove up to see our friends Andre and Missy on Gabriola, one of the Gulf Islands in British Columbia. Healing energy surrounded us there along with the consensus that our seven years of journeying with the medicines and of being on the road had exhausted us and we needed to rest. They invited us to stay, but we wanted to drive back east to celebrate Christmas with my family and Chris's kids at Timshel in Pennsylvania.

We left our friends and arrived just in time to be the last car on the ferry to the States. To our relief, we crossed the border without incident, sent on our way by a lovely young border control guard. Expressing happiness about our destination to visit family, she barely asked any questions about any contraband substances we might have on board except for firearms or liquor, which we were not carrying.

Chris started driving in heavy fog, but after an hour, I worried about his dwindling energy and suggested we stop for the night.

The next day, we shared the driving until Chris took over the last shift in heavy snow. We were relieved when we made it safely to Billings, Montana. After an unappetizing meal of frozen lasagna heated in the motel's microwave oven, Chris suggested sharing some Mother. We talked and cuddled, but there was no lovemaking. I found it hard to fall asleep.

We woke to a sunny, dry day and straight roads for our first uncomplicated day of driving. We spoke little. Curiously, I could think of nothing to say. The silence felt deafening. I ended up driving the last shift in the dark, fortunately on a road clear, straight, and not overly challenging.

I felt brittle with exhaustion when we arrived at a motel in Monticello, Minnesota, but sandwiches and long hot baths helped to revive us. As at each of our stops, we shared Mother before going to sleep. Although Chris participated and sometimes we made love, he faded rapidly. Still, I felt grateful for time we spent vibrating together.

The next day, my birthday, we stopped in Maumee, Ohio, after fourteen hours of shared driving. I didn't want to celebrate with sandwiches in our motel room, so we went for cheeseburgers and margaritas at a nearby restaurant—not a fancy dinner but satisfying enough as I relaxed with my beloved.

On Christmas Eve, I did almost all the driving on the last seven-hour leg of our journey. Chris seemed exhausted, and I didn't want to fatigue him further. We arrived at Timshel just before dark and settled into the little cottage on the edge of the property to rest and recuperate.

We did our best to participate in the holiday festivities, but Chris's vitality continued to diminish. His bright blue eyes had dimmed. He rarely laughed his once hearty laugh and lacked the strength to do the smallest of tasks. We continued a quiet life in the cottage, sharing meals with my father and Georgeanne in the evenings and making short visits with them during the day. I filled my days with playing my electric keyboard, writing, doing yoga and meditation, and talking to friends on the phone, but Chris seemed to lose more and more energy, even though he rarely complained of pain.

In late January, Chris thought visiting our friends Peter and Pam in Wendell, Massachusetts, would raise his spirits. He didn't feel up to driving, so I drove the dangerously slushy road from Timshel to Wendell while he sat listlessly in the passenger seat. In the past, Chris always drove when we had challenging conditions since he had more experience driving, but in the new times we had entered, I had to rise to the occasion no matter what we preferred.

We arrived safely in the afternoon and settled into Peter and Pam's living room. Peter, a trained psychotherapist, quickly noticed that Chris did not present his usual lively self and dove into finding reasons. Peter probed, but Chris seemed unreachable. The more Peter questioned him, the more Chris disappeared inside of himself.

Since Chris did not complain of physical pain, Peter suspected that Chris suffered from clinical depression. He interpreted the contraction of Chris's body as his attempt to shut down unacceptable feelings from childhood. Peter speculated that the process of integrating expansive mystical journeying of the past seven years could have brought old wounds to the surface.

I wasn't sure I agreed with Peter's diagnosis, but I didn't see an alternative. Chris willingly acknowledged he had unexplored wounds around a controlling mother, a distant father, and an abusive older brother, but little new information emerged.

We ate a delicious dinner, and at around nine-thirty, Chris said he felt tired, and we crossed the driveway to the cottage Peter and Pam had prepared for us.

Chris happened to undress for bed with the light on, and what I saw shocked me. For weeks, he had gone to bed before me and gotten up after me, so I hadn't seen him naked, although we still made love. Looking at him in the Wendell cottage, for the first time I really saw him. His skin color had turned ashen and I couldn't believe his muscles had diminished to sticks. He looked like a ghost. I felt terrified and confused. Before, I had seen only depression and despair. Naked in the light, I pictured him at death's door.

How could I have not seen what was now right in front of me? My mind bounced back and forth between the horror of recognizing the deterioration of Chris's body and the optimistic words that we had heard from his doctors that said he was simply tired or moving through a transformational process.

As I looked at Chris, a momentary thought flashed through my mind that he looked like my brother's partner, Anna, during the final stages of ovarian cancer. Terrified, I erased the notion as soon as it emerged. My beloved could not be dying. I wasn't ready to lose him. The doctors had said he was fine, and I preferred to hold to that story. I could not allow myself to think dark thoughts. Chris was moving through a healing process which would pass.

And then all would be well.

With that determination in mind but still filled with sadness, I got into bed with Chris. He felt so insubstantial lying beside me, and I felt helpless. Hoping to bring my life force into his weakened body, I wrapped my arms and legs around him. We cuddled and I whispered my love and finally—warmed by the heat of a wood-burning stove—we drifted off into dreamless sleep.

The following day, I left Chris in bed as he wished and went to have breakfast with Peter and Pam. After eating, Peter went to the cottage to talk with Chris while I stayed with Pam. I was grateful to fall into her warm energy, as I had felt alone since Chris had fallen into his mysterious withdrawal. Pam held me gently in her arms as she listened to my fears that Chris had fallen ill because of something I had done, although I didn't know what. I needed to talk, and Pam listened. I was grateful.

When Chris and Peter returned, Chris asked if we would offer him the love fest that we offer before mat trips at Shalom Mountain. In the ritual, we gather around a person and celebrate them by sharing memories.

Thrilled that he had asked for something we could provide, Peter, Pam, and I enthusiastically agreed. Chris lay on a mat in the center of the floor while Peter, Pam, and I sat around him with our hands placed tenderly on his body. We lovingly showered him with positive, caring affirmations and memories. The room's energy shifted immediately into a bouquet of love offerings, and Chris soaked them up like a dry sponge.

I spoke about the beauty of his art, the pottery pieces that he called earth grails to honor the mysteries of Mother Earth, and the phallic-shaped wood turnings he created to honor the masculine archetype. I thanked him for being an open channel where love moved, gifting not only me but so many of our loved ones. I spoke about how he didn't simply talk about gratitude but lived gratitude and how he had, in that way, softened my heart. I spoke of his love for his kids and their love for him. I talked about the men who loved him and the actions, strength, and groundedness of his tender heart. His eyes welled up when I mentioned his connection with men, especially our beloved friend Jack Kochner.

Peter and Pam also had beautiful things to say. Pam spoke of Chris's loving actions in the world, and Peter talked about his appreciation for the times he and Chris had worked together to bring beauty to Stone Oak, the land where Peter and Pam lived.

Later, as the four of us gathered for dinner in the evening, Chris said he felt as if he might either be dying or going crazy. He said that feeling so clueless and impotent was bringing him to a place of immobilizing despair. In that intense moment, he spoke and then fell silent with any remaining feelings locked away.

I found it excruciating to see him so hopeless. Chris and I had shared each other's company twenty-four/seven for the past seven years. We were a team and did things together, but I could no longer find him. He seemed lost in a place where I couldn't reach him. I felt terrified to think that we could lose each other.

As soon as we finished eating, Chris left the main house to walk across the driveway to the cottage. He said he needed to rest and be alone. I went over to join him an hour later and looked up into the sky spangled with stars that burned so brightly and so close I felt I could touch them. The beauty of that night sky lifted my spirits.

Chris had left the lights on, and when I reached the cottage, I got into bed. I found Chris asleep. He woke, and I curled up close against his still body.

"How are you feeling, my love?" I asked.

"I don't know. I have no idea what is happening. I wish I knew."

Sleep didn't come easily as my mind spun trying to understand the strange force that was taking Chris from me. How could we fight something we didn't understand? I slept that night wrapped around his body, clinging to him and hoping that some of my life-force energy would rub off.

The sun shone brightly on newly fallen snow in the morning, and crystalline beams of light flashed up from the ground. The clarity of the natural world contrasted sharply with the chaos of my inner world. I looked back at Chris sleeping fitfully in the bed, then walked over to join Peter and Pam in the main house.

Chris's lack of vitality frightened us all. We had found some comfort in the previous evening's affirmations and hoped to find a more effective response to his distress. Given that none of the doctors we had seen had recommended further medical testing, we felt Chris in the throes of depression rather than disease. We began to look at places that would support his emotional healing as he gained tools for reviving his energy for life.

We considered sending him to a psychiatric hospital, but we had all had negative encounters with hospitals. I considered the disastrous three months my sister had experienced in a psychiatric hospital. We doubted that a hospital would provide Chris the supportive healing environment he needed. In a wild leap of imagination, we decided that a twelve-step rehab would best provide community, support, and healing for Chris.

I never believed that Chris was an alcoholic or even that he had a problem with alcohol, but we could say that he had recently used alcohol to deal with his discomfort. That would gain him admittance. The three of us thought residential rehab would provide a safe place for Chris to work through unresolved issues. He would have a solid structure in the twelve-step program of Alcoholics Anonymous, and he would have a healing environment in community. We didn't consider it the ideal solution, but we didn't know what else to do.

We looked into rehab facilities and found one with an excellent reputation where both Peter and I had made previous client referrals. The inpatient program cost thirty thousand dollars for thirty days, and insurance didn't cover it. It seemed an outrageous amount of money worth every penny if it helped bring Chris back to life.

Chris walked in as we talked, and we shared our plan with him. His eyes brightened immediately, and he responded with a decisive yes. The mere possibility he could find help filled him with new energy.

Once we had Chris's approval, we called the rehab office. Everything went well until the admissions person told me that a place would not be available for three weeks.

In a horrifying moment, it occurred to me that he might not live that long.

"That won't work," I insisted. "Chris needs help, and he needs it now."

A calm voice replied, "Well, if you're willing for him to go to a new Texas facility operated by the Caron Foundation, we could admit him tomorrow. The price for that location would be only thirteen thousand dollars."

Finally, we felt the support of the universe and proceeded to set up Chris's admission to the rehab. My relief that Chris would get help put aside all my concerns regarding how I would feel about separating from him for a month and being on my own after our continuous companionship for the past seven years. It was not the time to think of such things. It was time to get help for Chris, so I pulled back my thoughts from my own worries and focused on him.

Peter finished making admission arrangements for Chris as I booked an airplane ticket for the flight from Hartford, the closest airport, to Dallas in the morning. I planned to get him safely on his flight, and when he landed, he would be met by a rehab employee who would take him to the facility.

We hurriedly packed our belongings and said goodbye to Peter and Pam. I was numb and in a place of limbo. Until Chris settled, I couldn't look at my own situation. I could only let the energy carry me and trust that Spirit guided us in the right decision.

We headed for Hartford an hour away where we would spend the night in a motel before Chris boarded the plane at six in the morning. Chris already looked better just knowing we had a plan. On the way, I gently probed about what he thought was going on, but he had little understanding of his strange symptoms or why he felt so lifeless. Since everything was back at the Timshel cottage but the clothes we had packed for a weekend visit, we needed to buy essentials to take Chris through his month at the rehab. We found a shopping mall with a department store and bought jeans, sweats, underwear, socks, and toiletries that he would need for his stay.

I watched him looking like a lost child as he walked through the aisles of the store. He told me he felt like a deer in headlights. Where had the Chris gone who had walked with me for so long? The man I saw in front of me looked like a shell of Chris. I missed my partner.

We quickly finished shopping and checked into a motel near the airport. Exhausted, we fell into bed enfolded in each other's arms for a moment of quiet connection before we entered a strange new chapter we could barely imagine.

I couldn't imagine what it would be like to live for a month without Chris, but in many ways, he had already been absent for the four months since his energy leaked out in October. As we prepared to separate, I knew that hard work for both of us was just beginning. Still, I trusted that the crazy plan we had concocted would bring healing, even though I suspected that we would both change during our month of separation.

Night fell, we got into the car, and I drove to a close-by chain restaurant. Cheerful, light rock music and friendly, attractive waitresses greeted us. The food did not inspire us, but we were both too emotional to eat much anyway. We sat side by side at the table for a couple of hours, our bodies pressed against each other as we talked about our feelings, concerns, and—most importantly—our love for each other.

I tried not to get tearful, but sometimes I couldn't help myself, and the tears leaked out, causing Chris to cry. I felt vulnerable expressing such tenderness in public, but we were so lost in each other and our uncertain future that we didn't care where we were.

On the way back to the motel, we stopped for gas so I wouldn't have to fill the tank in the morning. It felt surreal to do such a mundane task amidst our intense drama. Chris showed more energy since he had begun to see a potential way out of a death path, but I suspected that it was more cosmetic than real.

I trusted we had made the right decision, but it did seem like a crazy scheme. Crazy or not, it was the only option we saw, so I did my best to believe in the path we had chosen. Our tangled state of not knowing made me feel like I was going crazy.

I knew I needed to stay strong for Chris's sake. Falling apart would not help Chris in his fragile state. I didn't want to collapse until he was in a safe place, but my belly bubbled with anxiety. I willed myself back together and wondered how Chris had managed to stay calm during the past months of watching his body deteriorate.

We returned to the motel, got undressed and into bed. Feeling the pleasure of Chris's body entangled with mine, I felt the stab of remembering that we would not share a bed or feel the warmth of our bodies wrapped around each other for a month. A long chapter in our lives had ended, and we had no idea what new world lay ahead. I lay wide awake in Chris's arms and knew there was nothing to do but trust the process and our love for each other. After many hours, I slept.

The alarm woke us at 4:30 a.m., and I popped out of bed. We had done most of the packing the night before, and since I planned to return right after taking Chris to the plane, we didn't need to clear out the room. Getting up in the pitch dark of night to send Chris away felt like a dream. Everything had happened so quickly that I hadn't had a chance to get my brain around it. I knew only that we had finally found help and a shred of hope in our frightening situation.

My heart ached for both of us. I was grateful that Chris could do healing work he had not been able to do earlier in his life, yet I wondered how changes in him might affect our relationship. I could only trust that things would get better no matter what the turn of events.

Even though we weren't hungry, we headed to the motel breakfast room at a little after five o'clock. Caring little about the outside world, we nevertheless distracted ourselves by watching the TV blasting in the corner. Barely speaking, we waited for the airport shuttle. What could we say? How might we express the depth of our feelings at such a tender and vulnerable time? Chris's debilitated state hadn't decreased my love for him. In fact, I felt more and more love and respect for him and trusted deeply that he would find his way, since we at last had a plan.

A shuttle came to take us to the terminal less than seven minutes away. The drive felt too short. I wanted more time together before we had to separate. I insisted on helping Chris get the boarding pass inside the terminal, and I stayed with him through an endless security line. We clung in silence to each other's hands.

When we got close to the front of the line, we hugged and kissed and declared yet one more time our love for each other. I didn't want to leave him alone, but I could go no further.

Barely holding back our tears, we let go, and I turned to walk away. When I looked back, Chris had left the security line, and I watched as he stepped alone into the next stage of his life.

I went to a nearby ladies' room, locked myself in a stall, and cried softly until I felt ready to go out into the world. I found a phone and called the shuttle to take me back to the motel. A pleasant woman said I should stand in front of the terminal and flag down the driver when I saw the van. It was cold and dark, and my insides reflected the external chill. I waited fifteen minutes before I saw the shuttle pull up to the curb. I was surprised to be the only passenger and decided to engage with the driver rather than sit silently in my private world of despair.

The driver was a gentle, elderly African American man. I asked him about his work, and he told me that he had previously driven a bus for the motel for eleven years. When he started, he had a full-time job, and he drove a bus he loved. Times changed, and the motel needed him to work just five hours a day and downgraded him to a small van. Although disappointed, he said he felt grateful to have a job he enjoyed even though it was a shadow of his former situation. His dignified demeanor and heartful acceptance of his difficult life touched me and made my transition a little easier.

I was grateful.

Silence and loneliness enveloped me when I returned to the room I had recently shared with Chris. Lost with no idea what to do, I tried to sleep, but sleep wouldn't come. Hoping that meditation might benefit, I found a comfortable seat on the floor. Just as I started, the phone rang. It was Chris calling from the airport.

Several times, I had checked the 6:15 a.m. departure that I bought online. Pam had rechecked it before I booked the trip. However, when I picked up the phone, Chris said the ticket he held was for 6:15 p.m., not 6:15 a.m. Apparently, Spirit had wanted us to have more time to process the momentous change in our lives. I was grateful.

I got dressed, into our car, and to the front of the terminal to meet Chris so fast that he didn't recognize me when I honked to get his attention. I was thrilled to see him and relieved that we would have more time together before our extended separation and his adventure.

We drove back and settled into our room. It felt like one of the many ordinary motel stays of our seven years on the road, but we both knew we would soon move into uncharted territory.

Chris rested while I canceled scheduled appointments with his internist and acupuncturist. I tried to get an extension for our time in the room, but the front desk clerk told me we could stay until noon but then would have to leave.

I woke Chris at 11:45. We packed everything into the car and said goodbye to the place that had held us during our time of transition. A food wasteland surrounded the motel with few choices for lunch. We weren't hungry, but we needed a warm place to hang out.

We found a Thai noodle place barely more than a hole in the wall, but we could get hot soup that, while not gourmet, at least provided some nourishment and an excuse to sit indoors out of the cold. We went next door to a little shop to buy an alarm clock that Chris would need and enjoyed joking and laughing with the cashier. Things almost felt normal.

We had the whole afternoon ahead of us and decided to spend it watching a movie before Chris's flight. The easy part was finding a place to rent a DVD. The more challenging problem was figuring out how to view it. It hadn't occurred to us to book the motel room for another night for just a few hours so we would have a warm place to stay. That lack of foresight left us with only one option, which was to take refuge in our car.

We didn't want to stay in the mall parking lot, so I drove back to the motel parking lot, which had started to feel like home. We set the computer on the dashboard and covered ourselves with a blanket. We created a warm and cozy nest in our improvised movie theater. High snowbanks surrounded the car, and safe in our private world, we were happy to be with each other for a few precious hours.

We watched Woody Allen's *Midnight in Paris*, a light, frothy romance set in Paris that brought back sweet memories of our honeymoon almost sixteen years before.

The movie ended, and an hour remained before Chris needed to check in for his flight. I didn't want to leave him, but he convinced me that I would be safer driving back in daylight to my friend Adrian's house in Wendell, especially since freezing rain had started to fall.

We both cried because of the painful business of parting after the tender day. We knew that the separation had to happen eventually and waiting would not make it easier. The prospect of driving in the dark on Wendell's slushy roads frightened me enough that I finally acquiesced. I insisted that Chris call me when he got through security and settled inside the terminal. I assured him I would gladly turn around and return if he had any problem.

I reluctantly drove the car back to the terminal and stopped at a place where we could talk before we had to part. I told Chris he might find himself doing inner work that involved getting in touch with anger at me or other beloveds. I wanted him to know that I supported whatever would lead to his healing. I thanked him for the work he had done and would do. Over and over, we told each other of our deep and abiding love.

We pressed our bodies together as if our very lives depended on it. Then I watched as Chris walked through the terminal door and let go of a deep breath of relief and grief.

Weeping, I sat in the car until a security guard told me I had to move. I stopped a little past the loading zone and did my best to compose myself. Then with determination, I set out on my first adventure without Chris since my trip to Peru in 2006.

I felt the intensity of the energy I had held for the past four months but knew I had to keep things together for another hour and a quarter until I completed the drive to Adrian's house, where I could finally rest.

Twenty minutes later, I got a call from Chris. He said he had checked in with grace and ease and felt ready to start out on his own journey. From the sound of his voice, I trusted he would be okay. He had only to get on the plane and when he arrived, someone would meet him. He promised he would call when he landed.

Finally, I could take care of my own feelings I had so carefully guarded.

We had no idea where our separate adventures would lead. We really didn't know much at all. We knew only the strength of our love and trusted that we would meet any challenges with that love.

I took a breath and did my best to steady myself as I drove into the dark and frozen night.

Into the Dark

Dark and getting darker—nothing to do but to make of the body a home for
darkness to open every secret drawer where we hide our private darknesses.
—Rosemerry Wahtola Trommer

We had just ten minutes at 7:20 p.m. each day—just ten
minutes to share the events of the day and our love for each
other. It was such a short time after being with each other day
and night for almost seven years. The rehab had strict rules.
They allowed no contact for the first three days except for a
quick call that assured me Chris had landed safely and was in
good hands. After that, the rules limited us to a ten-minute chat
each evening. I did my best to convince myself that this restric-
tion was the necessary price for the possibility that Chris would
find healing.

Chris called me after the three-day blackout period and told
me his body still felt exhausted and that he wasn't sleeping.
Still, he hoped that being at Caron would help him heal. I felt
encouraged when Chris described finding his place in the
community, pushing himself a little at the gym, eating well,
and enjoying the companionship of the other men. He said he
had started working with a therapist he liked and trusted.

The news felt promising, and I began to have a shred of hope that our crazy plan would bear fruit.

I found it excruciatingly difficult to say goodbye at the end of the short call. I so loved wrapping myself around Chris's body at night and waking up with him. It felt impossible that he wouldn't return to my bed that night. We said goodnight as if everything were normal, but we knew that nothing was. I let the echoes of his deep voice reverberate in my body and then went into the kitchen to prepare a meal I knew I would not eat.

A week after Chris left, his therapist called to ask me whether I thought that Chris had an addiction to alcohol.

I answered truthfully, "Of course not!"

"So, what," she asked impatiently, "do you think he is doing here?"

Then I remembered. We sent Chris to Caron because he seemed depressed, and we couldn't think of a better place for him to get grounded while learning practical coping tools. Even though he enjoyed a Scotch now and again and a glass of wine with dinner, I knew alcohol was not the problem. No matter how strange a choice, we needed a safe place to hold Chris during his mysterious, spiritual emergency.

Regaining my balance, I said as if I had just had a momentary memory loss, "Oh, yes, of course I know he has a problem with alcohol. He must be using it to hide some dark feelings he can't yet express. His drinking has not interfered with our relationship or his relationships with others," I assured the therapist. "But yes. Of course, he has issues with alcohol."

I suspected that, probably accurately, she thought me in deep denial about my husband's condition. I didn't know what had caused his change, but I knew he wasn't an alcoholic. That said, I cautiously hoped we had found the place where he would find himself.

I decided to send an email to a small group of our beloveds. I told them that Chris was going through a challenging spiritual emergency and needed support. I explained that, beginning in October, he had gradually fallen into a state of depression that had become serious, although the doctors we consulted found nothing wrong. I told them that we knew he needed help beyond what the family or I could offer and that he had, therefore, entered a thirty-day treatment program in Texas. I shared that I understood that a comprehensive medical workup had been done but thankfully had found nothing notable.

I asked them to send prayers, affirmations, and healing thoughts for his recovery and rebirth into a more authentic expression of his beautiful essence. I also encouraged them to send love and healing to each other and to all beings. I hoped we could create an encompassing circle of love around Chris.

I missed Chris but didn't feel empty. I didn't even feel as if he were really gone. He had felt more absent when I watched him sinking further into depression every day. At least with him at Caron, I could imagine him as the Chris I once knew who laughed, got excited, made love, and seemed content. I had hope.

I couldn't imagine life with Chris when he returned, and I still found it hard to believe that he had collapsed into such a state. Talking to him during our limited phone calls, I realized he had gone back to his beginnings. Nothing was certain anymore. Everything was up for grabs. He barely remembered his life as a gifted potter and woodworker, an admired teacher, and a beloved parent. As for our relationship, I knew I would have to begin again with the man Chris would become in his time away.

Some of our friends told me they believed Chris had gotten lost in my sometimes-overpowering energy. Others thought his disease came from our spending too much time together. I had never felt a hint of Chris's unhappiness with our constant presence with each other when we lived on the road. In fact, whenever I shared the most minor fantasy of settling down, he quickly quashed the idea.

In the turmoil of my brain, I nevertheless wondered whether I had caused his distress. Maybe I had projected something onto him that had no reality. Perhaps I thought we were on a journey together, but he had merely tagged along. Thinking only of my own pleasure in our adventures, had I missed something? Was Chris really on board? Should we have ended our travels and looked for a home? Did Chris's crisis occur because he didn't know where home was? Had he gone out too far, not knowing how to return? And why had it taken so long for me to see that Chris was falling apart? I realized I had noticed but perhaps chosen not to grasp the seriousness of his condition.

Even if I had understood, I don't know what I would have done. I was lost in a tangle of questions that had no answers.

As I thought about our relationship, I recognized myself as more centered in my mind while Chris was more centered in his heart. Chris's love opened my heart and taught me about surrender and adoration. My need for exploration and understanding had cracked Chris open so that he could more readily express his true essence and delight. We had gifted each other well, but I had no idea how to help him in new territory. I knew that I must stay present and take care of myself in the best way possible. I had to look for joy and gratitude, even in the presence of things dark and frightening.

Although Chris had been at Caron for almost two weeks, he sounded as physically distressed as when I put him on the plane. Our friend Peter tried to encourage me by saying that his recovery would take time and that the two weeks were a drop in the bucket.

Deep anxiety floated in the back of my mind.

Almost three weeks into his stay at Caron, Chris made his customary 7:20 p.m. call. He sounded like the old Chris. He told me about his equine therapy and said he would be talking with his therapist about our use of marijuana.

I felt concerned. Our ceremonial use of Mother had been crucial in our spiritual journey and our sexual relationship. I worried that his therapist would not understand how it had opened vast, new spiritual realms. I had always assumed that that Chris and I were on the same page as we journeyed with Mother. What had Chris experienced during our journeys, and what would he tell his therapist?

I no longer knew anything for sure.

We hung up the phone, and I felt overwhelmed and shocked to feel so far apart from my beloved. How did it happen?

It wasn't that we hadn't shared with each other. We had always talked and made decisions together. How did things get so off track?

I believed in the importance of the Twelve Steps and Chris's work at Caron and felt committed to supporting him in whatever he needed. I also had plenty of work dealing with my own feelings. I couldn't believe that the person who had accompanied me in my life for the past fifteen years had disappeared. I kept hoping he would bounce back, but there were no guarantees. Remembering the pleasures of the good old days, I did my best to banish my fears.

The next night Chris called sounding happy. He told me he had been encouraged to tell the story about his ceremonial use of Mother and found people fascinated by the sacred way we used the plant. I felt relieved that he saw himself as a shaman who carried valuable experiences to share with the community.

It was the first sign that he remembered who he really was and that positive mirroring from other community members made a difference. I suggested that he was not just at Caron to be healed but also to be a healing presence. Undoubtedly, he would see opportunities to give and receive what we called pickup and delivery.

I went through my days on autopilot. Feelings came and went, but everything that had happened before seemed irrelevant as soon as the moment passed. I felt numb. I couldn't think about the future because I didn't know what that would look like, and I had no desire to dwell on the recent past. It felt too bleak. I remembered the joy of our traveling life, but even that seemed like a fantasy or a dream. Part of me didn't dare look back.

I found myself in the middle of a mysterious game of being on my own but still attached to Chris. I didn't know who he was or would become, what he was thinking or feeling, or what we were becoming. Thinking didn't help. I could only trust and take the next step.

As we neared the end of Chris's month-long stay at Caron, he called to discuss his reentry into the world. He told me that he looked forward to it and felt anxious. I had to admit that I felt much the same. Despite the emotional roller coaster, I understood Chris and I would have to get to know each other again almost from scratch. I suspected that both of us would need a lot of patience and capacity to surrender. We could only trust that we had the necessary tools.

After thirty days of treatment, Chris boarded a plane, and I met him at the Binghamton, New York, airport about an hour and a half from Timshel. As he came down the escalator, I saw the old Chris energy had returned. He was no longer the ghost who left for Texas a month ago.

We fell into each other's arms and held each other, sinking into our familiar energy. The month of separation already seemed a hazy dream. We were finally together as we were meant to be. All was well once again.

We had relaxed and easy conversations as I drove Chris back to the Timshel cottage. We could almost pretend that nothing dramatic had happened and that we had returned to ordinary life. As we got onto the highway, the sun began to set. It peeked through dark clouds that had covered the sky all day. A brilliant show of color and shape surrounded us, a hopeful sign of a positive future.

When we got back to the cottage, I headed into the house with an armful of groceries. Hearing a heavy thud, I turned around and saw Chris crumpled on the ground. Thinking he had simply missed a step, I helped him up. He made excuses for his fall, I suspect to put my mind at ease, but it frightened me to see him so unsteady. Still, I didn't want to believe anything was physically wrong with him, so I did my best to focus on welcoming him back. Thankful to have him with me again, I climbed into bed with him, and we wrapped ourselves around each other. It felt as if all were well.

We had canceled Chris's date with his doctor when he went to Texas, so the following day, I called for a new appointment in New Haven with Dr. David Melchinger, our physician and friend of twenty years. Since Chris's discomfort had intensified over the past month, we made an extensive list of symptoms. Fatigue kept him in bed much of the time. He experienced pain in his neck, ribs, and lower back and frequently threw up and fell.

We both felt anxious about meeting with the doctor. We didn't know if we hoped he'd order tests that led to a diagnosis so that we might have a cure or if we wanted him to have no diagnosis so that we wouldn't have to go through healing an organic illness. Neither option sounded good.

Chris sat quiet for most of the five-hour journey to the doctor while I drove, feeling sad and lonely. I longed for the old days when everything appeared to be blissfully easy.

Chris went into the examining room while I sat anxiously in the waiting room. An hour passed before Chris emerged with no sign of Dr. Melchinger. Chris said only that he had an appointment for a brain scan the next day.

That night, we stayed at my Aunt Ginny's house in nearby Branford. The next day, we drove back to New Haven for the MRI. We entered the address into the GPS and kept circling Smilow Cancer Hospital, looking for the right place. Then we realized with shock that we were at the right place. We had no idea that we had been sent to a cancer hospital. The building looked like a monstrous temple. Despite luxurious artwork and furnishings that filled the first floor, we felt a dark energy.

An engaging young man took Chris into his office to prepare him for the procedure. I was left in the waiting room trying unsuccessfully to calm my racing thoughts while the technician photographed Chris's brain in slices.

We made an appointment with Dr. Melchinger for March 8, a week later, to get the results as we continued to assume that Chris's nervous system was fried not just with medicines but with our intense life. Still, a week felt like a long time to sit in the unknowing.

We returned to the Timshel cottage for a few days before going back to New Haven to get the report. Meanwhile, Chris spent much of every day in bed, although he got up for meals and had enough energy to do the dishes. He told me that he experienced intense pain and felt staggeringly weary.

He wanted to know how I felt, and even though I didn't want to burden him with my fears and grief while he had so much pain, I wanted to speak as honestly as possible. It felt wrong for me to insist on full disclosure from him if I held back. I answered that I was relieved and happy to have him back home. Still, significant losses in the most recent months of our companionship, sex life, and our spiritual journey challenged me. I told him I didn't want to focus on my feelings until we knew more, but I also didn't want to be in denial.

After I talked to Chris about my pain for the first time, he thanked me for being truthful.

The week passed slowly. I felt lonely even though Chris and I had many sweet moments of connection and good talks. But I missed our energy that used to have a life of its own—positive, erotic, and exciting. Chris was back, but the once-so-alive way of being we had created together had evaporated. I struggled to feel good as I might on a cloudy, cold, nasty day. I could do it, but it took extra effort, and I couldn't banish the feeling that something dark lurked in the background.

We returned to New Haven for our appointment with Dr. Melchinger to hear the results of the MRI. A nurse ushered us both into his office. We sat and waited.

Dr. Melchinger walked in and told us the news we didn't want to hear. "Chris," he said gently, "I'm so sorry to tell you this. The MRI showed that you have twenty spots of cancer in your brain. We don't know the source, but with so many small sites scattered throughout, the cancer in your brain will not be operable."

The words hung in the air. I stood behind Chris and placed my hands over his shoulders to steady him. Chris maintained a stony silence as Dr. Melchinger pressed on, telling us that Chris would need to see an oncologist to determine where the cancer started for treatment with the most accurate form of chemotherapy. He also suggested that radiation might be offered, not to cure but to make Chris more comfortable.

The unnamable had been named and threw us into a new world of danger and uncertainty. Holding on for dear life, I willed my mind to shut down. I couldn't even find a way to say no to the terrifying news. Responding felt like it gave too much reality to the circumstance.

I could feel myself deciding. *From now on,* I thought, *I will not look ahead. I will simply do the next thing, the next, and the next.* The old life had shattered, and the present was all we had.

My mind went crazy trying to find a story to help make sense of the doctor's evaluation, but nothing came. If Spirit had chosen to call Chris to wake up, it wasn't clear whether he would wake up in this lifetime or the next.

It terrified me to think that he wouldn't overcome the challenge, and I resolutely chose not to consider that option. The question was, I decided, whether Chris wanted to live or not. I believed in miracles, and I wanted to support my beloved in whatever he required. But he had to choose.

We returned to the cottage grateful for familiar surroundings. Immediately upon our arrival, we climbed into bed and held each other close.

We talked a little, snuggled, and quietly tried to understand the shocking news.

We didn't know what organ had sent cancer cells to Chris's brain. Our best guess seemed that his painful rib indicated that cancer may have begun in his lung. But why would he have gotten lung cancer after quitting smoking more than twenty years before? Could one puff of Mother at night create cancer?

Nothing made sense.

I had always suspected that if anything happened to Chris, it would concern his heart, not his brain, since he had such a tender heart. Although we might make up stories along the way, I knew we would never really know. Still, I kept searching for a reason for the diagnosis.

We lay in each other's arms, talking gently about the new situation as we clung desperately to each other's bodies.

We turned off the lights and tried to sleep. I woke up at 2:30 a.m., hoping it was time to get up and out of my bad dream. But I knew that it was not a dream.

The heavy clouds drifted away, and the full moon shone brightly. The light on the field outside our bedroom window made me think that the new day had arrived. It was, however, still the dead of night, and I watched helplessly and in terror as Chris struggled for breath.

Melting into the One

At last, you have departed and gone to the Unseen.
What marvelous route did you take from this world?
Beating your wings and feathers, you broke free from this cage.
Rising up to the sky you attained the world of the soul.

—Rumi

Waiting for the results felt excruciating. Trying to figure out what was going on and what the future would bring seemed like a waste of time. I knew only the burning presence of the moment.

I found myself totally unprepared for the shock of the devastating news we received. The cancer had lodged not only in Chris's brain but in his lungs, liver, and lower back. Still, the oncologist recommended by Dr. David Melchinger sounded optimistic about treatment as he explained in detail that Chris would begin radiation treatments to relieve pressure in the brain. Further biopsies would find the source of the cancer and pinpoint the most effective treatment. The doctor told us not to worry about passing time in the absence of immediate crisis.

We felt concerned but hopeful.

Meanwhile, Chris appeared to be on a course of his own design. Although a sensitive and feeling person, he had rarely

313

taken time in the past to observe his emotional life in depth. I watched him grow fascinated with the multitude of feelings arising from his circumstances. He seemed in no rush to move out of his distress.

I wanted him to fight for his life, to say, "I belong here. I don't want to die." Instead, he told me he didn't want to leave the moment before understanding more about what he needed to learn.

I remembered that Chris often said he would just stop if he couldn't live life on his own terms. I feared that was what I was seeing.

I wrote an email to our friends letting them know of Chris's diagnosis, and I asked him to add something. He wrote:

> Thank you that I can speak, hear, see, taste, feel and move and that hundreds of people are sending me love and sharing in this moment of hope, inspiration, and gratitude. My preference is to be a worthy vessel as I explore my healing as it unfolds. I am grateful for the preparation our journeying has given me. I have judged my body harshly in the past and now am more filled with feelings than ever before. I am learning to be patient. Feeling that we are all One, I want to connect with everything. I am filled to overflowing with love for all my beloveds.

Chris's serenity amazed me, and I did my best to support him even though I longed for him to fight to stay in his body.

Being with Chris reminded me of how Carlos and Maria held space for us when we journeyed. Often when in the medicine, I felt sick in body and soul. I was grateful as they remained physically, mentally, and emotionally present for me while I did what I must to return to my body.

I did my best to provide similar holding for Chris, but it wasn't always easy. He spent much of each day sleeping, and even when awake, he seemed to inhabit a space where I couldn't follow. I wondered if he had the skill, resources, and longing to return to his body. I didn't know if he could heal or even if he cared.

On March 28, 2012, we moved into the Suites, a hotel affiliated with Yale-New Haven Hospital's Smilow Cancer Hospital, where Chris would receive treatment. After having no settled place to stay for the past month, we felt grateful for a well appointed apartment with a bedroom, living room, full kitchen, and free valet car service to the hospital.

As grateful as I was to have a place to live, Chris's rapidly depleting strength devastated me. He could barely hold himself up to walk to the bathroom and no longer cared to eat. I appreciated his efforts to stay connected with me, but he found conversation difficult. He hadn't yet started treatment. No support team of nurses or social workers had been set up for us, and we couldn't reach our doctor even after leaving multiple messages. We both felt lost and abandoned.

On a Sunday morning three days after we arrived at the Suites, Chris's thirty-year-old daughter, Hope, took the train from her home in New York City to help me and be with her dad. Our inadequate support and lack of knowledge felt overwhelming to both of us. At least I had Hope's loving presence.

Chris's treatment plan called for chemotherapy to start the following day, but I watched with alarm as he lay listlessly in bed. He refused food and barely had the energy to connect with the outer world. I didn't know much about chemotherapy, but I knew the importance of the patient's stability and sufficient hydration to withstand chemo's powerful, toxic attack. How could Chris start treatment if he was too sick to get out of bed?

We had heard nothing from our oncologist, and I doubted we could reach him for support on the weekend.

315

Panic-stricken, I no longer felt I could take care of Chris properly. I called the hospital, and the operator connected me to the doctor on call. He knew nothing about Chris nor his condition but told me that we should get an ambulance to take him to the emergency room where a doctor could evaluate him.

Hope and I talked to Chris about my concerns with his loss of strength and asked if he would consider going to the hospital. He agreed but didn't want the drama of riding in an ambulance. He preferred that we push him over the several blocks to the hospital in a wheelchair supplied by the Suites.

We settled Chris into the wheelchair and began our wild walk through New Haven traffic. The uneven sidewalk made every bump painful for Chris and agonizing for Hope and me. Thankfully, he took it as an adventure, and his spirits rose. We arrived at the hospital's back entrance, and after wending our way through a maze of corridors, we found the emergency room.

The admitting process seemed endless as Chris went through multiple tests and X-rays. Hope and I sat nervously and waited. After seven hours, a nurse finally came to accompany Chris to a private room where she hooked him up to an IV that hydrated him and provided morphine for pain. She also gave him oxygen to help him breathe. Visiting hours ended soon after Chris was settled. Hope said a tearful goodnight to her father and went to a friend's house. She promised to return in the morning and stay as long as I needed.

I wanted nothing more than to be close to Chris, but my heart ached. Watching him slip away, I wished I could find a magical cure that would shift the uncertain trajectory he had entered. But I didn't know what he wanted. Did he want to stay in this world, or was he ready to leave? I saw only an equanimous patience that flowed gently with whatever came along. He seemed in utter surrender, but I worried that he had surrendered to leaving his body rather than staying with me.

I longed to curl up next to him, but I sat properly on an easy chair next to the bed long after Chris went to sleep. Eventually, I tucked myself onto the sofa bed on the other side of the room and listened to his labored breathing.

The machines delivering meds and hydration beeped at intervals all night. Often it meant the IV lines had twisted. I had to get up over and over to walk down the cold corridors to summon help that arrived slowly. I spent a long, restless night with little sleep, but at least I was with my beloved.

To my relief, Hope returned at eight in the morning. Chris's rapid decline, the complicated hospital environment, and the countless decisions seemed too much for me to handle alone. I welcomed her company and support even as we shared our sadness and fear.

We had not been able to reach his oncologist, so the doctor on call, a small Indian man, stopped in to evaluate Chris. With little preamble, he told us that Chris was too sick to tolerate chemotherapy. The treatment plan, he said, would allow Chris to stay in the hospital for radiation that would continue for another ten days. After that, we would have to admit him to a nursing facility or hospice.

Hospice! People went there to die. No one had mentioned death. They spoke only of treatment. My head started spinning as I fought against the doctor's pronouncement. How could my beloved be dying? I wanted to hear that a miracle could still happen.

The doctor finished his speech and began to head to the door. I raced after him and followed him into the hallway. "I need to know what is going on with my husband. Is he going to get better?" I demanded.

Saying he didn't like to talk about such things, the doctor began to turn away

"What? You don't like to talk about such things?" I screamed. "This is not about you. I need to know the truth, and no one here will talk to me straight."

The man seemed to shrink as I bombarded him with my seething rage.

"You need to talk to me. I need to know. Is Chris going to get better?"

I watched as the doctor took a breath and found his voice. "No, he is not going to get better. The only thing that we can do now is to make him as comfortable as possible."

Finally, someone had said the words out loud that I had dreaded. My fury dissolved into cold terror as I asked, "How long do we have?"

He told me gently that someone with minor tumors might have six months, but he thought it might be more realistic to believe that Chris had two months.

I hoped we had more time, more possibility of healing, more time to love each other. Still, I felt grateful that this doctor had finally dared to speak the truth.

The moment had come. The time for hope in a miracle had passed. There was nothing left but to prepare for what would come and allow the possibility of death to become real. I had entered a passage that terrified me and could do nothing but trust in the power of love.

The same doctor showed up the next day to talk to Chris about his situation. He explained that in order to receive chemotherapy, a patient must be able to stay out of bed at least half the day and have adequate health to tolerate the toxic side effects of treatment. He told Chris he was too weak for chemotherapy, and without it, the disease would undoubtedly progress quickly.

Chris barely responded, and I asked if he had understood what the doctor said.

He looked at me quizzically. "No, what did he say?"

"Would you like me to tell you again?" the doctor asked.

"Yes," he answered, pulling his attention together.

"Chris, your body is too weak to tolerate chemotherapy. You are not going to get better."

"Wow!" he said, taking a deep breath, his eyes wide open. He drew the sound out long and deep as if to spread the reality into his body. He seemed genuinely surprised and amazed at the fate that had befallen him.

I asked him what he thought about the new situation and saw nothing but blankness. He was no longer of this world enough to engage with such earthly matters. He had more important work to do, the business of shedding the cares of this life in preparation for his upcoming adventure into a place beyond human awareness.

I felt lost and ungrounded when the doctor left and felt grateful when a lovely young woman named Gisela came unexpectedly through the door, offering a Reiki session for Chris, Hope, and me. Chris was lost in his inner world, but his body was tense and agitated. Gisela tended to Chris until he fell into a peaceful sleep. Then she turned her attentions to Hope, bringing her into a calm state. When she placed her hands on my shoulders, I wept, burying my head in her belly. When the tears ceased, I received her tender ministrations as I struggled to ground myself in a new world.

Since noon that day, Chris's chest had filled with fluid requiring that his lungs be drained several times. A beautiful new doctor, Ursula, came in to reevaluate the meds. Seeing so much fluid in Chris's lungs, she decided to cut off the IV hydrating his body. Horrified, I realized that without hydration, Chris would contract into the dying process.

We had entered the phase where comfort meant everything and maintaining life was no longer the priority. Everything had changed, and it took all my will to stay in the new reality.

I remembered the voice at my wedding telling me that we would be separated. Chris and I had always suspected that we would go through a death experience, but I had imagined I would be the one to get sick and die early.

That would not be.

As I pondered our impending separation, I wondered if Chris's dying had come as a lesson for me in loving beyond my ego. Perhaps I had to experience my beloved's physical death to know that love never dies. I wondered if we had asked for the devastating separation to learn the lessons our souls needed. With the price so extravagantly high, I vowed not to miss anything.

After Chris fell asleep, I pulled a recliner next to his bed and wrote in my journal for a couple of hours. Wrapping my feet around his legs comforted me. Chris's eyes were closed, and I doubted that he even knew I was there.

Or perhaps it was the other way around. We were so much a part of each other that he couldn't imagine that I wasn't there.

Time was so precious. I didn't want to waste a moment being away from the man I loved so dearly, the one who had given me so much joy. I couldn't believe that his body would no longer exist to walk with me and lie with me. I stayed in the pleasure of being close to Chris even as my heart was breaking.

I moved to the sofa bed for the third night since we had entered the hospital. I listened to Chris's labored breathing as

I tried to sleep. The discontinued IV drip no longer sounded through the night. Chris lived now on his own, letting his body shut down as it must, a body no longer of use to him. Despite my distress, my body and spirit insisted on sleep. With few thoughts, I drifted off.

I woke up early and listened to the rhythmic gurgling in Chris's lungs. He seemed to sleep comfortably, and I happily shared a moment of peace. Then I realized I had watched Chris close his eyes the night before. They hadn't opened. Chris had turned inward, and the transition out of his body, out of my world, had begun.

As I rested my hands on his still body, I breathed in the sweet essence of him and knew. Never again would I hear his voice, that wonderful booming laugh, nor the magical interaction of our energies. From that moment on, I would carry the substance of Kai and Chris alone.

I didn't know when on the earth plane Chris would choose to pass, but I did know that the process had begun with no turning back. Grief-stricken, I nevertheless had to find the focus to contact family and friends and tell them that they had to come immediately if they wanted to see Chris while he remained in his body.

It had never occurred to me that Chris was close to death when we went to the hospital three days before. I hadn't even considered gathering the family together to see Chris for the last time. I made numerous calls telling nearby friends and family that they should come quickly. Sadly, I had to inform those who lived further that Chris was dying and it was too late for them to make the trip.

People started arriving early in the afternoon. Chris's daughter Barbara from his first marriage arrived with her three kids, Madison, Katrina, and Grant. Her brother Kit came with his kids Lauren, Evan, and Ashton. My sister Ginger came with

Georgeanne. For some reason that he did not explain, my father chose not to come. Hope and Josh had been with me since early that morning. Somehow the word had gotten around, and half a dozen friends joined us, including Erik, one of Chris's closest friends and my friend since Chris and I had been on the road.

I had crawled onto the foot of the bed, facing Chris, my legs entwined with his. Stiff and quiet except for labored breaths, he barely inhabited his body. I clung to my memory of the life that had previously coursed through him.

An awkward party atmosphere filled the room as people shared stories, jokes, and sweet conversations. Occasionally, someone would burst into tears, fall into someone's arms, and then move back into the group energy. The hospital's housekeeping staff sent up coffee, soda, and little snacks as we carried out the time-honored tradition of supporting the transition of a beloved.

I pulled out my laptop and showed dozens of pictures of Chris, many from his childhood and adolescence. I'd never seen some of the photos Chris had scanned into our computer. Many showed young Chris standing at full attention with a worried, watchful look, his hands hanging in a clutched position by his side. Apparently, the family required the four boys to be good little soldiers. It didn't appear to have been a relaxed household for the brothers to thrive, but Chris had emerged as a passionate lover of life and those he met.

In the adolescent pictures, I saw a handsome, dashing young man with a sense of adventure, a captivating openness, and a great smile. The images showed the beginning of the Chris I knew, although traces of the scared little boy lurked.

Visiting hours ended at around eight in the evening, and the beloveds made their farewells. As people left, Erik stayed behind, saying that he couldn't leave me alone in such circumstances. It hadn't occurred to me to ask him to stay, but I was relieved. I had no idea what would come and felt grateful for his company.

I stayed cuddled in with Chris on the hospital bed. I tried to get as close to him as possible even as I knew he was already worlds away. Erik pulled up a chair, and we talked until one in the morning, sharing stories and reminiscing about times we had shared with Chris. We filled the room with as much love and gratitude as we could. I stroked Chris's almost inert body and talked to him, acutely aware that he no longer had anything to do with the earth plane or me.

Erik urged me to rest and said he would watch over Chris. I had no intention of going to sleep, although I feared I might. I knew I needed to rest my body, so I agreed to turn off the light. Erik retreated to the sofa bed, and Chris's labored breathing continued resolutely on.

I thought of the vigil that Jesus's disciples carried out, waiting while he prayed in the Garden of Gethsemane. His friends fell asleep, but I resolved to stay awake. I allowed myself to rest, but when Erik began to snore softly, I knew I had to remain even more vigilant so as not to drift into sleep.

At four in the morning, a nurse came to give Chris his meds. Erik woke up and came to sit by the bed. The nurse checked the morphine drip, and when she left, I noticed Chris's eyes open for the first time in twenty-four hours. They had rolled back in his head with only the whites visible. That I understood as a sign that he had begun the final stage of his transition.

Instinctively, I decided not to fall into grief but to surrender into supporting Chris's passing. I slipped out of my ego self and into the role of priestess and midwife. In an ancient and holy ritual, I put myself aside to offer a final gift to my beloved as he made the monumental metamorphosis.

As I witnessed Chris's transition from earth plane life to birth into something beyond, I felt that I, too, passed through deep cycles of Earth, of life and death. I was the priestess, not the woman losing her beloved. I was the Earth, giving life and then taking it back.

I went to the side of the bed and knelt by Chris's head. I sang some of our favorite songs.

> Oh, my Soul, you come, and you go through
> the paths of time and space.

and

> We've come to the place
> where everything is music.

and

> All I have to do is hold your hand.

and

> Lo, I am with you always.

and

> On the day that I die,
> being brought to the grave,
> don't weep. I cannot go away.

I sang songs long sacred to us, but they took on new meaning as Chris embarked on his final leave-taking.

I stopped singing and asked Erik to bring the computer so I could play some of Chris's favorite music. When I opened the laptop, a picture of Chris's seven-year-old granddaughter Katrina popped up—a gift. New life made its appearance as the old moved on.

I thought about what music to play but then realized that Chris didn't need it. His body and spirit seemed to know precisely what to do. Instead, I gently talked to my beloved, telling him he was going home, that I would always love him, and that I trusted he was taking his leave with grace and ease. Remembering Maria's words from the desert, I quietly and repeatedly reassured him, "All is well."

I watched his breathing slow and sometimes stop for long periods. When it ceased, I could see peace fill him. Then, something in his body struggled so he could take yet one more difficult breath.

Slow, ragged breaths came and went until something shifted. Chris inhaled a long, steady breath that seemed to carry him higher and higher, far out of his physical body. The breath reached its fullness, yet the exhale never came. Chris melted before my eyes in a tender letting go that barely created a ripple in the energy field. He exited this world with no resistance, as if he had returned to his only true home. I was in awe that death could be so gentle and organic.

Still waiting for closure, I turned to Erik and asked, "He's gone, isn't he?"

In a whisper, he answered, "Yes, he's gone."

And we both fell into deep silence that had no thought.

Sending Chris on His Journey

I was born when all I once feared I could love.

—Rabia

Chris took his last breath on this earth at 4:30 in the morning of April 5, 2012. It was Maundy Thursday, the day on the Christian church calendar that celebrates the night before his crucifixion when Jesus washed his disciples' feet and ate a Passover meal with them. While they ate, Jesus shared bread and wine, which later became known to Christians as the Eucharist or communion. And he gave a new commandment to his followers to love one another as he had loved them.

As I looked at Chris's inert body, I felt grateful that he had chosen such a day of love to take his leave rather than the next, Good Friday, the day that Christ was nailed to the cross.

I stood at the bedside of my beloved, gazing at him, hardly able to grasp the reality of his leaving. I thought back to the Rumi medicine journeys Chris and I had shared. As he took his last breath, I imagined Chris had been offered the sacred medicine pipe. I watched him inhale and fly far out into worlds beyond as I had many times before, waiting for his return. This time, however, I knew he would not return. He was off on adventures that would not include me. Chris's earth plane journey with me had ended.

The hospital room felt cold and empty even with Erik at my side. I longed to do something to honor the moment so far beyond my mind's ability to hold. But I had no idea where to begin.

After my brother's partner, Anna, died, I remembered that we saged and cleansed her, washed her body, and then dressed her. Though the soulless hospital room provided no sacred tools for a ceremony, I felt the urgency of sending Chris off not just with love but with a holy ritual.

When the hospital first admitted Chris to the room, I made an altar with several powerful crystals, but we had no sage or other cleansing smoke to bless Chris's body and no candles. It came to me to place a six-inch double-terminated quartz crystal in a glass bowl and ask Erik to shine the light of a flashlight I had found in the room through it, creating sacred light for the ceremony.

I blessed each part of Chris's body as Erik shined the light. With each blessing, memories flooded in of our journey together. I felt how we had shaped each other and grown with each other. I felt how our love had radiated out to the world. I thanked Chris for the many ways he had opened my heart and taught me about love.

Touching his flesh, I knew palpably that Chris no longer inhabited the body I ministered to so tenderly. At the same time, I had the eerie feeling that I had also left the earth and followed him into realms we had explored in our medicine journeys. Even looking at his lifeless body, I didn't feel apart from Chris. Feeling that we had been connected from the beginning of time and would be forever, I couldn't imagine what it would be like to be physically apart from him.

I completed the ceremony and felt the ground shake beneath my feet. I sat down with Erik on the couch and allowed myself to feel the confusion of the moment. Chris was gone, whatever that meant, and I had no idea what to do next. Chris and I had a shared purpose, most recently as a loving couple on life's journey. Alone for the first time in a long while, I didn't know who I had been or who I was becoming. I didn't know what the new story would require of me. I could hardly think an intelligent thought in the face of such shattering. I didn't even know how to grieve. The impossibility of the moment didn't allow for feeling.

I was lost.

Thankfully, no staff had entered the room during our ceremony. I took time to ground myself and then went to the nurse's station to report Chris's death. A kind nurse expressed her condolences and gently told me that we could take our time and be with his body as long as we wished.

I waited until eight o'clock for Chris's family to awaken in their rooms at the Suites to tell them that Chris had died. I wanted to offer his children and grandchildren the opportunity to be with his body before he was taken away.

Chris's daughters and youngest son declined to see his body, but his oldest son, Kit, wanted to come with his two older kids.

They came and spent half an hour at Chris's bedside. Kit gently invited his kids into the experience, and I watched as he modeled grief with his tears and his loving connection with Chris. He asked the kids to come close, touch Chris, and kiss him. Clearly, they trusted their father enough to engage.

I wished I had had such support when I came to say goodbye to my mother as she lay in the coffin.

After Kit and the kids left, I felt ready to wash Chris's body and dress him as my offering of gratitude and preparation for his final journey. Although many traditions empowered women with the ritual of sanctifying the body, Chris's daughters didn't want to participate, so I asked Erik to assist me.

Erik appeared leery about touching Chris's dead body, but I told him that he would only need to lift Chris's body when necessary for dressing. His primary responsibility would be focusing the light through the crystal as a cleansing tool. He reluctantly agreed.

Already becoming stiff, Chris's body remained warm to the touch. I got a basin of tepid water and started washing him. I talked to him as my fingers brushed his skin, even though Chris no longer inhabited the flesh.

I nevertheless felt his presence all around.

I thanked all of him, piece by piece. I washed his eyes, ears, mouth, head, shoulders, arms, hands, heart, genitals, legs, and feet. The body before me seemed a dim echo of the warm, loving body I had known so well. Rigid and filled with cancer, tumors, strange bones jutting at different angles, and genitals totally inert, Chris's body lay eerily still.

I gave his body all the love I could before sending it off with those who would see it taken eventually into the cremation fire, where it would be reborn into something very different from the form that had long supported Chris's soul. When I completed the washing, Erik and I began dressing him.

I didn't have the lightness of energy and laughter that my friend Qadira and I had when washing and dressing my brother's partner, Anna. Trusting that she was going to her beloved, who had died three years earlier, Anna looked forward to leaving this life. Unlike her, Chris had been filled with energy and dreams. He had so much to live for, and his leave-taking had come far too soon.

I performed the ceremony of washing and dressing more for myself than for Chris. He had already embarked on his new adventure, but I needed to find a way to ground the idea that Chris and his body had separated. I needed to grasp the incomprehensible reality that Chris's spirit had been set free from his body, never to return. Our love remained intact, but in a form that I would have to learn to recognize and interact with in new ways.

As I touched Chris's body for the last time, I realized that I faced a long and steep learning curve to forge a new relationship with my beloved. I sensed it would be my sacred path for the next chapter of my life.

Erik and I found it challenging to get the clothes around Chris's stiff and heavy body, but finally, we had him fully dressed in his signature jeans and black tee-shirt reminding me of the clothes he wore when I first met him at Shalom Mountain.

As we finished the ritual, two young women bounded through the doors and rudely announced, "You'd better get out of the room. We've got to bag him."

The crudity of the remark barely penetrated my numbed emotions, but it made Erik furious. I feared he would become violent toward the unthinking young women. I held him back while they quickly zipped Chris into a thick black plastic bag like something you put your clothes in when traveling. Their job completed, they left the room, leaving Chris in a bag on the gurney.

I took Erik out into the hallway, where he continued to seethe. I, however, felt a strange gift in the insensitivity of the two young women. It reminded me of the nitty-gritty reality of death so that I could begin to take in the truth that my beloved was gone and would never return.

I needed a task to ground me, so Erik and I started to pack the crystals, pictures, and other objects that had held us lovingly for the past few days. Two men showed up to take Chris's body away as we finished packing. Strangely, it did not wrench me as much as I expected since my mind seemed unable to grasp the reality of the moment. I watched numbly as the men wheeled the black bag out on a gurney. With Chris's body no longer in the room, we had no reason to stay.

The hospital social worker, Irene, came in before I left and asked if I needed anything. I told her that I didn't know how to go through the process of getting Chris cremated. I explained that I had no interest in paying a lot of money to show that I loved him and would accept the least expensive cremation. She recommended a funeral parlor and stayed with me while I called and made an appointment for noon, only two hours away.

Barely in my body, I asked Erik to accompany me to the funeral parlor to start the process. We arrived at a grungy one-room office where we had an impersonal, businesslike interview. I mechanically filled out forms with Chris's vital statistics and signed endless papers. The man behind the desk informed me that cremation would not occur until Monday, and I should return to pick up the ashes on Tuesday morning.

Chris and I had often talked about the possibility of following the Buddhist practice of letting our bodies lie undisturbed for three days before burial to allow the spirit time to separate from the body, life experiences, and attachments and to move more gently into the next world. I wouldn't have known how to make it happen, but our desire for transitional time occurred miraculously because those in charge did not transfer bodies on Good Friday or on weekends. Chris's body would rest in the hospital morgue for three days before entering the fire on Monday.

My mind couldn't grasp the finality of Chris's departure. Chris was dead. What did that mean? He was an integral part of my own body, and I was clearly alive and well. He still danced in the hearts of hundreds of beloveds in whom he would continue to live. Chris had become like a forest where life and death entwine intimately and challenge one's ability to tell them apart.

Regardless, I needed to move forward even though an integral part of me had been declared dead.

I tried to understand how it had taken so long for all of us to notice that Chris was dying. I imagined that Chris's higher self had put a spell on everyone he met, including himself, so we would not see or retain the fact of his profound illness. He lived his life with every bit of energy he had, and when that expired, he left in the most graceful way possible.

I remembered that I had watched my father go through the process of grieving his soul mate and partner when my mother died. His anguish had terrified me at the time, and now I had entered that same dark territory.

I imagined Chris and me still in a teaching role with our beloveds. Though he existed on the other side, it didn't mean that our work together had finished. Perhaps by his death, the two of us created the necessary breach between heaven and earth that I had seen in my vision at Estes Park when Chris had seen the Face of God. Even with Chris's death, I wanted to believe that the gifts of our union would continue.

I felt an urgency to continue our work together and to move forward, but that required that I experience and assimilate the material reality of Chris's death. I had the impression that the world as we knew it would move into a time of shattering and chaos in the not-too-distant future. I sensed that conscious people needed to prepare themselves uniquely for a radical shift we could not imagine. Facing Chris's death appeared to be part of my training and preparation. Choosing to make meaning of Chris's death gave me strength, love, gratitude, connection, and trust in the perfect unfolding, energies that would be necessary in a chaotic future.

As grief settled in, I chose to believe that love cannot die. That ground held me as I felt everything else slipping away.

Talking to God

What is your life about, anyway? Nothing but a struggle to be someone,
nothing but a running from your own silence.

—Rumi

I left the funeral parlor, dropped Erik off at his car, and
returned to the Suites and Chris's older kids. A necessary but
grueling ritual, the family get-together left me not a moment
by myself to feel my turbulent emotions. I spent most of
the afternoon trying my best to show up and finally made a
graceful exit just before dark. My friend Su graciously invited
me to spend the night. As if in a dream, I drove the forty
minutes to her house.

When I arrived, Su asked me what I needed. I said I needed
to sleep. She tucked me into bed, and I fell immediately into a
dreamless state, waking a couple hours later when she brought
me hot soup and crackers.

After breakfast the following day, I returned alone and numb to
the cottage. I made a sandwich that I hardly remembered to eat.

I tried to make the day seem normal. Everything around me
looked just as it always had, but nothing felt right. The sun had
come up, the birds sang, the furniture was where it always had

been, and I recognized Chris's presence everywhere. It didn't seem that different from the time Chris spent in rehab. In fact, he seemed a little closer than he did during his time at Caron. Wherever I looked, I felt him—his favorite, blue-flowered chair, the ukulele he liked to strum, his clothes scattered here and there, and his pillow on the bed.

But Chris was gone. Over and over, I reminded myself that Chris was dead, yet I found it impossible to believe. I knew I had seen him take his last breath, leaving his body lifeless, still, and empty of his spirit. I remembered washing him, dressing him, and thanking him for the love we had shared. I had watched the aides wrap his useless body in a black bag. Yet the reality that he was dead seemed impossible to grasp.

Who was I with him gone? I looked into the mirror shocked to see that I was still Kai as much as ever. How could that be when Chris, an integral part of my being, was no longer at my side?

We had walked through the world as Kai and Chris for almost sixteen years. We had kept our individuality, but we had also unified as a couple. We had embedded in each other, entangled and interpenetrated. How could that end? How could I be Kai and Chris now that Chris had left the physical plane? Could he continue to live in my body since he had become one with all that is? Would I feel more myself knowing that deeper union with the One? I was lost in the mystery of myriad possibilities. My utter bewilderment overwhelmed me.

Chris's presence remained so strong that it almost didn't make sense to grieve. I wondered if I was in denial. It had all happened so quickly that I couldn't access the shattering reality. Just a month before, we believed that Chris's discomfort was an energetic, spiritual emergency, and now he was dead.

As I lay in bed, the bed where I had shared in such pleasure with Chris, I felt him close with me just as always. I could almost feel normal. Storms of grief came and went, but they had an impersonal quality. The intensity of my sorrow was weaker than the feeling that Chris had not gone anywhere but that he had simply shed a body that no longer served him. I knew his spirit as wholly present.

I felt crazy holding two conflicting emotions—raging grief and quiet peace. I had just lost my husband, soul mate, and companion. Yet, I experienced us profoundly still together in a new and more mysterious form, an unfolding of unexplained perfection. At the same time, I knew I could, at any moment, crash from that lofty view into despair and deep grief.

Hope and I drove to Evergreen Cemetery five days after Chris died to retrieve Chris's ashes. I walked alone to the office, past stone monuments to those who had departed from this life. I felt calm and grounded, not really grasping what it meant to receive the remains of my beloved. As I walked back to the car carrying a plain brown paper shopping bag that held Chris in a green box with a gold tag, all my strength slipped away, and I fell into uncontrollable tears.

Hope held me gently while I wept. I knew the box's contents were not Chris but merely the remains of his beautiful body, yet I also had the crushing knowledge that my earth plane life without my beloved would never be the same.

I dropped Hope off at the New Haven train station so she could return home to New York City. Alone, I drove the five hours back to the Timshel cottage with the bag of ashes in the passenger seat. Expecting to see Chris's broad smile and hear his hearty laugh, I kept turning my head. The bag of ashes sat silently in his place.

I made up the story that my beloved had not left the rehab in Texas and would return at any moment. I did my best to convince myself that he didn't have clearance to call because of the blackout period and that I would hear from him in a few days. I knew it wasn't true, but it felt more reasonable than the story that his body could be contained in a small green box with a gold tag resting inside of a shopping bag on my car seat.

I hoped we would eventually find a way to communicate between the worlds. If not in words, then perhaps we might discover new ways that would allow me to feel our connection. But at that moment, all I felt was a dull thud of pain in my heart.

On the drive back to the cottage from Connecticut, I telephoned Chris's good friend Mike. We hadn't talked since Chris started to weaken five months before in Estes Park. Shocked at how quickly Chris's death had come, Mike asked why we hadn't seen a doctor for a diagnosis earlier. I told him we had seen a doctor, chiropractor, acupuncturist, and massage therapist. They had all assured Chris that he was strong and whatever was going on was probably not a physical issue.

I reminded Mike that Chris did not trust doctors or western medicine and that I only knew one instance when Chris went to a doctor. He had always said that he wanted to live his life full out until he could no longer have a healthy and autonomous life. Chris didn't want to be like his father, who had a heart attack at sixty-eight and then sat placidly in his chair until his death at eighty-four. Chris said he wanted to leave as soon as the party was over.

Piqued by Mike's curiosity, another story came to mind. In 2010, Chris and I had journeyed to Egypt. It had been an extravagantly expensive trip, more than ten thousand dollars for the two of us. We thought it worth the money because arrangements were made for us to visit a dozen and a half temples when they were closed to the public and only available to our group.

One of our first visits was to the pyramids of Giza. Our group had the exceptional opportunity to be allowed into the King's Chamber. A bare, unornamented room made of pink granite with a tiny entrance trapdoor in one corner, the King's Chamber contains only a large sarcophagus that reminded me of an oversized stone bathtub.

Our guide shared a story that the pyramids once housed a mystery school that taught initiates the secrets of the immortality of the human soul. After twelve years of arduous study, initiates faced a challenging test of the control of consciousness. One test required the initiate to explore higher levels of awareness outside the body after having been given a hallucinogenic medicine while lying in the sarcophagus in the King's Chamber. The task was to be able to return to the body. Sometimes initiates who had not fully mastered the skills of return died in the dangerous undertaking.

When we visited the King's Chamber, each of us had permission to lie in the stone sarcophagus for seven minutes while the rest of the group toned sacred sounds. When I had my turn to lie in the coffin, I dissolved into cosmic ecstasy as I often did in my Rumi journeys, although in the King's Chamber, I took no medicine.

Chris never shared his experience in the sarcophagus of the King's Chamber, but as I spoke to Mike, I wondered whether when Chris found himself shot out into the cosmos, he either could not or did not want to return.

I felt comfort from telling Mike stories about Chris. When we said goodbye, I was left to my own thoughts and the convoluted process of trying to make sense of something I would never understand.

I couldn't easily understand the many layers of my feelings. I had spent so much time with Chris in the dissolved state of our medicine journeys and Tantric explorations that I had often felt him energetically even when without his physical presence. That made it even harder for me to accept that he was really gone, since his energy felt so powerfully present to me.

At the same time, I felt horrified by the thought that he had left me permanently with a crucial part of me forever excised. I watched (and experienced) myself flung from one feeling to the other, none making sense to my exhausted brain.

A week after Chris's death, I heard a voice in my mind. "Wait a minute!" the intruder insisted. "Your beloved Chris has just died. He is gone. You'll never see him again. What is wrong with you? You never pleaded with God not to take him. You never raged. You simply midwifed him into the next world and got on with things. What is wrong with you?"

The accusation that I had failed to bargain with God felt heavy, and I feared I had failed Chris by letting him go so effortlessly. At the time of his death, I thought I had no choice but to support his transition and focus on his process. In light of the disembodied questions, my behavior felt cold.

I remembered that, as my beloved took his last breaths, I understood that I had been cast in the ancient priestess role of companioning a dying person through their process into the other world. But Chris was not just any person. Chris was my soul mate and one of my deep channels to God. At the time, I did what I felt I had to do. But with the intruder's voice reverberating in my ear, I knew I had to allow space for the grieving widow part of myself and put aside the priestess.

Chris's body had burned to ash in the cremation fires. No amount of bargaining could bring him back into his physical body. Still, I felt the necessity of bargaining with God for his life.

Sitting in the cottage living room just as dusk fell, I decided to take action and invite God for a chat. To my surprise, God appeared as the classic bearded older man, very different from my more familiar understanding of God as spirit. He sat down on the easy chair across from the couch where I sat. Putting aside my judgments about the form God had taken, I waited. After a long period of quiet, he asked, "So, what can I do for you?"

Grateful for the opening, I explained that, as with my mother's death, Chris's death came so quickly that I didn't have a chance to bargain for his life. I explained with tears in my eyes that I wanted my beloved husband back.

God settled back in the chair. He gazed deeply into my eyes with love that touched my heart, and I felt a deep sense of being seen and known. "So," he said in a long, drawn-out tone that felt hypnotizing, "I hear that you want Chris returned to you. Do you want him back the way he was in his dying moments, when every organ in his body had failed and when his consciousness was already going back to the other world?"

"Oh, no," I answered in horror. "Bringing Chris back to life in that body wouldn't be fair to him or to me. I wouldn't want him back if that was how he would be."

"Okay. Then, would you like to have Chris back the way he was in 1976 when you first met him?"

"Well, no. Not that either." Chris had grown since we married and even more in our years on the road. "No, I wouldn't want him back the way he was when I first met him."

God continued to ask about bringing Chris back at this time or that time, and I began to see that Chris had never lived as a stable, unchanging entity. He constantly shifted in small and significant ways. And the Chris I knew was not the Chris that others knew. He was a father, a son, a coworker, a friend. He was sometimes even a mystery to himself and others.

Who was Chris, anyway? Was he a projection of my longing? A teacher who had come with perfect lessons for me in my present earthly lifetime? Who was he when he wasn't with me, and who was he absent from the physical body I had known?

I saw the illusion of the solidity I had taken for granted in the past. I had lived a beautiful dream. Was it my dream, or had we dreamed it together? I knew only that one story had ended and another had begun.

Would the new unfolding offer anything more substantial than the last? If Chris had been just a dream, then so was I, and so was everything else. If true, I was a dream living within a dream. What could I do but dream the dream and, in that dream, be as awake as I could be?

As thoughts tumbled wildly through my mind, I realized that I was alone in the room. God had taken his leave, and I began the hard work of finding my way in a world without Chris's physical presence.

Grief

'Tis a fearful thing to love what death can touch—
A fearful thing to love, to hope, to dream, to be—to be.
And, oh, to lose—A thing for fools, this, And a holy thing, a holy thing to love.
—Yehuda HaLevi

Ten days had passed since Chris had disappeared into realms unknown, and I had fallen into the void of his absence. I rode a roller coaster of emotion. One minute I could be in ecstatic gratitude for my life with Chris. Then out of nowhere grief would have its way with me, and I would be overwhelmed by storms of anger and sadness that found me marching through the cottage, stomping my feet, and wailing, "No, no, no."

At the same time, the normalcy of the days shocked me. Each morning, I got up and made coffee and breakfast just as I had in the past. Everything was almost the same, yet Chris was gone and I sat at the table alone.

Every day I walked on the country road by myself, watching hawks glide in the sky, sending my greetings to cows lazily munching in the fields or catching sight of deer peeking out of the woods. It felt good to move in the fresh air, but my thoughts swung wildly as I tried to grasp the reality of Chris no longer at my side.

I found a lovely waterfall surrounded by flat rocks deep in the woods. Every afternoon, I sat and watched cascading water as my tears flowed with it. One day merged into the next as I wandered aimlessly in the new land of sorrow.

My friend Su encouraged me to sign up for a weekend grief ritual at Rowe Center in western Massachusetts. Sobonfu Somé, an African shaman from Burkina Faso who brought the traditions of the Dagara people, would lead the weekend. Less than two weeks from the time of Chris's death felt early to bring my grief into the public sphere, but I had followed Sobonfu's work for many years and wanted to experience her healing energies.

Twenty-five of us gathered at Rowe in a large meeting room that would serve as the center of our rituals for the weekend. Because traffic held up Sobonfu's arrival, we started our introductions without her, each of us sharing a little about ourselves and the place of grief in our lives.

When Sobonfu entered, the calm energy in the room became electric. She dressed in bright red and orange Burkinabé robes and a yellow scarf tied around her black hair. The blue ski jacket she wore over traditional garb gave her a quirky air. With bright eyes and a surprising round belly on her otherwise slender body, she combined youthful appearance and the wisdom of an elder. I immediately trusted her quiet and modest, yet powerful and commanding energies.

Sobonfu, whose name means Keeper of the Rituals, began her teaching. "Grief needs to be communal," she said. "It is more painful when it isn't shared. The person who dies opens a portal for all of us. If we refuse to do the work, we become a burden to ourselves and others, and the grief can grow into depression or violence. Conscious grieving is a portal for our healing and growth. We can't do it alone."

She said she could talk about grief all night but that it might put us all to sleep, so she sent us off to our cabins for the night.

The following morning after breakfast, we began our first activity of communally creating three shrines, one for holding our grief, one for forgiveness, and one for honoring the ancestors. Sobonfu had asked us to bring sacred objects, candles, and photos that we would place among the three altars to represent our grief.

Since Chris's Hindu name was Hanuman, I chose for my grief symbols a six-inch bronze statue of the monkey god of devotion, Hanuman, and a statue of a voluptuous, unnamed Hindu goddess. Chris and I had carried the figures with us on our travels as representations of our shared mystic love. After Chris's physical death, they represented my grief at losing my lover and friend. I also brought one of Chris's identifying trademarks, a red baseball cap he had worn daily for many years.

Sobonfu divided us into three working groups. I chose to work on the forgiveness altar and joined four other people. Holding hands, we closed our eyes and said prayers of gratitude before asking the spirits for permission to build.

We spread purple, gold, and green cloths over a long table and filled the altar with crystals, feathers, sacred statues, photos of ancestors, and other ritual items we had been invited to bring. Soon we had filled our creation with energy and beauty.

I placed pictures of Chris, my mother, my brother Dan, my grandparents, and even Bernie, my first husband, with the ancestors. I felt the profound weight that death had brought to my family. Death had been a powerful and demanding teacher from early in my life. Yet, I knew I had still much to learn in my time of grieving Chris.

I wondered about the appropriateness of putting my wedding picture with Chris on the ancestor altar since I still lived, but Sobonfu said we could be our own ancestors, which I took as permission. I wondered how others would hold me as ancestor after I die.

On a small stage just a foot off the floor in the front of the room, a group of seven people built the grief altar by lashing long, supple branches together in the shape of a teepee. They covered the six-foot structure with blue and black cloths, leaving a small opening in front for the grief bundles we would create. On top of the frame, they spread pine boughs to make it look like a forest cave. In front of the entrance where we would kneel to grieve, they placed a row of white candles.

Sobonfu outlined many layers of grief. She emphasized the importance of having representations of all aspects of our experience, including fear, anger, sadness, and any other emotion that might emerge. She asked us to go outdoors to find natural objects representing the various shades of our grief, including something emotionally neutral that would express unexpected emotions that might come up during the ritual. When we returned to the hall, we were to place the objects in bundles in the tent on the stage for later ceremonial burning.

I found a grassy knoll behind our building and collected a shard of pottery, a rusty nail, a sparkly rock, a yellow flower, and a feathery green piece of fern. The broken pottery represented the pain I felt for all the ways that, thinking I needed to feel superior to Chris to be safe, I hadn't been secure enough in our relationship. For my grief at needing to know, be right, and nail things down, thus sometimes creating distance between Chris and me, I chose the nail. The sparkly rock symbolized my sadness at having to be the shining one, sometimes at the expense of others, especially Chris. The yellow flower represented my unwillingness to accept that things change, have their cycles of beginnings and endings, and my resistance to accepting that Chris's death was part of the natural order of things. The sprig of fern served as the neutral object representing anything unforeseen.

I wrapped the objects I had gathered and the baseball cap into a cloth bundle. I found it startling that the hat I had brought from home caused an outpouring of my grief. It had been such a familiar part of Chris's life, and now I had to accept once more that he was never coming back and would never wear it again. I sat in the grass and, aware that the effort-less ease of my old life would never return, let the tears flow. Longing for Chris's energy to embrace me in my sorrow, I clasped the soft, faded red material.

When I got back into the hall, I placed my grief bundle in the opening of the tent. I sat and waited for the others to return. Before the room was half full, I felt energy moving from my belly into my throat. Was it grief or anger, fear or confusion? I had no idea. There were no thoughts, only raw emotion and agonized sounds.

Sobonfu gave directions to the group about the ritual process, but lost in my own feelings, I didn't hear anything she said. As soon as she finished the instructions, she pushed me up to be the first person at the shrine. I stumbled up to the front of the grief tent and, not knowing what I was supposed to do, knelt. I heard the powerful beat of Sobonfu's djembe drum, and the group began singing the words "Eh lala coo laya," the chant that would accompany us for the next two days. I didn't need to worry about what I should be doing. My body overtook all thought, and my energy rose to meet the wild anguish that coursed through me as I howled in pain.

Traditionally for the Dagara people, a West African ethnic group, a person is not left alone when at the grief tent. Sobonfu said each of us was always to be supported by another member of the community. Overwhelmed by emotional storms racing through me, I barely noticed the quiet presence of a young woman gently touching my back as I thrashed.

Crying, screaming, and moaning, I remained at the shrine for what seemed like an eternity. In the depths of my emotion, I knew that others had joined me at the altar. I could hear others grieving, each in their own way. Older people and younger people expressed their pain over recent deaths and deaths of long ago. We were a community of grief. Feelings moving through me felt not only personal but also universal.

Thoughts emerged as my sobs began to recede. It occurred to me that death helps us experience the full range of human existence. Maybe we grow by having the old wiped out in shattering ways so that we are forced continually to rebuild. I had no answers, but as my body quieted, I felt scrubbed clean and at peace. Relieved that I had been able to let go of some of the fatigue and pain of the past months, I stayed at the shrine for a short while longer to rest.

When I returned to my seat, I felt energized, cleansed, and awake. The radical reversal in my feeling state astonished me. Yet, a small part of me wondered, "What is wrong with you that you could get over something so monumental so quickly?" But I knew better. I wasn't over anything at all. I had simply taken another step into the long process called grief. I had moved energy ready to move and knew there would be more later. Still, I felt a new quiet inside and took my place in the group to support others just opening to their grief. The ceremony continued for the next two days as we drummed, chanted, grieved, and healed together.

After the weekend, I returned with an aching heart to the Timshel cottage and watched as the days ground relentlessly forward. In my lonely despair, I examined the many colors of my sorrow. As I mourned the loss of my beloved, I was aware of the bursting of spring all around, especially the myriad shades of green that occurred only at the time of new beginnings. I watched a tiny yellow bird move so fast it appeared to be nothing but a streak of yellow smearing the blue sky. And when I heard the transparent color of bird song, it touched a tender part of my heart, making me smile and grieve simultaneously. I watched the sun go down from my cottage deck and observed the colors of the day turn into deep black. Sometimes Venus shone through, and sometimes she played hide and seek in the clouds.

There was the color of Chris's scent that I had breathed in so many times in the past without a thought, a scent rich with shadow and light, dark purples and pastels so diaphanous they almost dissolved. And there was the color of my tears, milky white opalescence shimmering like the wind that brought ever-shifting changes of hue to all it touched. Washing over everything in my world, kaleidoscopic colors of my own internal emotions shifted from deep charcoal grey to the palest, almost white shades of violet and yellow.

I knew that Chris had died, but I was also aware that I, too, had died. The old Kai was no longer, and I watched as my new reality began its gradual unfolding.

Dreaming

Grief: it will lift you up, encase you in its powerful grip for its own time,
then let you go—sometimes gentle, sometimes harsh
again and again and again.

—Julie Cadwallader-Staub

I was grateful that my medicine work had allowed me to
develop an observer, the part of myself who could witness
all that happened from a distance and without judgment. My
observer gave me the little stability I had as I negotiated my
new life.

Still at the cottage almost four months after Chris's death, I
felt ready to engage actively with the world, but I had nothing
to return to. Not only was Chris gone, but I had no home,
community, or job. All I had was Silver Mystery Rider, the
car Chris and I had traveled in for the past three years, and a
resolute willingness to trust Spirit to take me where I should go.

When Chris and I arrived at Timshel for the Christmas
holidays, it never occurred to me that he and I would never
again set out on the road together. In a matter of months,
everything had changed. Chris had died, and I was alone. Yet
as long as I stayed in the cottage, I could imagine Chris off on
another journey, soon to return. If I left Timshel and drove off

in Silver Mystery Rider without him, however, I would take a significant step in accepting the reality that he would never return. As much as my mind knew the truth, my heart was reluctant to take the leap.

To open genuinely to the present moment, I had to accept that everything, whether agreeable or painful, came to me as a gift. Chris and I had practiced that teaching on the road, and his death provided a test of whether I really believed in those principles, a test I wished I could have avoided. Despite my grief, I could feel the stirrings of adventure and committed to saying yes to my continued unfolding.

I arbitrarily chose July 25 to head west on my solo odyssey. Coincidentally, I discovered that the date marks the Day Out of Time on the Mayan calendar, a day set aside for contemplation and worship before the Galactic New Year, celebrated on July 26. I saw Mayan New Year's Eve as a sacred bridge between the old and the new and the perfect time to begin my next chapter.

As I loaded bins into Silver Mystery Rider, I wished I had paid more attention to Chris when he packed. I once suggested that we occasionally switch jobs so we could each become proficient at all the necessary tasks, not simply the ones each of us had taken on. I proposed that I could pack, and Chris could cook. Chris scoffed at such an idea, clearly aware of the chaos that might result.

Alone, I had to learn as I went. I didn't do the accomplished job that Chris would have done, but I managed to cram all the bins and gear into the back of the car. Even as I saw how much I had to learn, I took momentary pride in my accomplishment.

I got into the car and, ready to begin my journey, turned the key. At that moment, I felt tightness in my throat followed by a torrent of tears. I raced back into the cottage, fell onto the bed, and wailed. The tears were intense, but when they came to an end, it was as if the feelings causing them had never passed through. The storm had come and gone. I didn't know what to make of it, but those wise ones who invented meditation teach that we are meant to watch—without attachment—the precious feelings we experience, and then we must let them go.

I returned to the car, drove down the driveway, and headed west. On that bright and sunny day, I set out filled with both excitement and fear at traveling alone for the first time. In the midafternoon, I stopped at a travel plaza for coffee. Chris and I had stopped at countless service areas in our years on the road, and the familiar place provoked a heart-wrenching wave of nostalgia that took me aback.

I watched couples holding hands, especially older couples who had grown to look alike and related in that casual way of people who had been with each other for a long time. Chris and I were once one of those couples. People noticed us for our couple-ness. I swallowed hard as I remembered that I had become a single woman, no longer a couple, let alone one that shined.

Standing in the plaza, I softly sang a few verses of "Hello, Young Lovers" to myself. I felt old and nostalgic remembering the tenderness of our time together, the ache surrounding Chris's passage, and the transformation of my life into something unknown.

I spent a month visiting friends in Illinois, Colorado, Utah, California, and Oregon. I wanted to go to places where Chris and I visited together and be with people who had known Chris and could grieve with me.

During the week of August 12, just a little more than four months after Chris's death, I attended the Sufi Camp my brother had helped found, where they blessed me with a special zikr ceremony in Chris's honor. A form of meditation chanted, sung, or danced, zikr repeats phrases or prayers designed to remember God as described in Sufi tradition.

Two dozen people sat in a circle surrounding me and Kalama, a Sufi friend who had also recently lost her husband. Singing began, and I began to cry. Soon I felt the arms of my friends holding me.

When I returned to Timshel after Chris died, I had only my father, Georgeanne, and my sister who, experiencing grief themselves at losing Chris, did not provide me a lot of support. Although I had many friends who loved me, they lived far away, and without community, I had to hold myself in my grief.

As I listened to the vibrations of the zikr and felt loving arms around me, I felt my body begin to soften. Finally, I could sink into their support. Finally, I could rest.

Sitting in the widow's seat, I saw myself playing an archetypal role as a living reminder in the community that death is part of life. That day, I took the role, but others would take my seat in the future.

After Sufi camp, I was ready to make my first foray into camping by myself. My nephew Shems, a fisherman of great skill, recommended a campground on a secluded lake in Washington state. I put the information he gave me into the GPS, which sent me onto a lonely logging road that went on for hours. I traveled through endless twisty, narrow trails surrounded by dense woods. I saw no road signs, only an ever deepening forest.

I started to fear I would never find my destination. With no other cars on the road, I worried about breaking down and needing help. It would have been a grand adventure if Chris had been with me, but my stomach started doing flip-flops as I pushed myself forward.

After four hours, I reached a small town and found a convenience store. A pleasant salesperson told me I still had to travel thirty miles on a forest road and another seven miles on gravel. I comforted myself with the thought that I had to end up somewhere, and from there, I would necessarily find my way. I couldn't be lost forever.

As I moved more deeply into the journey, I recognized that I had surrendered to a pilgrimage, not merely an adventure. It was an initiation into my new life. I was not just camping. I was entering a new territory I had never inhabited. I had camped before, but never on my own, and never without Chris. I had driven many times but not alone in an unknown forest unaware of the challenges ahead. I saw myself moving into a new relationship with death, grieving while simultaneously committing to life.

I let go of my need to get to the campground as fast or as efficiently as possible, yet I hoped I would arrive before night fell. I trusted that if no sites were available or if I found the campground unsuitable, I would simply return to the small town where I had gotten directions and find a motel. My backup plan gave me a little comfort, and I surrendered to letting go of any picture of how the adventure was supposed to turn out.

Thick green forest, snow-covered mountains, glorious blue sky peeking through the leafy canopies—the scenery stunned me. I felt simultaneously peaceful and anxious, excited by the beauty and quiet of the trees around me and fearful of the challenges of the drive.

The final seven miles demanded a lot. The gravel road felt like a washboard and shook the car so violently that I didn't know if it would make it in one piece.

Finally, I arrived at the Takhlakh Lake campground surrounded by a crystal clear body of water with majestic views of Mount Adams. I felt overflowing with gratitude to find such a peaceful sight after the rigors of my journey. I drove around the campground searching for an available spot and miraculously found a perfect empty site. Larger than most, it had views of the lake, mountains, and woods. And thankfully, it was private with only one other campsite nearby.

I started setting up the campsite as Chris and I had done so many times. Then, grief came charging through. I didn't know whether it came from feeling Chris's absence or his presence. It seemed no different from the many other times that Chris and I had set up camp together. As I set up the tent, I could believe that Chris had just driven back up to the entrance to pay for the site and would return soon. So why should I miss him? He'd be right back.

I watched myself waiting for Chris's return. Then the storms of grief overtook me, and I could do nothing but surrender. I climbed into the sleeping bag in the tent I had just set up, pulled the covers over my head, and wept. In time, the tears subsided, and I emerged ready to settle into my new home.

Without thinking, I followed my regular set-up routine and placed two camp chairs around the fire pit. Sitting and looking at the empty chair beside me, I lost my bearings. Where was my beloved, and why was I sitting alone? Chris should be sitting beside me. Where was he—the man who had walked beside me and filled the airwaves with his presence, who filled me with his presence? Where was the one who was so much a part of me that sometimes, maybe most of the time, he was me?

We were two beings, yet one. I loved Chris's body. His body was my body as mine was his. We played music with each other's bodies even when we sat beside each other doing nothing. It wasn't the doing that mattered but the being. Wherever we were, we were at home. We could make love by merely making breakfast together. It was all a celebration.

356

When Chris was alive, I didn't have to remember him. He was the air I breathed. He was the sound of the sky and the rumble of the earth. He was embedded in my cells and reflected outside of me as well. Back then, he was held physically in a body that I was attached to, one that I could touch and one that touched me in return.

With the empty chair, I sat by the fire alone.

I thought of the story of the Hindu god Krishna, the Source who preceded all that is. In his state of total oneness, wholeness, and harmony, Krishna was not satisfied and wanted something other to draw himself out, excite him, and bring him into new possibilities. And so he created Maya, the illusion of separation. She allowed him to forget himself and enter the mystery. She gave him the joy of finding himself over and over. But fearing that he might become totally lost in Maya and never return, Krishna swallowed a seed, the seed of the desire to remember his oneness. That desire to remember oneness thus embeds in all form and calls each of us back to remembering our true nature.

Was I Krishna creating my beloved to amuse and surprise myself? Was I playing hide and seek with myself and the desire to remember? Could it be that I was all that existed and that everything was a projection of myself?

What if grieving the passing of a beloved opens us to the reality that we were never two but were always one? Perhaps we simply dreamed or projected an image to play with, and when the play was over and the set was taken down, the truth shone through that we were always the One playing with itself. My whole life felt like a dream that had taken a circuitous route to bring me to that exact moment at the beautiful campsite on Lake Takhlakh, dwarfed by Mount Adams, a snow-covered giant in the distance.

While I remained lost in my reverie, a grey-haired couple stopped their vehicle next to my campsite. They introduced themselves as the campground hosts and explained that the site had been reserved for Labor Day. I could stay for three days but then had to move. I hadn't seen any reservation signs and hadn't thought about Labor Day, given that I no longer lived by the calendar, but my ignorance didn't change my situation. I would need to find another home.

They told me about another campground just five miles away. I decided to check it out before the schedule forced me to move. The following morning, I set out to explore the new possibility. To my dismay, I quickly discovered that the way to the new campsite followed a narrow gravel road that went straight up the mountain.

I set out nervously, aware that the car wended its way on a narrow space between rock face and abyss. Hardly breathing, I crept up the road as I gripped the steering wheel and prayed that I would make it to my destination.

My worst fear materialized when I saw a parade of three cars coming down the mountain toward me. The road seemed only wide enough for one car, and I had no idea what to do. The first vehicle stopped about twenty feet from me. Clearly, that vehicle and Silver Mystery Rider could not both pass.

A young woman dressed in a ranger's outfit sauntered down the road from the other car to my car.

"Honey," she said in a sweet southern drawl. "Honey, you have to back up."

Panic stricken, I could barely breathe. I had learned to drive as a teenager but had little use for a car during my thirty-two years in New York City. The idea of backing up on that narrow mountain road paralyzed me with fear. While I had done half of the driving on our travels, Chris had always made sure I did the straightforward driving. When driving got tough or required some degree of skill, he took over.

Chris could no longer save me, and the hard reality flashed that I had never learned properly how to back up a car.

The ranger patiently waited for me to respond.

"I am sorry," I said tentatively. "I don't back up. Maybe you can do it."

"I can't. It's against regulations for me to get into your car. You must do it," she said sweetly but firmly in her honey-like drawl.

I saw the drivers in the two cars behind the ranger's car and sensed their impatience while I bargained. Frozen, I couldn't move.

The ranger jumped into action.

"Okay, sweetheart, I will walk alongside the car so you will know that you are not falling off the mountain."

I was doubtful, but I didn't see a way out. I cautiously took my foot from the brake and set it on the gas pedal again. Frightened, I immediately stepped back onto the brake.

"No, no, honey. You have to step on the gas."

I tried, but my foot danced nervously between gas and brake pedals creating a stuttering motion.

"Okay, honey," she said with just a bit more impatience. "I'll keep walking beside the car and hold onto the steering wheel. All you need to do is keep your foot on the gas. Please," she begged.

With visions of hurling into the precipice, I slowly lurched back to a safe place on the shoulder. I thanked my angel with tears in my eyes, and she rushed off without a word to free the other two cars to continue on their way.

I didn't want to take the chance of meeting another car, so I continued up the road for another five minutes until I found a safe place to turn around. Alone in the car, I broke into heavy sobs. I missed Chris and felt terrified and unskilled at the simplest tasks ahead.

All of it made for classic dream material—crisis, fear, inability to act, and an angel appearing who saves the day. As I awoke from what felt like a nightmare, I saw the road open with nothing more threatening than several passing motorcycles that quickly gave me a wide berth.

I returned to my campsite and discovered new neighbors, a couple in their early eighties. Before the husband left to go fishing, he told me of another campground nearby. His wife and I continued chatting. I told her that my husband had recently died. She expressed her condolences and began to tell her story.

She wistfully told me of her husband's macular degeneration, bad hips, their endless round of trips to doctors, and the likelihood that they were making their last trip to Lake Takhlakh. I could hear the combination of her terror that he would die and leave her and at the same time, her exhaustion from the life they lived.

We talked a little longer, and I realized that Chris and I would never share the experience of getting old together. I wondered why Chris was taken from me while still in the prime of his life. Perhaps we didn't need or want the lessons of getting old. But what lessons had we signed up to learn?

As I returned to my tent, I felt blindsided by that twist in our story and wanted to find a way to figure out what it all meant. I suspected that I couldn't know until time passed and I could see turns that my life took. After my conversation with the woman at the campground, I had no idea where I wanted to go or how I wanted to direct my life forward. Maybe a wiser part of me would do the steering. I hoped so because I had no map.

The camp hosts recommended another nearby campground that did not require my return to the narrow mountain road, and the following day, I moved into a new campsite. By sheer chance, I set up the opening of my tent to frame the gradually rising full moon.

In the light that shone through the darkness, I thought about dying and wondered if death had been devised by humans afraid to breathe. What was breath but taking in and letting go, living and dying with a still point in between, that delicious moment at the end of the exhale and before the inhale, a moment of nothing, nowhere?

So why should the big story be any different? The breath constitutes the height of simplicity yet also the unknowable. Anything might happen between inhale and exhale. Any dream might be dreamed only to dissolve in the waking.

Chris went gently into the dream with no resistance, only letting go. He had already entered the next realm. Why create so much drama about something so simple? Perhaps the responsibility of having that much freedom to choose the dream overwhelmed us humans as we got more attached to form.

Could it be that what we call death merely means returning to infinite dreaming?

Letting Go

Go down to your deep old heart, and lose sight of yourself.
And lose sight of me, the me whom you turbulently loved.

—D. H. Lawrence

I returned to the Timshel cottage at Christmas and settled in. I desperately needed quiet and a place where I could rest and heal. I enjoyed being with my family and made short visits to see friends, but the journeys ended quickly when I sensed I needed to hurry back to my safe nest. I had planned to get back on the road by early spring, but as I watched days and weeks roll by, I couldn't find the energy to move forward. Winter passed and then spring. Soon, it was June.

It began so slowly that I hardly knew anything was happening. One hot day, I felt cold—not the kind of cold that comes from a sharp wind on the skin, but a bone-chilling cold. Even worse, I felt exhaustion that quietly sucked away at my life force.

I thought a nap might comfort my aching body and bring me back to life, but it brought no relief. As hours drifted on, I felt myself nailed to my bed with my energy so depleted that I could barely turn over and reach for the glass of water next to my bed.

I dragged myself to the bathtub, but the heat of the bath barely touched the cold coursing through my body even as I returned to the steaming water every couple of hours.

I couldn't imagine what had brought my body to such a state. Extreme pain in my head, muscles, and bones felt like punishment for an unknown crime. The hours dragged on. In agony, I wondered if I was doomed to endure such suffering for the rest of my life. If so, how could I live?

I told my father and Georgeanne that I didn't feel well, but they seemed not to take it seriously and offered no help. I wished I had someone to take care of me, but I felt too miserable to want anyone around. I missed Chris, who would have provided quiet, loving, and helpful presence and no burden on my already stretched nerves. I couldn't remember having such pain and had no story to explain it. I tried to think, but my brain had shut down.

The following morning I awoke feeling even more uncomfortable. I couldn't get underneath the pain and wondered what it must have been like for Chris to live for months with such a level of discomfort. I wished he could have shared more about what he felt, not that I could have done anything to alleviate it.

Lost in a body that seemed to have run amok, I realized that I knew little about the physical form that I lived in. I had some skills to live in harmony with it, like brushing my teeth, eating well, sleeping, and doing yoga, but when I tried to think about why my head hurt or where chills came from, I had no idea.

I decided to distract myself by watching the slideshow my friend Erik had made for Chris's celebration of life a couple of weeks after he died. I hoped it would bring me some relief. Erik had collected photos of Chris and arranged them to the accompaniment of Sheena Easton singing "When He Shines."

The pictures of Chris showed him as a child, a teenager, at our wedding, and on our travels. His bright smile beamed out of the screen, and he did shine.

After watching the slide show, I looked out the French doors into the gradually darkening sky. Wind whipped wildly in the branches of trees in the woods around the house. Once Chris had left his body, I felt his presence whenever the wind blew. I followed the turbulent energy coursing through my body and outside the house. Tears leaked, and my weeping soon turned into wails, shrieks, and unworldly sounds as I thrashed around the bed in a gut-wrenching this-can't-be kind of grief. I let the rawness of my feelings overtake me and surrendered to the flood of feelings.

I knew all the emotion was just the stuff of life. Some life stuff hurts, and some feels ecstatic. That's what I signed up for when I birthed into this embodiment. If I had wanted nothing but grace and ease, I probably wouldn't have been gifted with Chris. We both must have said yes to the full range of experience, because that was what we got. Still, the intensity of the grief that persisted more than a year after Chris's death surprised me.

Gradually I quieted along with the wind outside my window, and calm prevailed inside and out. Release felt good. I had been holding on for dear life in my profoundly contracted body. Having surrendered to the storms raging through my being, I felt lighter, but the pain in my body continued.

Five days into what seemed like unendurable misery, I wondered if my agony contained a message. What was I holding on to that needed to be set free?

And then I heard the answer. Even though had Chris died more than a year before, I still wore my wedding ring and had not spread his ashes, ashes I insisted had no meaning for me.

I realized I persisted in acting as if Chris lived and traveled somewhere, soon to return to me and our life as we had known it. Excruciating physical pain had thrown me back into my earth plane self where I could no longer find comfort in the mystical connection I held with Chris. I had to face the truth. Chris was dead. He would never return.

I had continued to think of myself as married, but I was married to a person who was dead.

Enough! The time had come to return to the real world. I loved Chris deeply and always would. But Chris was dead, and I could no longer be married to a man who was not alive.

I considered calling my friend Su, who did shamanic work, to help me create an appropriate ritual for unmarrying Chris, but all of the planning soon became irrelevant.

In a moment without thought, my right hand came down on my ring finger, seized the simple gold band, and off it went. Surprised at seeing my naked finger, I held the ring in my hand, turning it over and over as if it were a foreign object that I had never seen before.

Something had changed. I was no longer married to my beloved Chris.

At the very moment I separated from my ring, the symbol of our marriage, a little orange tabby kitten raced by the French doors. She scampered toward the shrubs just out of my sight. A young spotted fawn appeared seconds later and, clearly aware of another animal's presence, sniffed the air.

I watched as the kitten came bravely out of her hiding place in the greenery to meet the giant stranger. For ten seconds, I held my breath as the two stood still just feet apart, their eyes locked in strange communion.

The moment ended abruptly when the kitten casually took her leave and walked around the corner of the house. The deer, evidently surprised at being abandoned by his new playmate, turned and leaped into the woods.

I wondered about the message from the two visitors and looked up the meaning of their animal totems. I checked Ted Andrews's *Animal Speaks* and discovered that Cat represents magic, mystery, and independence. Cat also foreshadows meeting new ideas and new places with courage and confidence.

My other friend, Deer, brings gentleness and new perspectives. He urges letting go of old patterns and behaviors that no longer serve. Deer's antlers mean regeneration and new life.

In that transitional time, I appreciated the generous support of those animals. With Chris no longer of the earth plane world, he and I were of two different species. In the kitten and deer's meeting, I received a visual symbol that Chris and I could meet—I, in my earth plane body, and Chris, in his spirit form. I had no idea how it would play out but chose to believe our relationship had been blessed by the spirit animals.

Still full of pain, I went to sleep that night. I woke starving at 2:30 a.m. Instead of lying in bed unable to move, I bounced up, walked to the kitchen, and made scrambled eggs and toast. It felt like a proper feast. It was the first time I could eat at the table in almost a week. I felt like I had just popped back into my body and was home again.

The following day, happy to sit on my deck soaking up the sunshine, I felt as if I had made a miraculous recovery. Since I no longer had severe symptoms, I thought going to a doctor would be a waste of time. I casually picked up a newspaper and turned to the astrology reading for the day. A surprisingly specific message awaited me. "June," it said, "is an important time for Capricorns to take the opportunity to see a doctor."

I couldn't ignore such clarity, so I called Dr. Melchinger for an appointment. Two days later, I drove to New Haven to get examined. He called three days later and told me to begin a ten-day course of antibiotics. I had Lyme disease.

The medicine started working immediately, and I soon returned to the circus of life almost as if nothing had happened. I knew, however, that something radical had happened, a shift that seemed to change everything. I felt infinite gratitude as I had not for some time for even the most minute things—being able to fall asleep at night and wake up refreshed, walk around upright, sit on the deck, listen to the birds, and watch the wind.

I acknowledged so many blessings. The most minor experience felt like an enormous gift, and the largesse kept tumbling forth. I couldn't believe how lucky I was to be able to exist without pain. I knew millions of people didn't have that gift, and for almost a week, I hadn't. But I had become healthy again. How could I not keep saying, "Thank you, thank you, thank you"?

I was grateful for the Lyme disease. Being ill forced me once again to accept that Chris no longer lived on this plane and would never again. A disruption in my ordinary life reminded me once again that everything changes. Clearly, the time had arrived to forge a new relationship with my beloved. I had put it off for as long as possible but could no longer pretend. The ring no longer graced my finger, and I would soon spread the ashes.

I hadn't wanted the day to come, but it had, and there was no going back. I trusted that grace would carry me as it always had, but I found the feeling of bewilderment hard to live with. It was painful to realize that I could barely remember how Chris and I had lived in the carefree way we had enjoyed. Once an easy and delightful celebration, our life together had become only a memory.

Memories couldn't support my new life. I needed to start living in the now. Anything not happening in the present wasn't real, and Chris wasn't part of my present reality. I felt him real in the wind and the cosmos, but he did not exist in my physical world on the earth plane.

I had a lot of work to do, but I trusted that whatever I needed would come when I was ready for it. The time had come to look to Chris not as my husband but as a teacher and guide.

With my wedding ring absent from my finger, I had one more task. I had to spread Chris's ashes.

My father, Georgeanne, Ginger, and Chris's kids, Hope and Josh, gathered for the ceremony in a flower garden my father had tended on his property next to a small gurgling stream. Before the ceremony began, I created an altar on a large flat stone in the garden's center. I spread a green velvet cloth over the top and placed a candle, a singing bowl, the little fabric frog Chris had given me when we first got together, pictures of Chris, and a wooden snake he had carved.

I brought rattles for everyone and asked them to shake them to raise the vibrations of the ceremony. I called in the directions and cleansed each person with sage. I appreciated that everyone was willing to surrender to the unfamiliar ritual.

We held hands in a circle to create a strong container. It had rained for the past three days, leaving the ground soft and muddy. I loved feeling the mud between the toes of my bare feet. I set up the computer so we could watch the slideshow Erik had made. Seeing Chris in his many guises made us cry as we heard Sheena Easton sing, "When he shines, he shines so bright." When the song ended, we all sat in tender silence.

I asked for stories, and they tumbled out, moving us back and forth from tears to laughter. We took turns emulating Chris's deep and full-bodied laughter and felt his presence close by. Thinking of Chris when he laughed made it hard to be sad, and we all delighted in remembering how blessed we had been by the sound of his deep roar.

I was ready to move on from the stories when Josh quietly spoke and said he had something he wanted to share. Saying he had wanted to keep his father's art close to him, he lifted his shirt and proudly revealed a tattoo. Inked on the right side of his torso, he had an exact eight-inch copy of one of Chris's unglazed white earth grails, a dragon supporting itself over a chalice. Josh's tender vulnerability moved me and made me grateful that that part of Chris lived on in him.

I had put most of the ashes in a blue velvet bag and invited everyone to take handfuls. Hope started, and we all joined in spreading them to the winds. Josh took his handful of ashes to the stream and performed his own private ceremony. Soon the bag of ashes was empty, and we each sat quietly with our own thoughts.

Hope looked bereft, and I asked her to come and sit with me on a bench a short distance from the stream. We held each other and wept.

"I know that this is an ending," she said through tears, "but now that Dad is gone, I don't want to lose you, too."

Her concern that she thought I would go anywhere surprised me.

"Oh, my darling, it was not only your father who held us together. I love you dearly. You will always be family, and more importantly, you will be my friend."

I felt her body relax against me, and we sat in silence.

We returned to the group, and I called everyone together. We wrapped ourselves into a tight ball and together chanted three Oms. The vibrations of Om faded away on the wind, and the ceremony came to an end. The ritual had not wrenched me as much as I feared, and its gentleness made me grateful.

A chapter had ended, but I couldn't envision the new one. I faced so many unanswered questions. Where should I go? What should I do? What would the future bring?

I knew I had to be patient and trust that I would be guided as I always had been. I looked into the vast open sky, took a deep breath, packed up the altar, and headed back alone to the house.

The Burn

Take, eat: this is my body, which is broken for you:
this do in remembrance of me.

—1 Corinthians 11:24

Two months later, I had not found the energy to get back on the road and remained stuck at the Timshel cottage. Feeling that I needed company and support, I invited my friend Louise to visit. We had first met at an Ayahuasca medicine circle that Chris and I attended in 2007. She and I had stopped to say hello on the driveway of our meeting place. We casually shared minor details about our lives, and soon our souls spoke together in a familiar language as if we had been reunited after a long absence. Later, we discovered that we shared a birthday on the same day and year, making us feel almost like twin sisters.

A lawyer from British Columbia, Louise had devoted her career to working with Indigenous Peoples to reclaim their territories from the British Crown. It was slow, challenging work that included much love and reciprocity.

In gratitude, people of native communities often invited her to local ceremonies, and Louise gratefully received spiritual knowledge and four sacred Indigenous names from different

Nations. In her long robes and beaded jewelry, Louise looked more like an Indigenous person than a Jewish woman from the suburbs of Toronto.

Every spring after we met, Louise invited Chris and me to stay for a month at her vacation house on Mayne Island, a tiny outcropping floating between Victoria and Vancouver. There, we watched eagles fly past her deck, whales swim through the channel below, and deer and other animals pass by the house. Although Louise rarely joined us during those magical stays, her energy connected me with precious memories of times with Chris, and I felt grateful that she could accompany me in my grief.

On our first morning together, we shared a hearty breakfast on the cottage deck as we looked out onto the Endless Mountains rising gently before us. Though the middle of August, it was cool, almost cold. I had felt disoriented since Chris's death, and even the weather seemed out of order that day.

After eating a light lunch of soup and salad, we settled quietly, each in a corner of the living room, to attend to emails. I looked out the French door leading to the deck and, to my surprise, saw a mottled grey boxer dog with his nose pressed against the glass, begging to be let in. Louise said he looked hungry and that we should feed him. I, however, was reluctant to give him food since I would be leaving for the road soon and didn't want him depending on me. I also didn't think I could take the responsibility for an animal when I could hardly care for myself. I hoped if I ignored him, he would go away.

Hoping to distract the dog, I suggested that Louise and I walk up the gravel road next to the cottage road. Ignoring my resistance, the dog jumped off the deck to follow us. He trotted beside me and happily wagged his tail as if we had walked together for lifetimes.

When we reached the top of the road, we sat in a small family cemetery under an old oak tree with our feet buried in soft pine needles. The dog sat comfortably at my feet and looked at me adoringly.

Louise was convinced the dog had a message. Since it was not long after the year anniversary of Chris's death, she thought Chris might be asking for a Burn. She explained that a Burn is a sacred ceremony performed by Indigenous Nations where food enjoyed by a departed loved one is prepared and then given to the fire, its smoke sending transmuted nourishment to the departed soul.

Louise told me she had attended large and smaller Burns conducted by spiritual leaders with the burning of favorite foods for departed loved ones on the anniversary of their passing or when a loved one had appeared in a dream to a family member.

Never previously responsible for a Burn, Louise did not profess any expertise but said she could replicate what she had witnessed.

When I agreed to the ritual, Louise said we would seek guidance by asking questions with a pendulum. Louise trusted the pendulum to speak the truth. She told me that even when in court in her fancy English robes, she often checked it to determine whether a witness had lied or told the truth.

Since Louise didn't have access to her own pendulum to inquire about the Burn, she used the pendant that our friend Sherril had made of moldavite for Chris. A unique green gemstone, moldavite fell to earth more than fourteen million years ago during a meteor impact that formed the Bohemian plateau. We considered it perfect that Louise used a crystal that connected earth and sky as she spoke to Spirit about creating the ceremony. We had many questions to ask the pendulum.

Where should we make the fire? Who should we invite? What food should we offer? And what was the most auspicious time?

All of it was new to me, and I watched as Louise held the pendulum still in her hand while asking yes or no questions. The pendulum was clear. When the answer was yes, it moved in a direct line in front of her. When the answer was no, the pendulum moved in a circle.

The pendulum assured us that Chris had requested a Burn at an auspicious time and that we should invite Chris's parents, Lucas and Eldora, who had passed, as well as my departed brother Dan, called Ishaq, and our beloved dog, Alia. The pendulum circled when we asked about inviting my mother and brother John Mark, indicating they would not be called to the ceremony. The guest list was complete with Chris, his parents, my brother, and our dog.

We invited each one separately and received answers through the pendulum. All of the invited guests happily accepted.

The pendulum told us that we needed to make a fire at the far end of the yard, and it had to be especially hot.

Next, we had to work out the menu. Through the pendulum, Eldora and Lucas told us they would share the pasta with raw tomato sauce that we breathing humans would eat.

We learned that we should serve Chris three courses, starting with Scotch, followed by the main course consisting of a strip of bacon, mayonnaise, Brie on a cracker, and a piece of shrimp. His dessert course included ice cream, a square of chocolate, and a cigarette.

My brother's plate would include ice cream, a clementine, and a square of chocolate, sweets that, as a childhood diabetic, he was not allowed to eat. Having left this life, he could have as much as he wanted.

And for Alia, our beloved dog, we offered a thick pork chop with a bone.

The pendulum communicated that we should serve the food on paper plates and the Scotch in a paper cup. It then directed us to a spot near the edge of the woods for the fire. On the ground, I laid the large garbage can lid that Chris and I used to contain fires when we camped. Louise built a stone ring around the lid while I split wood, a job that Chris usually carried out since he was more skillful. I took a deep breath and followed guidance from a voice within to say "Thank you." I struck with the ax, and the wood split effortlessly into pieces.

I made a nest out of twigs and leaves to start the blaze. Louise and I sat on the ground and blessed the fire as it began to burn, creating the coals that would burn the food.

The ceremony began as Louise offered black tobacco to the fire and the spirit helpers who would guide our work. The flames brightly consumed the tobacco, and we concluded that our gift had been accepted with pleasure.

Louise said I should present the guests to the spirit helpers, and I started with Chris, introducing him as my beloved soul mate. Then I introduced his parents and Ishaq. When I spoke Alia's name, one of the logs in the fire blew up in a fiery explosion that ruptured the center of the log, sending sparks all around.

Alia, Alia. What are you trying to tell me? The dog's presence all afternoon and the explosion seemed to indicate a message, but I couldn't unlock it. For the moment, I could only say thank you and move on.

We put the paper cup filled with Chris's favorite Scotch in the center of the fire on the coals. The cup burned slowly, but the alcohol caught with a bright burst of appreciation. Then we fed Chris's parents the plates of spaghetti, and I thanked them for bringing Chris into the world.

Sizzling bacon created a joyful sound when we put Chris's plate on the fire. Ishaq's plate melted into a beautifully shaped bowl that held the ice cream while it bubbled, but the clementine took the fire longer to consume. We saw no sign or message when we gave Alia her pork chop, just happiness as flames surrounded the juicy meat with loud crackling.

Finally, we served Chris his dessert. Amazingly, the plate slipped to an almost vertical position while all the food stayed firmly fixed. As we watched the dessert plate burn, the cigarette lit at the tip and burned down its length as if Chris had actually smoked it.

When our other-worldly guests had eaten, it was time for us to eat the spaghetti I had prepared with raw tomato sauce, pesto, and mozzarella cheese. The hot fire burned down to glowing coals as we finished the last bites of our dinner. The embers looked like gems coming up from the earth as the moon rose perfectly framed by two trees behind the firepit.

I asked Louise to inquire of the pendulum if I had fulfilled my obligations in the ritual. The pendulum answered that I had not. I sat quietly and heard an inner voice say, "You must speak to Chris."

I assured Chris of my commitment to listening to his messages and that I understood that we still had work to do together. I promised to do my best to be awake and aware and polish my listening skills. I thanked him for sending the message through the dog that we should provide him with a Burn. When I felt complete with our conversation, Louise checked again. The pendulum then assured us of the perfection of the Burn.

Several days later, walking up the hill, I was surprised to see the grey dog sitting in the yard of the only house on the road. I had never seen him before nor after his visitation at my home, and I expected he would be happy to see me. I wanted to thank him for the message and apologize for not being kinder when he showed up at my door.

I called out to him, but he ignored me, not even turning his head in response. His lack of recognition supported my story that Chris had borrowed the dog's body to bring me a message. Having fulfilled his mission, the dog had no more interest in me.

Pilgrimage

I did not die, and yet I lost life's breath.

—Dante Alighieri
The Divine Comedy

The night after the Burn, I watched the sun go down. As the sky darkened with fireflies twinkling in their wild dance, I wondered what would become of me. I worried that I wasn't getting anywhere, but I didn't know where I should be going. Slogging through my days felt like walking the Camino de Santiago in June 2008, four years before Chris's death.

The Camino de Santiago, a five-hundred-mile pilgrimage, crosses Spain from the border with France to the Atlantic Ocean. At the beginning of our thirty-four days of walking, Chris and I considered a pilgrimage the same as a glorified walk. Instead, we found it a serious commitment that required discipline and willingness to change radically.

Hiking eight hours a day at our own pace, we needed to surrender our desire and comfort to the demands of a higher purpose. The defined goal meant reaching the Cathedral de Santiago. However, the spiritual goal involved facing inner demons that arose physically and emotionally as we faced the journey's challenges and limitations of our bodies. The Camino meant committing to our intended path no matter the challenges. Even so, we encountered ample pleasure and beauty.

At night, we stayed in albergues, inns expressly set aside for pilgrims. Each day started just before dawn to avoid the sweltering heat of midafternoon. We gathered our sparse belongings into our twenty-pound backpacks and set out on a path marked by scallop shells painted on trees, sidewalks, buildings, or boulders. It felt like an elaborate scavenger hunt.

Every day, we covered between twenty-five and thirty kilometers, between sixteen and nineteen miles. Some days we walked in the beauty of mountains, forests, and rivers. On other days, it felt like drudgery when we walked through dusty, treeless plains or busy cities. Some days, we sweltered in hot sun, and others, we shivered in cold rain. Often, bloody blisters covered my feet, but we woke each day, faced the unknown, and continued forward no matter what.

We met extraordinary people also on personal pilgrimages. On the road, we walked together, ate together, and shared stories of our triumphs and failures. We were a community of people, together but on separate journeys.

We learned quickly that we couldn't waste energy looking to the end goal. On the first day of walking, a steep climb in deep mud up and down the foothills of the Pyrenees, we couldn't find comfort in saying we had walked 30 miles and had only 470 to go. That would merely sap our energies. Instead, we understood we would have to take the journey step by step and stay as present as possible to reach Santiago. Often, it wasn't easy, especially when we walked in the rain or had to slog our way through a city or found ourselves lost with no one to ask.

Though sometimes a challenge, it helped us to remember the perfection of everything. Still, we chose to believe that all was well no matter what. Gratitude helped immensely, and we always found something to be grateful for if we chose to look. Looking for opportunities to place our appreciation became a game.

As Chris and I walked, we shared stories about our beloveds. We found that even without them with us physically, we experienced their presence so intensely that sometimes we felt they actually walked with us.

The themes of presence, gratitude, and connection were powerful, and we practiced them every day. As we walked, we embedded the lessons quite literally in our bones. Four years later, I felt grateful for the skills learned on the Camino that supported my engagement with grief as I experienced Chris's physical absence.

I chose to look at the chapter I lived through following Chris's death as a pilgrimage. I had to walk the path, trust Spirit, and let go of the story that my ego was in charge. I had to surrender—not to a goal but to something I didn't understand. I had to be willing to wake up morning after morning to walk into the mystery. I had to trust that I was on the right path even when I felt lost in the dark, knowing I could always make a U-turn if I found myself going the wrong way.

But as fall approached, I felt like I was wasting away at the cottage. I wrote daily in my journal, practiced the piano, took long walks alone up the adjacent hill, and occasionally shared meals with my father and Georgeanne. I made short trips to visit friends but returned quickly to the quiet safety of the cottage. Nothing kept me from leaving and returning to the road, but days turned into weeks, and I couldn't find the energy or focus to go.

Finally, at the end of October, I packed up the car and made my farewells. Surprisingly, I didn't feel the same heavy sadness of leaving as I had in the past. Excitement stirred as I set out on the road again.

I spent almost two months visiting friends, partaking in a series of Ayahuasca ceremonies, and returning to places Chris and I had loved. Before Christmas, I drove up the coast to Portland, Oregon, for a winter solstice party with old friends Chris and I had met at Sufi Camp.

I enjoyed the first hour of the party, catching up with people, eating good food, and sipping wine. Then the solstice ritual began. My dear friends Daniel and Rahmana started to sing, "Out beyond ideas of right and wrong, there is a field. I'll meet you there," a Rumi poem they had set to music. Chris and I had often taught the song in our work at our retreat center in New Haven. At first, I felt the slight moistness of a tear at the corner of my eye, but as the music continued, tears streamed down my cheeks.

I felt confused by the wave of grief that came over me. I thought the storms of the past year and a half had come to an end. I had thought myself once again on firm ground, but the tears said otherwise.

The music entered every cell in my body, and I longed for Chris's touch, for the ease and companionship we had together, and the simplicity of knowing that we held each other in love.

The room was almost dark with only the wavering light of candles. My body ached with longing for my beloved. *Chris, Chris, how could you have left me? How can I go on? Where is the life that we once had?* There was no room for thought. My anguish stretched out into infinity. The nothing that felt so heavy clamped down on me.

Dimly aware of the forty people in the room, I didn't want to create drama. My yearning and pain felt too intimate for public viewing. Still, those around me knew something was happening, and I felt a hand gently placed on my thigh. I had no idea who had come to sit with me in my grief and longing.

It didn't matter since I wasn't in my body or even in the room. I had taken no mind-altering substance, but I found myself flying around the cosmos searching for my beloved and finding him nowhere.

Yet something felt different. Before, I had felt Chris so intensely at my side that the full impact of his death had not penetrated. I had continued to live the familiar life that Chris and I had shared on the road, visiting the same people and places. I could pretend that my life was marginally intact.

But at that moment, I felt a shattering. I could feel my life no longer fulfilling my needs. It was not just Chris who had died. The foundations of my life were in ruin. How had I not noticed until that moment? Perhaps my ability to feel Chris with me, even without his physical form, had made it possible for me to survive the devastation of his death. But suddenly, it felt that I held on to him in a way that prevented me from making a new life.

I felt myself enter a new phase of tender yet seemingly bottomless grief. Perhaps it was time to miss Chris in that way, but I found it excruciating to recognize another level of the reality that he was gone. I had expected that we would have a mysterious, cosmic connection. Sadly, that had not come to pass, or if it had, I had not received his messages.

I felt bereft. I wanted to cry but couldn't go deep enough. Even if I could, it would have done no good. My life was gone, and I was lost.

Although being mystically connected with Chris in his formless state had comforted me, I couldn't deny the truth. I was shattered. I was dying, and my only hope was to find a way to root into the earth. Whether my dying was physical or the slow seepage of the life force in a body that simply continued on didn't matter. I looked straight into the face of death and had to do something.

I needed to come down from the heights and commit to this earth plane existence. I needed to find a home. I needed to find roots, community, and a reason to continue. But where to start? I had no idea how I created the old life. How would I go about creating a new one?

Feeling as if a silent retreat would help me regain my center, I accepted an invitation from my friend Louise to stay at her home on Mayne Island in British Columbia. I drove to Port Angelus, Washington, and took the ferry to Victoria and then another ferry to Mayne Island.

I arrived with deep anxiety, but I committed to facing my demons through writing and meditation. I felt lost, not knowing who I was and what I wanted. Was it because Chris was no longer at my side? Was it because I had been away from structure and continuity on the road? I felt fulfilled when Chris and I traveled together, but now I felt dry, without passion, and without purpose. I hoped that focusing my attention inward in the next two weeks would help me find a way to live in my truth—alive, radiant, contented, blissful, a song unto myself.

If I could name my fear, I thought I could vanquish it, but I realized that what felt like fear was part of my grief. I had assumed I would be finished with grief when the sadness of losing Chris became more bearable. Instead, I experienced a new and unexpected level of pain as I faced the death of my old life.

Longing for Chris's return promised no possibility of fulfillment. I grieved the old days but wasn't sure I wanted them back. I had changed significantly in the past two years and was no longer the same woman who traveled with Chris on the road. Yet, I didn't know the new Kai or what she might need.

I still had many of the same friends, but my relationships with them had changed. I also had new acquaintances Chris had never met. Unlike the old days, I did all of the driving, and I went where I wanted to go without negotiating with anyone else.

More and more, I felt a yearning to find solidity, know myself, and have a purpose. I recognized that I had to allow myself to move back into a life in the world, but I didn't know where I fit. The possibility of making the wrong choice terrified me, yet I felt equally concerned that I might fail my destiny by doing nothing.

I was stuck.

With little creative energy and excitement, I felt numb and debilitated. I likely accomplished more than I thought simply by living, breathing, and moving through the grieving process as consciously as possible, but it didn't seem like enough. I wanted to bring more fire into my life.

Alone in the empty house, I spent the next two weeks looking out at the ever changing sea. I processed two buried feelings, but the future nevertheless looked dim. As the days glided by on my solitary island, my panic increased.

I took long walks to the beach, spent meditative hours in a Japanese garden, and watched sunrises and sunsets, deer, and eagles. As I let beauty nourish me, I watched my grief begin to heal, but deep in my body, I was exhausted. I had been traveling alone back and forth across the country for almost two years, but I no longer wanted to do it. My inner voice told me I had to find a home, roots, and community. I needed to belong to someone or something.

I could no longer stay in the Underworld.

Testing

Try corralling a lightning bolt, containing a tornado.
Dam stream, and it will create a new channel.
Resist, and the tide will sweep you off your feet.
Allow, and grace will carry you to higher ground.

—Danna Faulds

After my three weeks on Mayne Island, I took the ferry back to the States and rested for several days at the home of my friend Alan in Humboldt County, California. Since 2006, Alan had provided Chris and me with journey quality Mother that had fueled our cosmic explorations. He grew his plants with love and skill, and the product was matchless.

Alan and I spent two days before I started my drive back to Timshel. We took long walks along the Pacific coast beach with deep spiritual conversations accompanied by a lot of good red wine and tasty food. As a parting gift, he gave me a couple of lovely buds in a small tin. I had been living out of my car for almost ten years and had collected quite a bit of contraband. After the pressure of crossing the border from Canada with all that I secretly carried, I had gotten sloppy. I took the tin Alan had given me and dropped it into the overnight bag, which I kept under the passenger seat.

The drive was challenging from the start with foul weather and below zero temperatures. After spending the night in a motel in Wyoming, I stopped at a service plaza. Soon after I got on the highway, I noticed a police car following me. Distracted by a glitch in my GPS, I had only been going seven miles over the speed limit, but I suspected that my out-of-state plates made me an easy mark.

The cop asked for my license and then, to my shock, noticed an opened bottle of gin sticking out of my overnight bag in the front seat. Hoping a drink would help me relax and sleep quickly so I could wake up at dawn to begin my fourteen-hour stint, I had taken the bottle into the motel the night before. With the frigid temperatures, I thought it would be easier to tuck the bottle into my overnight bag rather than in the back of the car. When I left the motel, I tossed the bag unthinkingly onto the floor under the passenger seat.

The cop didn't care that it was 7:30 a.m. and was not interested in my protestations that I had not and would not drink while driving. He left me with a $150 ticket for carrying an opened bottle of booze and left without bothering to cite me for speeding.

I returned to the road the following day, and around noon, I noticed the check engine light flashing. My GPS guided me to a Volvo repair station out in the middle of nowhere in Illinois, and I walked out two hours later with a $350 charge and no flashing light.

I found my way back to the highway, and as soon as I crossed the state line into Indiana, I noticed a police car following me. I knew I wasn't speeding. There were no flashing lights, but the vehicle seemed to be following me, making me nervous.

Soon, the anxiety of not knowing what was happening overtook me, and I decided to pull over onto the side of the road, hoping the police would pass by. Something in me knew it was not a smart move, but I did it anyway. The patrol car pulled up behind me, and two cops walked over to my passenger window.

I was terrified.

One of the cops was a round-faced fellow of about twenty-five, the other a dark-haired guy in his late thirties with a military look. The younger one signaled me to roll down my window and asked in a friendly tone, "Do you need help?"

"No, thanks. I'm fine."

"Let me see your license,"

Panic flooded through me. I fumbled around my wallet and handed over my credit card by mistake. Not a good start. I tried again, and successfully pulled out my license. The young cop studied it, and then the unthinkable came to pass.

"I smell pot," he said.

I thought about the priestesses in the Mists of Avalon who could make a person see whatever the priestess wished.

"No, you don't," I said with as much authority as I could muster. My dissembling did nothing to dissuade the cops. One of the best growers in Humboldt County, Alan produced tiny buds that even in the tightly closed tin broadcasted a delicious green aroma that left no doubt.

"Get out of the car," the young cop demanded.

"No, I want to stay here," I said, vaguely remembering something I saw in a YouTube video that said when stopped by the police, you don't have to leave the car. I wished I had paid more attention.

"I've got a taser gun, and if you don't get out, I'll shoot it, and it will hurt."

I didn't like the idea of being shot with a taser or anything else. Trembling from the violence of the moment, I reluctantly relented and got out of the car.

The older cop took my arm and escorted me to the police car. It was ten below zero, and the cold intensified my terror of what would happen next. He opened the door and gently pushed me into the backseat of the car. I heard the door lock and knew I could do nothing to change my dangerous situation.

The back of my Volvo station wagon was piled high with bins of clothes, books, food, camping gear, drums, and other necessities that made life on the road possible. And then there was the contraband. I watched in horror from my seat in the locked police car as they searched through every bin. They couldn't miss anything, I thought to myself, and they didn't.

Out of the patrol car window, I saw the young cop find a hidden item and raise it up so his partner could see it or perhaps so that I could see their success. The jar of mushrooms, the Mother I'd so carefully hidden along with the incense, the powdered San Pedro cactus tucked in with the food, and a little more Mother in the clothes bin. They would not find a large quantity of anything, but many little packets of considerable variety were hidden among my belongings.

Shivering with cold and fear, I sat in the car. I had expected to be back at my father's place in two days. How would I explain being in an Indiana jail? How could I get out of my frightening dilemma?

I placed pillars of light for protection around the car and myself as I'd been taught by my Sufi teachers. I repeated mantras over and over. I whispered to myself, "Thank you that all is well, that I am safe, and that I can continue my journey in peace." I told myself that I could call Ed, a family friend and lawyer. He would find a way to get me out of the trouble I had found myself in. I watched the cops in their relentless search as I feverishly repeated my prayers and mantras.

Time dragged on, and I thought they would never finish.

After ten minutes, the older cop came over to the car and told me they had almost finished and not to worry because everything was okay.

I couldn't imagine how anything could be okay, given that they had found all my carefully hidden stashes. Still, he seemed kind and continued to check in with me, telling me they would be finished soon.

I kept watching my breath and saying my mantras. "Thank you that all is well, that I am safe, and that I can continue my journey in peace. Thank you, thank you, thank you, thank you." I did my best to clog the channels of my mind that screamed, "Danger, danger, danger."

Finally, the two cops came to the car and let me out. The young man said sternly, "You know, we found things in your car that you shouldn't have."

I waited to hear what was going to happen to me. Shocked, I saw the young cop held only three items. It didn't surprise me to see the tin with Alan's lovely smelling buds, but the other two objects struck me as absurd. Along with the Mother, he had a small grinder painted with green camouflage colors and an empty glass bottle of herbal tonic.

"Yes, you're right," I admitted. "I shouldn't be carrying such things."

"You have to throw them away," the young cop said. "Throw them in the bushes."

"In the bushes?" I asked incredulously. Arguing would have been ridiculous, but it seemed like a strange form of play-acting.

I clumsily threw each item toward the bushes lining the shoulder where we had parked our cars. One by one, I heard a gentle plop as each hit the ground falling just short of the greenery. Not understanding the point of the charade, I slowly realized I might not spend the night in jail after all.

When I finished throwing the last item, the older officer said, "Get back into your car and drive safely." I could hardly believe my ears. They were letting me go without even a ticket despite all they had found.

I thanked the officers politely and got into my car. I put on my seat belt and started to adjust the rear-view mirror, but in the back I could see only a jumble of bins and belongings totally obscuring the back window.

I jumped out and called the cops. "You made a mess of my car. I can't see out the back. I can't drive if I can't see."

The older officer didn't apologize for the mess, but he did say they would wait to be sure I was safe while I made some order. I couldn't do much, but I did my best to pile things to clear the back window.

My mind quickly snapped into action. Leaving behind my fear, I took care of the business of organizing my belongings. My body felt calm, and my mind concentrated on getting the car ready to drive away. I didn't allow myself to consider the possibility that the drama might have taken a darker turn. I could do that later when I was far away.

I finally brought enough order to the car to feel safe to drive.

"Okay, I'm set," I called.

The older cop walked back to my car and stood by my open window.

"Lady," he said, looking me straight in the eyes, "I don't know how old you are, but I just want you to know that when I'm your age, I want to be like you and do the things that I want to do."

I wanted to weep—not from sadness but from feeling the complexity of human emotion and the possibility that we all can rise above what we think we are. I realized how privileged I was to have gotten special treatment, but at the same time, I was touched by the older officer who wanted to celebrate the life I was living.

When I got to the motel that night, I was astonished to find every bit of contraband I had packed. Although they had created havoc with my neat packing, they had not taken anything, and except for the herbal tonic, the tin of Mother, and the little grinder, my stash remained intact.

A day and a half later, I arrived at the Timshel cottage, eager to begin my search for home. My return trip marked my initiation into the next chapter of my life. I had run the gauntlet and survived.

A new world awaited me.

Finding Home

A house is not a home.

—Polly Adler

Ready as I was to find a home, I didn't know how to begin. Thinking I would enjoy being close to culture and good restaurants, I was drawn to the stimulating life of college towns in the Happy Valley of western Massachusetts. Yet, the idea of being surrounded by people's noise and cars no longer appealed to me after my years on the road.

I wondered how to find a home when I didn't know what I wanted. I wished for someone to swoop down and present me with the perfect place, but every real estate agent I talked to said rentals were handled online and I was on my own. Houses for rent were scarce, and the few I saw were expensive, unattractive, and didn't feel like home.

Georgeanne told me she had dreamed about the house that would become my home. "I saw it, and it's beautiful," she said. "It's tucked away in the woods, and there's an iron gate near a barn in a shady spot surrounded by moss and rocks. I know you'll find it. I saw it."

Hoping he would have the key to finding my longed-for home, I drove to Wendell to visit Adrian. He met me at the door, and Gracie, his Miniature Schnauzer, happily greeted me with excited barking as her compact body shook with joy at seeing me.

I plopped on the sofa and started my sad story. "I'll never find the right place. I've looked and looked, but nothing seems right."

"Well, you might not be able to find a home today, but you can get a bed."

"What do I need a bed for when I don't even have a place to put it?"

"That will come in time, but this bed is exceptional. You have to buy it before someone else gets it."

I had no interest in buying a bed, but I knew Adrian had an eye for the beautiful and a good deal, so I finally gave in.

It was a short ride along the Miller's River to the antique store. We entered the musty, overcrowded store overflowing with seas of china, knickknacks, and furniture of a certain age. We found the owner, who showed us the headboard and footboard of the bed leaning against a back wall of the store. Even in its unassembled state, I could see that it was a bed for royalty. Thick brass pillars on each of the four corners had aged to a handsome patina and finials that looked like mushrooms capped the posts. Smaller tubes in between displayed delicate fleur-de-lys patterns.

Adrian agreed to store the bed until I had a home, but as I returned to the Timshel cottage the next day, I felt disappointed that a bed had appeared, not a home.

Two weeks later when I visited Adrian, he announced jubilantly, "I've found the perfect house for you."

Intrigued, I asked, "Really, where?"

"It is just up the street. It's my ex-wife Donna's house. Well, not exactly yet. She's buying out her sister's share and hopes to finish the deal in a couple of months. But don't worry about that. This is a place of healing, and it's the place you need to be. I know it. There's just one tiny little thing, though, that you would have to do to make it work."

"What's that?" I asked.

"All you'd have to do is let her use your shower and laundry room since she lives in the back of the property in a yurt without running water. There won't be any problem. Donna's great," he assured me.

"That would never work, Adrian. I don't like sharing my private space with strangers, and I only met Donna once. I can't even remember her. There's got to be another way."

That ended the conversation for the moment, but over the next week, Adrian did not give up. He relentlessly insisted that I at least look at the house. Meanwhile, I felt like a balloon floating above the ground, held by a thin string. I needed a home, and I needed it soon. Though ambivalent, I finally agreed to drive back to Wendell from the cottage to look.

Adrian and I rode from his house up and down the hilly road to Donna's house through pine, oak, and birch forests. As we parked, I remembered that Chris and I had often passed the place on our trips to see our friends, Peter and Pam. We always wondered who lived in the shockingly blue house with pink flamingos gracing the lawn.

My feet touched the ground, and I felt solidity and familiarity. Could this be home? I hadn't even gone inside the house, and I already knew the land had called me. I knew this was where I belonged.

I entered the house to an assault of walls painted in a mishmash of horrible colors— red, turquoise, purple, and a sickly beige, with pieces of furniture crammed together in chaos. It didn't look great, but I could see through the challenges.

Walking around the house, I found a large, open living room with a wood-burning stove and ample space for my seven-foot grand piano, which I had stored at Timshel. There were two guest rooms, an eat-in kitchen, a laundry room, and a bedroom with a spacious view of sky and trees. The house had an excellent layout, and the land offered wide open spaces for gardens and a shaded area at the side for quiet.

On the other side of the property was a small barn, and to my delight, I found nearby the gate Georgeanne had seen in her dream. I laughed when I saw it. An ornate wrought iron square swung between two poles, but unlike a typical gate, it lacked rails on either side, which would have enclosed a space. It was no ordinary gate. It was a gate to nowhere and everywhere.

How could I not see it as a sign? I had found my home.

Donna's closing on the house went through without complications, and I moved in three months later on the first of July. I spent two weeks lovingly bringing my new home to life. I painted the walls soft, nurturing hues of slate blue, buttery yellow, and sage green and arranged furniture and area rugs to add color and comfort. I emptied the many boxes that Chris and I had packed almost ten years before and filled rooms with Chris's pottery, wood grails, and paintings made by talented friends. I created altars with sacred statues, feathers, candles, and photographs on almost every flat surface.

Even as my home took shape, I sensed that nothing was real. Every morning when I walked into the kitchen, I had a distinct feeling that I was not myself but a hired actress who had lost her script and didn't know how to improvise. I had landed and had a house, but I still had not found that elusive thing called home.

I experienced pleasure and excitement in the new, but with every move forward, I felt I was losing another piece of Chris.

I grieved, but it was an expression of grief that didn't resemble the dramatic episodes of the past when I felt bombarded by violent emotional storms. I felt more like I was carrying a heavy weight that crushed all joy.

Fortunately, I had countless reminders that brought me back to myself—the beauty of the land, momentary connection with a new friend, or contact with a beloved from the past. But even in moments of pleasure, I felt deadened by sorrow.

My house gradually began to feel like my own, but since the new mattress that I ordered for my brass bed took several weeks to arrive, I had chosen to camp out in the downstairs guest room in my sleeping bag on a foam mattress. I hadn't yet committed. I felt more like a transitory guest just passing through.

When the new mattress arrived, I placed it on the brass bed frame in the middle of my bedroom, where I could see the beauty of trees and sky through a large picture window. However, my fancy bed brought little happiness or comfort. Rather, it served as a stark reminder of my aloneness. My beloved was gone, and I was being carried forward whether I was ready or not.

I had entered a new phase. No longer a traveler, I had a home with a bed that was mine, and only mine. A new life had begun, but it was a life that would never include Chris in his physical form.

Awakening

A free bird leaps on the back of the wind and floats downstream till the current ends and dips his wing in the orange sun's rays and dares to claim the sky.

—Maya Angelou

With little more to do to make my house livable, I sat alone looking ahead at empty days. In the past, I longed for such free time to fill with creative projects. In my new reality, the emptiness felt more like a trap than a gift. I felt heavy and disoriented, emptied out and untethered. I bounced around in time and space, lost, with no way to find myself. I didn't even know what I was looking for.

Much to my surprise, Donna had become a blessing in my new life. Part fairy, part artist, part pioneer woman, and a delightful, energetic woman in her late forties, Donna had lived in the yurt behind my house with no running water for the past twenty years. Only twelve feet in diameter, her home was a sparkling jewel crammed with her paintings, sculptures, and sacred objects. Creativity oozed out of her.

Despite my previous worries about her coming and goings in my home, she became a bright light, checking with me almost daily and offering support on my otherwise bleak and frightening days. I appreciated her excellent boundaries and never felt that she invaded my space. In fact, I looked forward to her visits to my shower and laundry room.

Two days after the arrival of my bed, my friend Esu telephoned me early in the morning as I prepared to drive two hours to New Haven for a haircut. Esu was a student of Malidoma Somé, an African shaman married to Sobonfu, the leader of my grief retreat. Chris and I met Esu before we went on the road while studying African shamanism.

"What's up?" I asked.

"Next week, we're having a Ritual of Ancestralization on the sacred land in Cherry Plain, Massachusetts, where you and Chris helped Malidoma build one of the temples.

"Ritual of Ancestralization? What does that mean?"

"In the Dagara tradition," he said, "a person is not considered an ancestor until this ritual has been carried out. Once completed, Chris will be more accessible to you for communication and guidance. It's time for him to be an ancestor."

I'd longed to connect with Chris and hoped he would reach out from the other side. So far, it hadn't happened.

As we talked, it became clear that I had too little time to collect the required articles of Chris's clothing and other ritual items and to travel to Cherry Plain for the ceremony. Although Esu offered to carry out the ritual for me, we agreed that it would be better for me to do it personally the following year when I would have more time to prepare.

As we said goodbye, I noticed my resistance to acknowledging Chris as an ancestor. As much as I knew Chris was dead, never to return, I didn't feel ready to formalize it with a ritual.

I realized my process around accepting Chris's death resembled a roller coaster. One minute I recognized the reality, and the next, his death seemed impossible. I suspected I might never fully comprehend the mystery of his death.

The phone call had taken too long, and I feared I would be late for my appointment. I took a deep breath, gathered my belongings, and got into the car. On the drive, I listened to a podcast by Terrence McKenna, my favorite psychedelic philosopher. As he talked about the slipperiness of time, my eyes got heavy, and I had to concentrate on staying awake. Since I was only ten minutes away from my appointment, I trusted that it was safe to continue down the four-lane highway.

A loud screeching sound jolted me out of a faraway place. A thunderous sound felt almost supernatural. As the sound receded, I felt a strange, almost ecstatic sense of the ineffable in my body.

In a state of shock, I had no idea what had just happened. I knew only that my car had encountered the car in the next lane. There was no hard crash, only a brief meeting of the two vehicles as they touched each other in passing, thus creating a piercing and eerie wail. My car careened out of control. It took everything I could muster to stay in my own lane, but I succeeded. In a quarter of a mile, I found a safe place to drive onto the shoulder.

I parked and got out to assess the damage. I was not hurt, but the door on the driver's side had bashed in. I didn't know if any other damage had occurred. The crinkled metal on the door gave me a cold chill as I realized I could have died or caused another person's death. My mind shut down so as not to have to face the terror of the moment.

I called 911 from my cell phone and reported the accident. The woman who answered told me that the police would arrive shortly. I looked back on the highway, barely able to see the other vehicle parked on the shoulder. I wished I could be closer to talk to the passengers and know they were safe, but I had to stay until the police arrived. Meanwhile, I was left alone and terrified with dark thoughts.

I stood impatiently on the side of the highway for twenty minutes. Finally, a policeman came and parked next to my car.

"Are you okay?" he asked kindly.

"Yup, although the side of my car is bashed in. What about the people in the other car?" I asked, not sure I was ready to hear the answer.

"As far as I could see, they're all okay," he said, "just a little shaken. By the way, there were witnesses in the car who said that it was you who drifted into their lane."

I felt a stabbing in my chest as I considered the possibility that I had been the cause of the accident. I knew I had momentarily nodded off, but it didn't seem long enough to lose control of the car. It frightened me to think I had been so unconscious.

The officer asked for my license and insurance papers, which I gave him with shaking hands. He disappeared into his car and left me for what seemed like an eternity. When he returned, he gave me a ticket for $150 for drifting out of my lane.

"Can you drive?" he asked.

"Yes, I think so," I said shakily.

"Then get on your way."

I got back into my battered car, and he blocked the left lane while I got safely back on the road as if nothing had happened. In fact, I didn't know what had happened. I knew only that the guardian angels had protected me in some unfathomable way. I was alive, the other driver was seemingly uninjured, and I could drive Silvy, my beloved car, even though she had been hurt.

I got to my haircut appointment and tried to ground myself as Robyn, my hairdresser of twenty years, snipped off three inches of hair. As she gave me a new hairstyle, I remembered when two and a half years before, she had cut Chris's hair to prepare for chemotherapy he did not live to receive.

After the haircut, I felt unsteady and wanted desperately to get back to the safety of my home. I decided to cancel the rest of my plans, including a luncheon date with Irene, the social worker at Smilow Hospital who helped me after Chris died. Before I left Robyn, I called my insurance company to report the accident and heard with surprise that the agent assigned to me was named Chris. Was that a strange coincidence, or was I being reminded that Chris was always with me?

Driving home, I felt alert and extraordinarily awake even though I no longer trusted myself nor my ability to know what I was doing. Whatever had happened wasn't from carelessness. I had experienced an unconscious moment out of control. The accident reminded me that my whole life was now out of control, and I was afraid.

From the road, I called Adrian and told him what had happened. Hearing how terrified I was, he offered to pick me up when I got home and bring me to his house for dinner.

On the way back to my house, I stopped at a gas station near the end of an exit. When I tried to get back on the highway, the entrance was blocked. I tried to find an alternate route, but my GPS took me on a ten-minute wild goose chase that brought me right back to where I had started. I felt caught in a maze and was afraid I might never find my way out.

I didn't know where to go, so I just kept driving straight and soon passed the Wellness Center in Northampton, where Chris and I had gone for one visit, futilely hoping for a miracle after his cancer diagnosis. Then, I passed the restaurant where we had eaten with Adrian after Chris had gotten a vitamin C treatment. I remembered that we had parked a mere two blocks away from the restaurant and that Chris could barely manage the walk. I remembered his courage in staying present as he moved step by step, teetering as he tried to negotiate a body that had run amok. He must have been terrified, but he kept moving bravely forward.

That's how I saw him walk toward his death—courageously, with his whole heart and energy and without complaint. I would never know of another story inside of him, but what I saw presented a deep and trusting movement toward the unknown.

I don't think anyone could feign that kind of courage under such challenging circumstances. It made me wonder if our whole life together trained me (and maybe us) for Chris's courageous walk into dying. What a possibility to think that one's living serves one's dying.

Looking back at the accident, I felt I had walked up to the portal of death where I was asked to decide. The open doors beckoned. I could have followed Chris to the other side. The question loomed. "Do you want to live or die?" I chose, and I decided to live even with grief and unknowing. I had been offered a way out, yet I decided to stay.

Eventually, I found the highway entrance and made my way back to my new home, which I called the Blue House, where Adrian promised to meet me. I didn't know what to do until he arrived. I thought about taking a walk but decided it would be better if I stacked wood. I felt relieved to find a concrete project, a rarity then. As I held each piece of wood in my hands, I began to feel a little more grounded but still far from settled.

An hour later, Adrian picked me up and took me back to his house. When we had made ourselves comfortable in his living room, he said he was concerned about my state of mind. He said I needed to find things to do that would bring passion into my life to find my way back. I heard his words, but I felt lost in a new town with few friends and no activities. I didn't know how to engage or what to engage with. I was clueless.

Adrian tried to comfort me and told me gently that I was now home and safe. Hearing those words, I cracked, and all of the terror and confusion of the day came tumbling out in wails and sobs. In the depths of agony and grief that felt too big to contain within my frail human body, I tried to move the energy through with my tears. But my weeping had little effect.

Although Adrian came behind me and put his hand on my back, it brought no comfort. My grief seemed endless with no apparent way out. Lost in my heartache, I recognized his comforting hand as a reprieve, not a final solution even when my tears stopped.

I rubbed my third eye, and Adrian put a cold cloth on my forehead. I doused myself with an essential oil made of white fir, black spruce, ylang ylang, and pine to help me ground. I sat silently in a state of inward concentration. With my eyes closed, colors collided wildly, and I felt like I bounced off rubbery walls willy-nilly around the cosmos.

Adrian sat next to me and quietly held space.

My body ached. I wanted to run away, but I stayed—engaged in a mysterious form of healing. I felt my entire being transform as it dissolved and reorganized in pulsating waves. As much as I wanted to regain control, I could do nothing but let go. Surrender was the only medicine for the moment.

Adrian brought me a mug of soup, and after barely touching it, I knew I needed to return alone to my home to process the grueling day. I tucked myself into my fancy brass bed, but sleep didn't come easily. I tossed and turned throughout the night until sleep finally came and I drifted into oblivion.

When I awoke in the morning after precious few hours of sleep, I felt swallowed by grief—sick, nauseous, and light headed. I didn't want to do anything, but I thought I should move rather than disappear into the darkness. I decided to go out and continue stacking wood. I loved the weight, the individuality, and the satisfying plop of each piece as it found the perfect place. For a short time, my mind was at peace.

Lost in my project, I heard Donna's voice calling me. She came around to the woodshed. Still tender and teary, I greeted her.

"What happened?" she said, looking at my tear-stained cheek.

"Come see," I said as I brought her to my bashed-in car to look at the damage.

I told her about my nodding off and sliding into the other car.

"I'm so sorry about poor Silvy, and I'm relieved that you weren't hurt. But there is good news. At least you got a really great haircut."

I tried to smile at her effort to cheer me up, but it didn't help.

"I'm really not doing well, and I'm scared because I don't know what to do to make things better."

"I do have a suggestion if you're interested."

"I'll do anything. Just tell me," I pleaded.

She was precise in her instructions. "Every morning at 7:30 a.m., you must come to the Country Store and just sit until 9:30 a.m."

The Country Store was where Donna worked as a cashier and honorary master of ceremonies, entertaining customers with stories, advice, and diversion when things got dull. As one of Wendell's few businesses, it was a place where people gathered around several tables to meet and share local news.

"Bring your computer so you have something to do if nothing else is happening, but otherwise, you just have to sit and watch. This way, you'll meet the locals, hear the stories, and gradually be known." She spoke with authority, and I was willing to take any guidance at this tender moment.

"And you know what?" she continued. "Within a year, your life will be so full that you'll be amazed."

I doubted that my life would make such strides. Still, I felt a faint spark of optimism when I heard that Wendell offered numerous activities, including yoga, reading, and meditation groups. I also heard that it had a zealous spirit of helping that brought people together in times of need. Donna told me that Wendell's town motto is, "We're all here because we are not all there," which sounded promising in my current unbalanced frame of mind.

I asked Donna if it had to be 7:30, and she told me it was the only way I'd meet everyone.

"Okay," I said, fear quivering in my heart. "I'll be there tomorrow."

I kept thinking about the accident, wondering about its message. Had it been my fate, or was it punishment? Did I want to die? Did I regret that I had survived?

I'd never know for sure. I could only make up a story that would hopefully serve my healing.

I didn't remember going into that blank space that led me to slide into the left lane, but I remembered coming out. It was as if I were being born, coming from the void, from the bright formless light. There was ecstasy in that awakening even though it coincided with the crashing of my beloved car.

Is that what it means to be born? In a moment, the old is destroyed, and something new and unfamiliar takes its place.

I chose to believe that the accident constituted not just a wake-up call but an awakening, a new way of standing on the earth that felt vulnerable and frightening, yet exciting.

Still, I walked around with nausea in my gut. Perhaps my body had to acclimate to the new atmosphere. Not even sure why, I wept uncontrollably. Perhaps beyond my present sorrow I felt sorrow for the whole human dilemma. Humans are such tender, vulnerable creatures facing monumental challenges with far too little information. Yet, we persevere.

Experiencing so much grief gave me immense love and respect for all of us humans as we muddle our way through our destinies. My heart opened to the possibility of someday expressing such love and compassion to myself as I moved forward.

I felt so naked, small, lost, and alone. At the same time, I felt powerful, beautiful, courageous, and creative. It was a lot to hold in a tenuous new place, but I knew it was what I came to do and be in this lifetime, and I wasn't going to give up.

I followed Donna's suggestion and showed up the following day and every weekday after that. Sometimes, meeting people felt like play, but other times, it challenged me so that I wanted to run. Even in the most pleasurable times, I sensed a bass note of sadness no matter the harmonies or dissonances wending their way above. I sat in the store. I watched, listened, engaged, and got to know the place where I lived, in a dawning new world.

One day in the Country Store, I heard a woman I had chatted with occasionally calling, "Kai, Kai." It shocked me when I heard myself think, "Oh, my goodness, she actually thinks I'm real."

A warm glow entered my body at the acknowledgment of my presence, but my tender response told me that I was more lost than I thought, even to myself.

I feared I had a long way to go before I could recreate a solid foundation for myself.

A Love That Has No End

In the early morning, a lover asked her beloved,
"Do you love me more than yourself?"
"More than myself? For sure, I have no self anymore—
I am you already. The I has gone; the you has come about.
Even my identity is gone. The answer is taken for granted.
'You and I' has no meaning.
The I has vanished like a drop into an ocean of honey."

—Rumi

Three months later, I made an appointment with Charles Cooper, a local acupuncturist. Trained in many traditional and esoteric healing methods, he had an excellent reputation. I liked and trusted him immediately. He seemed to understand the relationship between the contraction in my body and grief, so I made a second appointment.

When I arrived a week later, he asked me how I was doing. I told him that after the first session, I had felt more grounded and less anxious, but a few days later, I crashed hard, falling into what felt like depression.

I wasn't sure Charles had taken me seriously when he responded that such emotional states come and go, but he told me he had an ancient treatment that could help me let go of some grief.

It surprised me when he asked me to get on his table and lie on my belly. I had never had needles placed in my back. He said he would position the needles to draw negative energy out of each of my organs. He said the needles leave large red circles when they started working to move the blocked energy from each site.

Most of the needles went in painlessly, although when Charles inserted a needle into the one connected to the liver, I felt excruciating pain. In Chinese medicine, the liver reflects excess stress or emotions, and it made sense that it would feel most tender. I couldn't see my back, but Charles told me the spots around the needles got bright red and as big as half dollars. When he started lightly massaging my neck and head, I began to weep and couldn't stop.

He confirmed I was okay and left me alone to allow energy to flow. He checked on me repeatedly as I wept for most of an hour. Grief waxed and waned in what seemed like a never-ending cycle. I felt totally dissolved in sorrow with all thought erased. In its place, I felt only despair.

Face down on the table, I had wet cheeks and a nose so clogged that I could barely breathe. Charles came into the room and kindly reached under the face support to hold a tissue so that I could blow my nose. It felt tender, sweet, and intimate, almost as if I were a child being tended.

Too far gone to be embarrassed, I felt only gratitude.

My body started to feel exhausted and tense from all-consuming emotion.

"Find the softness in your body and breathe into it," Charles said.

I found nothing but contraction, yet I continued the search. Eventually, I found a small soft place in my belly and gradually imagined spreading softness and gentleness throughout my body. I even started laughing a little as I felt a warmth moving upward and throughout me.

Charles left me alone again, and I was aware that I no longer felt Chris's physical presence as I had for so long.

"Chris, where are you? I can't feel you. Something is changing. What's going on?"

I heard nothing but silence, but I knew that Chris couldn't be far from me.

Suddenly I felt a brief pop in my third eye, and a dime-sized blue circle appeared in my field of vision. Geometrical shapes in many colors spread out from the center. Astonishingly, I was thrown deep into a medicine journey without any medicine. My head burst with energy, and all feelings of sadness disappeared. I continued watching my breath, observing all that was happening as if I were viewing a movie.

"You are my beloved," I heard from somewhere above.

I felt awake with energy almost too much to hold. It reminded me of how I felt when Chris and I made love. We first met in our bodies in the physical, the sensual, and the vibratory of the earth plane world but then passed through to something beyond, something familiar, yet not of this world, a blessing beyond words. Love ruled, harmony reigned, and everything had its place. There we celebrated our beloveds, the ones who had loved us, shaped us, and brought us to the present moment. Our bodies dissolved, but sensation remained, and we danced light and free through the universe.

"Chris, my love, now that you are no longer in a body, how can I experience the cosmic energy we used to share?"

"You know," I heard in his familiar booming yet tender voice, "we can still dance as we did when I had a body."

"What do you mean?"

He answered simply, "All you have to do is remember that you are more than your physical body. We can meet in the oneness of All That Is."

I listened, not sure what he meant.

He continued, "I am like Krishna or Shiva or like the wind. I am in everything that is. Wherever and whoever you love, you love me. When you dance, you are dancing with me. And when you grieve or ache, celebrate or heal, I am with you. There is no place for me to go. Come, my beloved. Let us make ecstatic love."

And so it was and is and is to be.

I am the dreamer,
I am Shiva
chasing across the universe,
looking for myself
only to find
infinite shattered mirrors
reflecting blinding light.

Acknowledgments

Less than a year after Chris died, I consulted a psychic. She was clear. "You have to write a book about your travels on the road, but don't worry. Spirit will help you."

Years passed until one day, in my memoir class, I wrote the first chapter. At that moment in a flash of inspiration, I resolved to present a new chapter to my fellow writers every week. Miraculously, I kept to my commitment, sometimes staying up into the small hours of the night to finish.

So, yes, Spirit helped write *Life of Kai*, but more importantly, many friends helped birth it into being. That first draft has grown through the love, skill, and support of many people. Without their help, I could not have finished writing the book.

Those present from the beginning include members of our memoir-writing class—our teacher, Ruth Flohr, Morning Star Chenven, Shell Hines, Nan Riebschlaeger, Nancy Spittle, Ilina Singh, Sharon Tracy, and Mez Ziemba. Their honest feedback and loving curiosity kept me writing, rewriting, and rewriting again until the book took shape.

I am grateful for the support of my many early readers—Mara Bright, Mateo Pallamary, Deb Flying Horse, Louise Mandell, Stephanie Roy, and Sara Schley, to name a few. Their encouragement kept me going when I feared I had lost the strength to move forward.

My first editor, Eva Stulberg, helped shape my somewhat dry prose into a story that reflected my love and passion. Her skill and gentle touch were invaluable.

Thank you to my publisher Marcia Gagliardi for endless hours assisting me in wrestling with the text into its best expression and for bringing *Life of Kai* to the world. Thank you to Mary-Ann DeVita Palmieri for copy editing, to Joellyn Ausanka for her help with copy editing, and to Richard Bruno for proofreading.

Thank you to Jean Miele, whose cover portrait captures the moment; to Carol Guasti, Jean's wife, who helped with the concept for the cover; to Erik Johnson for his photos of Chris and me; and to Adrian Montagano for the elegant glyph at the beginning of each section. Thank you to Mark Wright for designing the book cover, helping with the ebook, and supporting me in my vision and to Peter Acker, who encouraged me with his skill and compassion as we recorded the audiobook. Of course, there would be no story without Chris, my beloved soul mate. We traveled the world and the beyond, meeting friends and teachers while connecting with and learning from the natural beauty of our planet. I will be forever grateful that Chris came into my life, touched my heart, and brought me joy.

Thank you to all the unnamed friends, family, beloveds, and unknown beings who generously gifted Chris and me as we journeyed through our life together. I am profoundly grateful.

And to you, my reader, thank you for sharing the adventure with me.

photo by Erik Johnson

Kai Carol Jud

About the Author

Kai Carol Jud is a mystic, wanderer of the cosmos, traveler on the edge, and storyteller. She is a psychotherapist and tarot reader whose embodied spiritual path and study of shamanism have taken her through the ecstasies and challenges of life and death.

Kai brings decades of experience to Core Energetics, Gestalt, and shamanic journeying with special interest in body energy, sexuality, spirituality, and group process. Her work is inspired by a mystical path that takes her deeply into the realms of Spirit and connection with the earth.

Kai has a bachelor of arts degree from Columbia University and a master's degree in social work from New York University. She trained with John Pierrakos for four years at the Institute of Core Energetics in New York City. In 1988, she founded the Institute of Process Therapy which offered yearlong training for therapists and healers in the techniques of process work. She has been in private practice since 1985.

kaicaroljud.com

Colophon

Text for *Life of Kai* is set in Palatino, an old-style serif typeface designed by Hermann Zapf, initially released in 1949 by the Stempel foundry and later by other companies, most notably the Mergenthaler Linotype Company.

Named after the 16th-century Italian master of calligraphy Giambattista Palatino, Palatino is based on the humanist types of the Italian Renaissance, which mirror the letters formed by a broad nib pen reflecting Zapf's expertise as a calligrapher. Its capital Y is in the unusual palm Y style, inspired by the Greek letter upsilon, a trait found in some of the earliest versions of the letter such as that of Aldus Manutius.

Unlike most Renaissance typeface revivals, which tend to have delicate proportions such as a low x-height—short lower-case letters and longer ascenders and descenders—Palatino has larger proportions, increasing legibility. Palatino was particularly intended as a design for trade or "jobbing" use, such as headings, advertisements, and display printing, and was created with a solid, wide structure and wide apertures that could appear clearly on poor-quality paper, when read at a distance or printed at small sizes.

Titles are set in Apple Gothic. Gothic was a popular typeface style in the Middle Ages from 1200 to 1500. The term originated from the Italians who used it to refer to the "barbaric" letterforms of Blackletter.

Printed in the USA
CPSIA information can be obtained
at www.ICGtesting.com
LVHW091910271023
762391LV00008B/33

9 781948 380898